Why the United States Lacks a National Health Insurance Program

Recent Titles in Contributions in Political Science

Why the United States Lacks a National Health Insurance Program

NICHOLAS LAHAM

Contributions in Political Science,
Number 331
Bernard K. Johnpoll, *Series Editor*

Greenwood Press
WESTPORT, CONNECTICUT • LONDON

Library of Congress Cataloging-in-Publication Data

Laham, Nicholas.
 Why the United States lacks a national health insurance program / Nicholas Laham.
   p.   cm.—(Contributions in political science, ISSN 0147–1066;
 no. 331)
   Includes bibliographical references and index.
   ISBN 0–313–28745–7 (alk. paper)
   1. Medical policy—United States.   2. National health insurance—
 United States.   I. Title.   II. Series.
 RA395.A3L34   1993
 362.1'0973—dc20   93–3167

British Library Cataloguing in Publication Data is available.

A paperback edition of *Why the United States Lacks a National Health Insurance
Program* is available from Praeger Publishers, an imprint of Greenwood Publishing
Group, Inc. (ISBN: 0–275–94779–3).

Library of Congress Catalog Card Number: 93–3167
ISBN: 0–313–28745–7
ISSN: 0147–1066

First published in 1993

Greenwood Press, 88 Post Road West, Westport, CT 06881
An imprint of Greenwood Publishing Group, Inc.

Printed in the United States of America

The paper used in this book complies with the
Permanent Paper Standard issued by the National
Information Standards Organization (Z39.48–1984).

10 9 8 7 6 5 4 3 2

To my mother, Laure, and Martha,
with love and appreciation

Contents

List of Tables

Preface

"Comprehensive health insurance is an idea whose time has come in America," President Richard Nixon declared in a message to Congress on February 6, 1974, that urged the establishment of national health insurance. "Let us act now—in 1974—to assure all Americans financial access to high quality medical care."[1] President Gerald Ford was no less determined than Nixon to secure the establishment of national health insurance in 1974. "Why don't we write a good health bill on the statute books in 1974, before this Congress adjourns?" Ford asked lawmakers in his first presidential address to Congress on August 12, 1974.[2]

Nixon and Ford were not the first Presidents to urge the establishment of national health insurance; nor were they the last. Harry S. Truman was the first to do so; and Jimmy Carter the last former president thus far. Both Truman and Carter left office deeply disappointed that they had failed to secure the establishment of national health insurance. "I have had some bitter disappointments as President," Truman lamented in his memoirs. "But the one that has troubled me most, in a personal way, has been the failure to defeat the organized opposition to a national compulsory health-insurance program."[3] Carter was no less disappointed than Truman. "The fight for equitable health care was one of my major efforts and one of my great disappointments," Carter lamented in his memoirs.[4]

This book addresses a single, central, overriding question: Why is the United States the only advanced industrial democracy without national health insurance? The fact that virtually all the countries of Western Europe, as well as Canada and Japan, have national health insurance programs suggests that a typical government in an advanced industrial democracy considers guaranteeing universal access to affordable health care to be politically, socially, and morally desirable, if not vital. As a result, we should expect the United States to have a national health insurance program. Why it does not remains a puzzle.

A rapidly growing uninsured population and soaring health care costs jointly threaten the very foundations of the medical system. As the health care crisis has worsened, the medical system has increasingly failed to adequately serve the health care needs of the public. Perhaps the worst failing of the health care system relates to its provision of primary care, which adds to normal and productive life. Primary care allows doctors to treat illnesses when they begin, before complications set in, if not prevent ailments altogether. Illnesses treated in their early stages can be cured with minimum pain to the patient and minimum cost to the third-party payer.

Due to its failure to provide universal, comprehensive coverage, the health insurance system imposes substantial financial barriers that impede public access to primary care. Inadequately insured individuals must pay either practically all or the entire cost of their primary care out of pocket. As a result, when illness strikes, they have financial incentives to avoid seeing a doctor until complications develop, resulting in unnecessary pain and suffering, deformity, disability, or even death. Lacking sufficient access to primary care, inadequately insured individuals are especially susceptible to suffering catastrophic illnesses, which are costly and difficult to treat. Without enough income and coverage, the inadequately insured must rely heavily upon uncompensated care provided by charitable hospitals. The insurance system inflicts unnecessary pain and suffering on the inadequately insured and needless financial loss, work, mental stress, and emotional burdens upon the medical profession.

On the surface, the best alternative available to sick, inadequately insured individuals is to seek uncompensated care from charitable hospitals. However, uncompensated care is usually provided only by public hospitals. As a result, public hospitals have stretched their resources to the very limits in assuming the burden of treating substantial numbers of inadequately insured individuals.

Overburdened with heavy patient loads, public hospitals are ill equipped and staffed to provide sufficient care to their patients. As a result, they must often stringently ration care, limiting their provision of services to the treatment of catastrophic illnesses. Accordingly, inadequately insured individuals are usually unable to receive primary care on an uncompensated basis from public hospitals. If they cannot afford to see a doctor in private practice, sick inadequately insured individuals must wait until their illnesses develop complications and become catastrophic before they are able to receive uncompensated care from public hospitals. Such individuals are only one illness away from unnecessary pain and suffering, deformity, disability, death, or an unpleasant, and even life-threatening, stay in a poorly equipped and staffed public hospital.

We could ignore the plight of the inadequately insured by directing our attention to the well insured. They generally receive comprehensive health insurance coverage, with only minimal patient cost-sharing requirements. On the surface, it would seem that the adequately insured are being well served by the insurance system.

However, access to health care even among well-insured individuals remains tenuous. Health insurance is not a right of American citizenship, but primarily a privilege of employment. Practically all individuals who are well insured receive their coverage from their employers.

Working families can easily lose their health care benefits and become inadequately insured. Since health insurance is mostly employment-based, they may lose their coverage when they lose their jobs. True, losing a job does not necessarily mean loss of insurance. They may find new employers willing to provide insurance. However, less than half of employers do so. Working families may lose their jobs with firms providing them insurance only to find new employers who do not extend them any coverage. Moreover, when working families lose their jobs, it usually takes weeks, if not months or years, to find new employment. They may lose their insurance with their former employers during this period.

Even working families who are fortunate enough to maintain their group health insurance cannot rely upon their health care benefits. As a result of soaring health care costs, employers are increasingly reducing coverage offered by their group plans as a means to cut their business expenses. Working families are having to assume an ever-greater responsibility for the cost of their health care. An increasing number of them are becoming underinsured.

The current health insurance system fails to adequately serve the health care needs of society, regardless of how well insured individuals may be. It needlessly exposes all but the wealthiest individuals to the risk of being uninsured, and deprived of access to health care. Health care is a right of citizenship in every advanced industrial democracy except the United States. This nation needs to guarantee this same right to its citizens through the establishment of a national health insurance program.

However, every effort to establish national health insurance has ended in abysmal failure due to the fierce and unrelenting opposition to the program mounted by the health care industry, especially its most politically powerful member, the American Medical Association. National health insurance cannot be instituted on an economically and fiscally viable basis without stringent health care cost-containment measures, which are certain to impose financial losses upon every segment of the medical industry. As a result, the industry has waged a pitched battle against national health insurance since 1920, when the AMA first announced its opposition to the program.[5]

The most important resource the health care industry has used in recent years to prevent the establishment of national health insurance has been financial. Since the mid–1970s, Congress has come increasingly under the influence of interest groups, which wield substantial political power on Capitol Hill through the significant financial contributions their political action committees (PACs) make to incumbent lawmakers.[6] Perhaps no interest group has taken greater advantage of the congressional campaign finance system to gain political influence on Capitol Hill than the health care industry. Since 1968, health care industry PACs, beginning with and led by the AMA's American Medical Political Action Committee, have contributed tens of millions of dollars to members of Congress. Those contributions have allowed the industry to consistently thwart efforts by such Democratic Party leaders as President Carter during the late 1970s and Senate Majority Leader George Mitchell of Maine during the early 1990s to secure passage of national health insurance legislation.

Despite representing overwhelming majorities in both houses of Congress during the Carter and Bush Administrations; Democratic lawmakers were willing to defy the wishes of their party leaders, not to mention public opinion, and refuse to take action on national health insurance. Financially beholden to the health care industry, congressional Democrats cannot pass a national health insurance bill without antagonizing members of the medical system. The health care industry will use its financial power to defeat congressional Democrats who defy its wishes and support the establishment of national health insurance. As a result, congressional Democrats have had no choice but to reject the appeals of their party leaders for action on national health insurance.

However, the health care industry cannot continue to prevent the establishment of national health insurance indefinitely. During the 1990s, health care costs have been soaring out of control. In the absence of corrective action, the public will no longer be able to bear the increasingly onerous financial burden of skyrocketing health care costs by the turn of the twenty-first century, resulting in a massive rise in the uninsured population, the financial bankruptcy of a large part of the medical industry, and a collapse of the health care system. To avert this collapse, Congress will have to establish a national health insurance program, guaranteeing universal access to affordable health care, by the turn of the century.

I hope that this book will contribute to fostering a full appreciation of the responsibilities and challenges Americans face in collectively providing for their health care during the 1990s.

During the course of writing this book, I have accumulated substantial debts to a number of individuals, without whose support this work could not have been published. I am grateful to three members of the Center for Politics and Policy at the Claremont Graduate School—Thomas R. Rochon, Lamont C. Hempel, and Daniel A. Mazmanian—for having read and critiqued earlier drafts of this book. I am also grateful for the editorial support and assistance I received from Mildred Vasan and Nita H. Romer at Greenwood Press.

Finally, I would like to express my appreciation to my mother, Nadia Laham; my aunt, Laure Abu-Haydar; and my sister, Martha Laham, for the moral and financial support they provided me during the course of writing this book. The real sacrifice in the development of this book was made by them, not by me. I hope that this book proves worthy of the sacrifice they made in assisting me to write it.

Why the United States Lacks a National Health Insurance Program

CHAPTER 1

Introduction

The debate about compulsory national health insurance (NHI) has extended over fully one-third of the United States' life as a nation. Teddy Roosevelt first made national health insurance an issue in the Bull Moose campaign in 1912. Since then, with varying degrees of intensity, the issue has held a place on the national political agenda.[1]

Theodore R. Marmor, political scientist, Yale University

National health insurance has been on the political agenda intermittently since the turn of the twentieth century. It received especially serious consideration in Washington during the 1940s and 1970s. Efforts to establish national health insurance failed during both decades. The defeat of national health insurance can be best addressed through an analysis of the policymakers and the issues that shaped the debate on the program during those two decades.

THE FAILURE TO ESTABLISH NATIONAL HEALTH INSURANCE DURING THE 1940s

The failure of health care reformers to establish national health insurance during the 1940s was largely due to the intense and unrelenting opposition to the program mounted by the American Medical Association (AMA). It launched its National Education Campaign to prevent adoption of the program after its primary sponsor, President Harry Truman, won a stunning upset victory in the 1948 election. The campaign was well financed, through special fees the AMA imposed upon its affluent members, and expertly managed by the San Francisco public relations firm of Whitaker and Baxter. It produced an avalanche of publications highlighting the AMA's arguments against national health insurance.

The debate on national health insurance occurred during the onset of the Cold War, when anticommunist sentiment was rising. This provided the AMA an opportunity to mobilize public opposition to the program on ideological grounds. A key tactic the AMA used in its campaign against the program was to define it as "socialized medicine." This tactic was effective, given the fact that any program with a conceptual linkage to socialism, like national health insurance, was politically unpalatable. As Monte M. Poen notes, "Anything or anyone remotely associated with the word socialism became immediately suspect, and health reformers could never rid their national health insurance proposal of that onerous title."[2]

The AMA reaped substantial political dividends from its success in defining national health insurance as "socialized medicine." Over 65,000 firms and nearly 10,000 interest groups opposed to "socialized medicine," joined the AMA in its campaign against national health insurance. The conceptual linkage between national health insurance and "socialized medicine" had an especially powerful effect in mobilizing congressional opposition to the program. This became evident during 1949–1950, when Truman recommended that the Federal Security Agency (FSA) be elevated to a cabinet-level department of health, education, and welfare. Congress rejected Truman's proposal. Congressional opponents of the Truman plans charged that a cabinet-level FSA would provide the administration with a high-profile department to use in mobilizing public and legislative support for "socialized medicine."[3]

The AMA had ample political resources to prevent the establishment of national health insurance. Chief among them was money. As an interest group with an affluent membership, the AMA had substantial financial resources unmatched by supporters of national health insurance. Moreover, the AMA's financial resources were bolstered by significant contributions from the business community.

Consider a comparison between the AMA and its business allies, on the one hand and the Committee for the Nation's Health (CNH), the primary interest group supporting the program during the 1940s, on the other. From 1949 to 1950, the AMA spent $3.75 million on its National Education Campaign. In addition, the business community spent over $2 million on an advertising blitz against national health insurance in October 1950, which was an important part of the campaign. By contrast, the CNH spent $140,000 in support of national health insurance during 1949 to 1950.[4]

While AMA opposition is an important reason why national health insurance was not established during the 1940s, it is not the only one. An even more important reason is the rapid expansion in private insurance. During 1940–1950, the share of the public covered for hospital care rose from 9 to 51 percent; for surgical care, from 3 to 36 percent; and for physician services performed in the hospital, from 1 to 14 percent.[5]

With a rapidly rising share of the population enrolling in private health insurance plans, a majority of the public saw no urgent and compelling need for a government program during the 1940s. As a result, popular support for the program was weak, as reflected in 1945 polling data, which showed the public evenly divided in their preference between government and private insurance. By providing coverage to a swiftly increasing segment of society, especially full-time working families, while giving the public an alternative to national health insurance, private plans defused popular support for a government program, depriving Congress of any immediate and overriding need to establish it. As Rashi Fein puts it:

Many Americans believed their problems and those of others had been or would be solved through the voluntary purchase of affordable health insurance. There was little middle-class pressure for a compulsory health insurance system. Middle-class voters were reaping the benefits of the postwar economic expansion, of the increase in jobs and employer-provided health insurance.[6]

THE FAILURE TO ESTABLISH NATIONAL HEALTH INSURANCE DURING THE 1970s

National health insurance received the support of a number of political leaders during the 1970s, including Presidents Richard Nixon, Gerald Ford and Jimmy Carter. However, their efforts to secure the establishment of the program were complicated by a number of factors. During the 1970s, the overwhelming majority of the public was insured through private plans, Medicare, or Medicaid. As a result, a majority of the public continued to see no urgent and compelling need for national health insurance. Public support for the program remained weak, with polling data showing the population continuing to be evenly divided in their preference between government and private insurance.

However, the most important reason for the defeat of national health insurance during the 1970s was Congress's refusal to impose stringent measures to contain soaring health care costs. By providing universal coverage primarily through an expansion in public insurance enrollments, the program promised to reduce financial barriers impeding access to health care, thereby raising patient utilization of medical services, especially among the poor and uninsured. In the absence of health care cost-containment measures, the program threatened to increase both inflation and the federal budget deficit.

To avert this possibility, Carter recognized that any economically and fiscally viable national health insurance program had to be coupled with health care cost-containment measures. Accordingly, in 1977 he recommended passage of the Hospital Cost Containment Act, which would have imposed stringent federal controls upon hospital costs. As a result, the bill promised to inflict substantial financial losses upon the hospital industry, which responded by mounting an intensive lobbying campaign to defeat the bill. The campaign was led by the American Hospital Association (AHA) and the Federation of American Health

Systems (FAHS), representing the for-profit sector of the hospital industry. The AMA joined the industry in opposing the bill. In 1979 the House of Representatives bowed to opposition from the hospital industry and the AMA and voted to defeat the bill, which dealt a fatal blow to prospects for the establishment of national health insurance. In the absence of health care cost-containment measures, national health insurance is politically and economically unviable, given the adverse inflationary and budgetary consequences it would have.

THE LATEST CAMPAIGN TO ESTABLISH NATIONAL HEALTH INSURANCE

During 1991–1993, health care reformers launched yet another campaign to establish national health insurance. Unlike the 1940s and 1970s, when the effort to institute national health insurance ended in abysmal failure, health care reformers will succeed in their latest campaign to establish the program, given the current medical crisis. In the absence of corrective action, soaring health care costs are certain to result in a massive rise in the uninsured population and the financial bankruptcy of a large part of the medical system by the turn of the twenty-first century. As a result, thousands of communities will lose their access to health care, provoking a collapse of the medical system. To avert this collapse, Congress will act to establish a national health insurance program, guaranteeing universal access to affordable health care, by the turn of the century.

The argument that the establishment of national health insurance is a virtual certainty contradicts prevailing wisdom that the United States is incapable of adopting comprehensive social reform programs to address vexing national problems, like those to overhaul the country's ailing and failing health care system. Critics of the American political system argue that interest groups wield enormous power on Capitol Hill, through massive campaign contributions to members of Congress. Financially beholden to interest groups, members of Congress are incapable of establishing broad social reform programs to rectify intractable national problems in a comprehensive manner, particularly those that undermine the narrow interests of financially powerful groups.[7]

Critics of the American political system are correct in their argument that interest groups have the capacity to wield their financial clout on Capitol Hill to prevent the establishment of comprehensive social reform programs that address broad national problems. Perhaps nowhere has this been more true than in health care. Since the late 1970s, the health care industry has used its financial clout on Capitol Hill to prevent adoption of national health insurance.

However, conditions in health care have changed radically since the campaign to establish national health insurance during the 1970s. By today's standards, health care costs were minimal during the 1970s; they did not pose any threat to the medical system at that time. During the 1970s, there was no urgent and compelling need to establish national health insurance. As a result, the health care industry was well positioned to prevent establishment of the program.

However, since the beginning of the 1990s, health care costs have soared out of control; they threaten the very foundations of the medical system. The health care industry is facing financial bankruptcy because soaring medical costs are pricing an increasing share of the public out of the insurance market, leaving them without the financial means to fund the cost of their health care. Health care providers will find it increasingly difficult to find patients capable of compensating them for their services. As a result, many, if not most, health care providers will go out of business. To avert this possibility, the health care industry is certain to support national health insurance when medical providers come to the realization that their survival will depend upon the political system's willingness to reform the current sick and troubled health care system.

The case of health care suggests that the narrow interests of pressure groups at times conflict with the wider interests of the public. The public has a rational interest in the establishment of national health insurance, which is the only means to guarantee universal access to affordable health care. The health care industry has an equally rational interest in opposing national health insurance, since it cannot be instituted on a fiscally and economically viable basis without stringent cost-containment measures, which would impose substantial financial losses upon every segment of the medical system.

However, it is possible for a convergence of interests to exist between pressure groups and the public. This is becoming increasingly the case in health care. Both the public's access to health care and the capacity of medical providers to be compensated for their services will become increasingly linked to the achievement of health care reform.

An overwhelming majority of the public recognizes the need for health care reform. Domestic public support for the American health care system is lower than in any other advanced industrial democracy, with the possible exception of Italy. American public support for the establishment of national health insurance stands at an all-time high.

However, unlike the overwhelming majority of the public, the health care industry stubbornly clings to its opposition to national health insurance, fearing the adverse financial consequences the program will have on members of the medical system. Nevertheless, as we have argued, that opposition is certain to dissipate by the turn of the twenty-first century, as the health care system begins to collapse, removing the final remaining political roadblock to establishment of the program.

Critics of the American political system assume that pressure groups are capable of rationally managing their own political interests; they use their financial influence on Capitol Hill to extract benefits from the political system. This has been the case in health care, where the medical industry has amassed substantial income through the capacity to use its financial clout on Capitol Hill to prevent health care reform, including stringent medical cost-containment measures. However, by driving up health care costs to the point where they have made medical services virtually unaffordable for an increasing share of the public, health care providers are pricing themselves out of their own market and risking financial bankruptcy. The case of health care suggests that interest groups do not always know how to manage their political interests; if allowed to amass overwhelming political power, unchecked by countervailing authority from any public or private institution, they can inadvertently take actions that undermine their own interests.

THE PLAN OF THIS BOOK

To summarize, the defeat of national health insurance during the 1940s may be attributed to AMA opposition, the expansion of private plans, and the lack of strong public support for the program. Its failure during the 1970s may be explained in terms of the fact that the overwhelming majority of the population was now insured, the continuing lack of strong popular backing of the program, and Congress's refusal to impose health care cost-containment measures. However, the current health care crisis and the increasing likelihood of a collapse of the medical system by the turn of the twenty-first century make it a virtual certainty that health care reformers will succeed in their latest campaign to establish national health insurance.

The remainder of this book attempts to develop in a comprehensive and systematic manner each of the explanations for the defeat of national health insurance provided in this chapter. It also analyzes in greater detail the current prospects for the establishment of the program.

Part I analyzes the politics of national health insurance during the 1940s. Chapter 2 focuses on the AMA. Its campaign against national health insurance during the 1940s is perhaps the best-known feature in the long and arduous debate on the program. Chapter 2 addresses two overriding questions: Why did the AMA oppose national health insurance? What were the political resources the AMA used to single-handedly prevent the establishment of the program?

Chapter 3 concentrates on the development of private health insurance. It argues that the expansion of private insurance was due to two overriding factors: AMA support; and the provision of federal and employer financial backing for group plans, the coverage firms provide their working families.

Part II examines the politics of national health insurance during the 1970s. Chapters 4 turns to the legislative battle over the Hospital Cost Containment Act. It addresses a single central question: Why did the House reject the Hospital Cost Containment Act, and thereby effectively thwart Carter's efforts to secure the establishment of national health insurance during the late 1970s?

Chapter 5 deals with the politics of national health insurance during the Carter administration. It analyzes the national health insurance plans sponsored by Senator Edward M. Kennedy of Massachusetts and President Carter during the late 1970s. It addresses two overriding questions: Why did Kennedy and Carter fail to negotiate agreement on a compromise national health insurance plan both could support? To what extent did other, less visible but no less important, political actors—Carter administration officials and congressional leaders—influence the debate on the program?

Part III discusses the latest campaign to establish national health insurance, which occurred during the 1990s. Chapter 6 analyzes the reasons why the program returned to occupy a prominent place on the national agenda during 1991–1993. Chapter 7 examines the efforts to pass a national health insurance bill in the 102nd Congress. Chapter 8 turns to the national debate on health care reform during 1991–1992. Chapter 9 concludes with an assessment of the long-term prospects for establishing national health insurance during the remainder of the 1990s and through the turn of the twenty-first century.

PART I

The Politics of National Health Insurance during the 1940s

CHAPTER 2

The Power of the AMA, 1945–1950

The American Medical Association is perhaps the strongest trade union in the United States.[1]

Milton Friedman, senior research fellow, the Hoover Institution

Perhaps the best-known aspect of the politics of national health insurance is the campaign the AMA launched against the program during the middle of the century. It first announced its opposition to national health insurance in 1920, five years after the Association for Labor Legislation launched a campaign to secure the establishment of the program.[2] During the 1930s, the AMA successfully thwarted renewed efforts undertaken by influential members of the Roosevelt administration to obtain the adoption of the program.[3]

The AMA confronted its most severe challenge during the 1940s, when Truman actively campaigned for the establishment of national health insurance. From 1945 to 1948, Truman repeatedly failed in his efforts.[4] However, prospects for the establishment of national health insurance received a substantial boost following Truman's stunning upset victory in the 1948 presidential election. Truman had a unique opportunity to use his election as a mandate to secure the adoption of the program.

The AMA responded to Truman's election by launching its National Education Campaign, a public relations drive that successfully mobilized popular opposition to national health insurance.[5] The collapse of public support for the program ended whatever chances existed for its establishment in the wake of Truman's election. In 1950 the program abruptly disappeared from the national agenda. It would not receive serious consideration in Washington again for two decades.[6]

Table 2.1
The Average Cost of a Visit to the Doctor's Office in Selected Advanced Industrial Democracies in 1989 in American Dollars

```
------------------------------------------------------------
United States    31
Switzerland      24
Luxembourg       18
Germany          14
France           13
Belgium          12
Denmark          11
Japan            10
------------------------------------------------------------
```

Source: Michael Wolff, Peter Rutten, and Albert F. Bayers III, Where We Stand: Can America Make It in the Global Race for Wealth, Health, and Happiness? (New York: Bantam Books, 1992), p. 126.

THE AMA'S OPPOSITION TO NATIONAL HEALTH INSURANCE: PRESERVING THE FINANCIAL INTERESTS OF DOCTORS

The AMA opposed national health insurance because it believed that the program would reduce physician incomes, deprive doctors of their professional and entrepreneurial freedoms, and reduce the quality of health care.

Its opposition to national health insurance during the 1940s came at a time when the medical profession was enjoying rising affluence, after suffering the same economic hardships experienced by the rest of the public during the Great Depression. After declining from $5,806 in 1929 to $4,470 in 1940, the mean net physician income rose to $15,262 in 1950.[7]

National health insurance would have threatened the financial interests of the medical profession. By reducing financial barriers impeding public access to health care, the program raises patient utilization of health care, resulting in increasing medical costs, which add to overall inflation. To the extent that health care is financed through the public sector, the program undermines the ability of governments to maintain balanced budgets. No national health insurance program can be fiscally and economically viable without health care cost-containment measures. As a result, the national health insurance programs of virtually all the countries of Western Europe and Canada impose stringent health care budgets, which include tight controls on physician fees and income.[8] This is in sharp contrast to the United States, where, due to the absence of a national health insurance program, the government maintains no effective health care cost-containment measures and doctors are, for the most part, free to charge whatever the market will bear. As a result, physician fees and income in the United States are substantially higher than in every other advanced industrial democracy, with the possible exception of Switzerland, as Tables 2.1 and 2.2 show.

Table 2.2

The Average Net Physician Income in Selected Advanced Industrial Democracies
in 1989 in American Dollars

```
Switzerland     150,322
United States   132,300
Germany          91,244
Canada           76,541
Japan            56,436
France           56,403
Denmark          50,585
Finland          42,943
Britain          40,544
Australia        36,943
Norway           35,356
Belgium          33,776
New Zealand      32,880
Sweden           25,760
Ireland          20,488
Italy            14,192
```

Source: Michael Wolff, Peter Rutten, and Albert F.
Bayers, Where We Stand: Can America Make It in the
Global Race for Wealth, Health, and Happiness? (New
York: Bantam Books, 1992), p. 127.

One could argue that the substantial fees and income American doctors earn are due to the existence of a physician shortage. Because they are in short supply, doctors have the capacity to raise their fees and income higher than would otherwise be the case. International comparative analysis shows that the United States has relatively few doctors, ranking fifteenth in its physician-to-population ratio among the advanced industrial democracies, as Table 2.3 shows. Nevertheless, the physician-to-population ratio in the United States is higher than in Canada, Luxembourg, New Zealand, Britain, Japan, and Ireland. If the significant physician fees and income in the United States were due to the existence of a physician shortage, then American doctors would earn less money than their counterparts in those six nations, which have a greater scarcity of doctors. However, the opposite is the case; Tables 2.1 and 2.2 show that American doctors earn considerably higher fees and incomes than physicians in the six nations. As a result, no discernible correlation exists between the substantial fees and income American doctors earn and the physician supply in the United States.

The substantial fees and income American doctors earn are due not to the existence of a physician shortage but to the absence of national health insurance. The practice of medicine is more lucrative in the United States than in any other advanced industrial democracy, with the possible exception of Switzerland, because this country lacks a national health insurance program that includes stringent health care cost-containment measures and severe controls over physician fees and income. This is in sharp contrast to the other democracies, where national

Table 2.3
Doctors Per 1,000 Residents in Selected Advanced Industrial Democracies in 1989

Italy	4.2
Spain	3.5
Belgium	3.1
Austria	3.0
Greece	2.9
Germany	2.7
Sweden	2.7
Denmark	2.6
Iceland	2.6
France	2.5
Netherlands	2.5
Portugal	2.5
Australia	2.2
Finland	2.2
United States	2.0
Canada	1.9
Luxembourg	1.8
New Zealand	1.7
Britain	1.6
Switzerland	1.6
Japan	1.5
Ireland	1.5

Source: Michael Wolff, Peter Rutten, and Albert F. Bayers III, Where We Stand: Can America Make It in the Global Race for Wealth, Health, and Happiness? (New York: Bantam Books, 1992), p. 118.

health insurance programs combined with health care cost-containment measures have served to restrain the growth of physician fees and income.

The AMA had a rational interest in opposing national health insurance, given the reduction in physician fees and income which would have resulted from the program. Its desire to protect the financial interests of the medical profession was especially strong during the 1940s, given the substantial income gains doctors were making. The AMA's opposition to national health insurance during the 1940s can be explained largely as an attempt to protect those gains.

THE AMA'S OPPOSITION TO NATIONAL HEALTH INSURANCE: PROTECTING THE ENTREPRENEURIAL INDEPENDENCE OF DOCTORS

Though the AMA opposed national health insurance primarily because the program represented a threat to the financial interests of the medical profession, much of its opposition was based on nonfinancial considerations. During the middle of the century, 90 percent of doctors in private practice were AMA members.[9] Consistent with the interests of private medical practitioners, the AMA was committed to preserving the professional and entrepreneurial freedoms of doctors: to practice when they wish, to accept the patients they are willing to take, to provide the services they believe necessary, and to determine their fees and how they are paid. The AMA feared that those freedoms would be threatened by the establishment of a government bureaucracy to administer national health insurance.

As the AMA feared, supporters of national health insurance were determined to impose federal regulation on the health care system. The 1949 version of the Wagner-Murray-Dingell bill, the national health insurance measure introduced by supporters of the program during each session of Congress from 1943 to 1949, would have established a new federal agency, the five-member National Health Insurance Board, to administer the national health insurance program provided for by the measure.[10] Creation of a federal health insurance bureaucracy was a major argument the AMA used against the program during its National Education Campaign. In its best-known publication produced during the campaign, a fifteen-page, question-and-answer pamphlet entitled "The Voluntary Way is the American: Fifty Questions You Want Answered on Compulsory Health Insurance Versus Health—the American Way," the AMA gave perhaps its most succinct summary of why it opposed the program.[11]

Because the Government proposes to: Collect the tax; control the money; determine the services; set the rates; maintain the records; direct both the citizens' and the doctor's participation in the program; assume control not only of the medical profession, but of hospitals—both public and private—the drug and appliance industries, dentistry, pharmacy, nursing, and allied professions; dominate the medical affairs of every citizen— through administrative lines from the central government in Washington—down through State, town, district, and neighborhood bureaus.[12]

THE AMA'S OPPOSITION TO NATIONAL HEALTH INSURANCE: MAINTAINING THE QUALITY OF HEALTH CARE

Of all the arguments against national health insurance made by the AMA, none is more potentially compelling, from a public-interest perspective, than the claim that the program would reduce the quality of health care. It is based upon the fact that by reducing financial barriers impeding public access to health care, the program will lead to a rise in the utilization of medical services, especially among the poor and uninsured. Doctors would presumably be overburdened with heavy patient loads. They would be unable to devote the time and energy necessary to meet the needs of each patient. A decline in the quality of health care would result.

The AMA is unlikely to mobilize much public opposition to national health insurance on the basis of the charge that it would reduce physician fees and income, and threaten the professional and entrepreneurial freedoms of the medical profession. Few lay individuals care about physician income and freedoms. However, almost everyone cares about maintaining high-quality health care. A convincing argument that national health insurance would reduce the quality of health care is likely to elicit substantial public opposition to the program.

True, poor and uninsured individuals who have either little or no access to health care are likely to support national health insurance, no matter how low the quality of medical services might be under the program. Full access to low-quality health care is better than little or no access at all. However, well-insured upper- and middle-class individuals who have full access to health care will be unlikely to support national health insurance if it reduces the quality of medical services. This is apt to be too high a price for them to pay to allow the poor and uninsured access to health care.

The claim that national health insurance would reduce the quality of health care was based upon the British experience. At the turn of the century, representatives of American business, labor, and the insurance industry visited Britain to view its newly established national health insurance program firsthand. They did not like what they saw.

In 1914 a delegation from the National Civic Federation, an interest group representing business and labor, visited Britain. Following the group's return to the United States, its members published a scathing critique of the health care benefits provided under the National Insurance Act. They concluded that the "greatest defect in the operations of the Act is the utter inadequacy and comparative inefficiency of the medical treatment provided." They charged that doctors did little more than "feel the patient's pulse, look at his tongue and prescribe for him some medicine to pour down his stomach." They warned against "any spirit of impatience in America to copy these doubtful experiments."[13]

Following its decision to oppose national health insurance in 1920, the AMA emerged as the major critic of the British program. Beginning in the mid–1920s, the *Journal of the American Medical Association* (*JAMA*) published a regular column on the program, which ran for about fifteen years. It cataloged the alleged waste, inefficiency, and high cost of the program. For two years the column frequently carried a subsection entitled "The Troubles of Medical Socialism."[14]

The AMA stepped up its attacks against Britain's national health insurance program following the establishment of the National Health Service on July 5, 1948.[15] For the AMA, the institution of the National Health Service could not have come at a better time—at the height of the debate over national health insurance in the United States. It seized upon the National Health Service as an example of the low-quality health care that would allegedly exist under national health insurance.

The AMA wasted no time in attacking the National Health Service following its establishment. In 1948 *JAMA* declared that the program was "a severe blow to the standard of medical practice." It charged that doctors were too overburdened with heavy patient loads to provide competent medical care. It concluded that the British government had established "a nationwide health service without hospitals, doctors, nurses, drugs or money to supply what they promised."[16]

During the late 1940s, Walter Martin, a representative of the AMA, and former Governor Harold E. Stassen of Minnesota visited Britain to view the newly established National Health Service firsthand. They returned to the United States with reports that the program had proven to be a dismal failure. In a 1950 report to the AMA's board of trustees, "Medical Care in England Under the National Health Service," Martin argued:

Abuses of the service are evident everywhere, and they must lead to more and more regulations, tighter enforcement, greater penalties for violation, further limitations on freedom and further deterioration of the quality of medicine. In the end the great consumer group will suffer most. Sad as is the state of the practitioner of medicine in Britain, the plight of medicine itself is more serious; but what is most to be deplored is the present and future effect of the quality of medical care received by the English people.[17]

Martin's charge that the National Health Service had resulted in a decline in the quality of health care was supported by Stassen. After completing his tour of Britain, Stassen launched a campaign of scathing attacks against the program, which appeared in three articles published in *Reader's Digest* in January, February, and April 1950. He charged that the program had resulted in a rise in illness and mortality rates. He claimed that elderly individuals were unable to enter the hospital because the beds were filled with chronically ill patients who had been referred there by overworked doctors. "The British program has resulted in more medical care of a lower quality for more people at higher cost," Stassen concluded. "Any plan such as that now advanced by the President to imitate the British program would be a serious failure, resulting in more deaths, more illness, lower-quality health service and a breakdown of the health professions in America."[18]

Gary Land argues that the critique of Britain's national health insurance program made by its opponents during the first half of the century created a negative American public image of national health insurance, which became "indelibly stamped with the characteristics of excessive expense, bureaucratization, and poor quality."[19] During the National Education Campaign, the AMA sought to reinforce this negative stereotype of national health insurance, repeating the familiar charge that it would reduce the quality of health care. The AMA's efforts in this regard were embodied in the most powerful work produced during the campaign. Ironically, this work came from that "notorious" bastion of "socialized medicine"—Britain.

On the north bank of the Thames in London, near the House of Commons, stands the Tate Gallery. Housed in the gallery is a painting, produced during the 1840s by Sir Luke Fildes, entitled "The Doctor." Rashi Fein has perhaps provided the best description of the powerful images etched in that work:

"The Doctor" . . . shows a physician at the bed of a sick child. The hour is late, the room is dark, the only light that of a dim oil lamp. The child sleeps with a fevered brow; the concerned doctor sits beside the child watching, thinking, waiting. The parents are in the background. It is a quiet painting.[20]

In April 1949 Whitaker and Baxter sent the 201,277 doctors in practice that year 1 million copies of a foldout pamphlet entitled "Compulsory Health Insurance—Political Medicine—Is Bad Medicine for America!"[21] It was prominently displayed in the waiting rooms of doctors throughout the United States. The cover of the pamphlet was a color reproduction of "The Doctor."[22] Underneath the painting was the following text:

KEEP POLITICS OUT OF THIS PICTURE
When the life—or health of a loved one is at stake, hope lies in the devoted service of your Doctor. Would you change this picture?
  Compulsory health insurance is political medicine.
  It would bring a third party—a politician—between you and your Doctor. It would bind up your family's health in red tape. It would result in heavy payroll taxes—and inferior medical care for you and your family. Don't let it happen here![23]

During the four decades preceding the National Education Campaign, American critics of Britain's national health insurance program succeeded in giving national health insurance a bad name in the United States through their accounts of the low-quality health care Britons were allegedly receiving. During its National Education Campaign, the AMA acted to bolster public doubts concerning the program that already existed. "Don't let it happen here!" cried the AMA as it warned the public of the alleged dangers of British-style national health insurance. The AMA's case against the program must have struck a responsive chord among the tens of millions of patients sitting in the waiting rooms of their doctors and gazing on that stark Whitaker and Baxter poster warning of the supposed threats to the health care system posed by the program.
    In addition to doctors' offices, the AMA saturated the print media and airwaves with an avalanche of advertisements opposing compulsory health insurance during the National Education Campaign. During the media blitz of October 8–22, 1950, the AMA spent $1,110,000 on advertising opposing the program, which totaled 1,186,594 inches of print space. AMA advertisements appeared in 10,033 newspapers with a combined circulation of 115,630,487 and in 35 magazines with a combined circulation of 55,202,080. In addition, the AMA broadcast messages opposing national health insurance on 1,600 radio stations, with a combined audience of 108,205,034.[24]
    Given the massive scope of the National Education Campaign, only a small minority of the public could have escaped exposure to the AMA's opposition to compulsory health insurance. The overwhelming majority of the public found the AMA's case compelling. The National Education Campaign had a powerful effect in turning public opinion against compulsory health insurance. Among

those who knew of Truman's support for national health insurance, backing for it plunged from 58 percent in 1945 to 36 percent in 1949. Three-quarters of those who knew of Truman's support for national health insurance were also aware of the AMA's opposition to the program.[25]

With the collapse of public support for national health insurance during the late 1940s, all hopes for its establishment rapidly disappeared. The AMA's success in turning public opinion against national health insurance was due to the interest group's ability to drive home the one potentially credible argument critics have used against the program: that it would reduce the quality of health care.

NATIONAL HEALTH INSURANCE AND THE QUALITY OF HEALTH CARE

The argument that national health insurance reduces the quality of health care— so prominently made by the AMA during its National Education Campaign—is based upon the assumption that the program would lead to a substantial rise in patient utilization of medical services, especially among the poor and uninsured, thereby overburdening doctors with unmanageable patient loads. However, this did not occur in Quebec, which established its compulsory health insurance program on November 1, 1970.[26] The data show that there was no overall increase in visits to doctors in the Montreal metropolitan area from 1962 to 1972. True, visits rose by 18.2 percent among families with annual incomes of $3,000 or under and 9.1 percent among households making from $3,000 to $4,999. However, visits declined by 3.9 percent among families earning from $9,000 to $14,999 and by 9.4 percent among households making $15,000 or over. There was no change in visits among families earning from $5,000 to $8,999.

Quebec's compulsory health insurance program substantially reduced financial barriers impeding public access to health care among the lower class. This allowed them to increase their visits to the doctor. However, this increase was offset by a reduction in access to health care among the middle and upper classes. Because the middle and upper classes now had to compete with the lower class for access to physician services, waiting times for appointments increased. Discouraged by longer waiting times, many middle- and upper-class individuals paid fewer visits to the doctor. Under Quebec's compulsory health insurance program, access to health care was redistributed from the middle and upper classes to the lower class, with little or no overall increase in the utilization of physician services.[27] Theodore R. Marmor concludes:

On the basis of Canada's experience, we should expect relatively modest changes in the overall utilization of hospitals and physicians. The fears that "cheap" care will foster runaway utilization thus appear unrealistic; they ignore the impact of pre-existent health insurance, the barriers to care that financing will not change, and the rationing that doctors will impose. The Canadian experiment contradicts projections of sharply increased use (or crowded offices) based on estimates of the elasticity of demand for medical care in the United States.[28]

The Quebec experience suggests that the AMA's most potentially compelling argument against national health insurance—that it would reduce the quality of health care—was false. American doctors would not have been overburdened with unmanageable patient loads, since the evidence from Quebec indicates that the program does not lead to excessive patient utilization of health care. If the AMA succeeded in turning public opinion against national health insurance during the 1940s on the basis of the charge that it would reduce the quality of health care, then this is most unfortunate. It suggests that the public was swayed by an unproven argument, emotionally exhibited on a poster displayed in doctors' offices, rather than by sound and reasoned judgment.

THE POLITICAL RESOURCES OF THE AMA

The AMA had four kinds of political resources it used to defeat national health insurance during the 1940s: it served as the authentic and legitimate representative of the medical profession, and it had a socially respected and economically powerful membership, substantial financial resources, and a solid network of alliances with other interest groups. During the 1940s, the AMA was the true and genuine "voice of American medicine."[29] This resulted from the fact that an overwhelming proportion of doctors were AMA members. That was true of over two-thirds of all doctors during 1947–1949.[30] Given the fact that an overwhelming majority of doctors were AMA members, the interest group could legitimately claim that its opposition to national health insurance was representative of physician opinion on the program.[31] This provided substantial credibility to the AMA's opposition to the program.

The AMA benefited from the fact that doctors had social status. A 1947 poll conducted by the National Opinion Research Center found that the medical profession and governors were tied for second place in occupational prestige, behind only the justices of the Supreme Court.[32] In 1953 the Gallup Poll found that the medical profession ranked first among the careers the public would recommend to young men. Twenty-nine percent of those polled said they would recommend that young men pursue careers in medicine.[33] Given the prestige and status of its members, the AMA's pronouncements on health care policy were likely to find a sympathetic audience on Capitol Hill and among the public.

The AMA also benefited from the possession of substantial financial resources and a powerful network of interest-group allies. With physician income tripling during the 1940s, AMA members had significant funds to provide the interest group in support of its campaign against national health insurance. The AMA took full advantage of the medical profession's newfound affluence by tapping into the financial resources of its wealthy membership to finance its National Education Campaign. Without the unprecedented post-Depression affluence the medical profession enjoyed during the 1940s, the AMA would have lacked the funds to finance the campaign. And without the campaign, it is questionable whether it could have successfully mobilized public and congressional opposition to national health insurance during the late 1940s.

The AMA could not have mounted a successful campaign against national health insurance alone. It needed allies. Perhaps the most valuable asset the AMA possessed was its powerful network of interest-group allies, composed of business and other conservative organizations, which it developed during the National Education Campaign. A total of 65,246 firms contributed $2,019,849 million to finance the October 1950 advertising campaign against national health insurance sponsored by the AMA.[34] In addition 9,829 interest groups signed resolutions, introduced by the AMA, opposing the program during the National Education Campaign.[35]

The AMA succeeded in securing support for its opposition to national health insurance among business and other conservative interest groups on ideological grounds. A key tactic of the National Education Campaign was to link national health insurance with "socialized medicine." Consider the following excerpt from "The Voluntary Way Is the American Way":

Would socialized medicine lead to socialization of other phases of American life?

Lenin thought so. He declared: "Socialized medicine is the key-stone to the arch of the socialist state."

Today, much of the world has launched out on that road. If the medical profession should be socialized, because people need doctors, why not the milk industry? Certainly, more people need milk every day than need doctors. On the same erroneous premise, why not the corner grocery? Adequate diet is the very basis of good health. Why not nationalize lawyers, miners, businessmen, farmers? Germany did, Russia did, England is in the process.[36]

As this excerpt shows, the AMA publicly regarded national health insurance as the opening wedge in the nationalization of other industries. This charge represented a scare tactic designed to exploit anticommunist sentiments that existed during the early years of the Cold War. The AMA had two reasons for doing this. First, by linking national health insurance not only to "socialized medicine" in particular but also to socialism in general, it intended to mobilize opposition to the program among the overwhelming majority of the public and members of Congress who were anticommunist.[37] Second, by warning that national health insurance would be followed by the nationalization of other industries, the AMA sought to win corporate support for organized medicine's opposition to the program, on the premise that its establishment would threaten the survival of private enterprise.

The AMA's linkage of national health insurance to "socialized medicine" was effective, at least insofar as business and other conservative interest groups were concerned. This linkage was largely responsible for its success in eliciting support for its opposition to the program among those groups.

In addition to ideological considerations, the business community had economic reasons to oppose national health insurance. The Murray-Wagner-Dingell bill would have imposed a three percent payroll tax on wages of up to $4,800 to finance the national health insurance program provided for by the measure.[38] As health care costs rose, so would have the payroll tax. As a result, the payroll tax provided for under the Murray-Wagner-Dingell bill would have dramatically raised business expenses.

True, most firms already bear a substantial share of the financial burden for health care through the group health insurance plans they provide their working families. The premiums they pay for those plans are functionally equivalent to the payroll taxes which they would have had to pay under the Wagner-Murray-Dingell bill. However, firms have the freedom to determine the scope of the coverage they provide their working families and the amount they must pay for their group health insurance plans. To control their health care costs, firms need only reduce the coverage they provide.

Under the Murray-Wagner-Dingell bill, business would have been required to pay payroll taxes for a package of federally-mandated health care benefits which most of the public would have received and would have been deprived of the right to alter those benefits to reduce their health care costs. To insulate themselves from having to bear health care costs beyond what they were willing to accept, tens of thousands of firms supported the AMA in its opposition to national health insurance.

The AMA's success in building alliances with so many interest groups, especially within the business community, was a major factor in its success in defeating national health insurance. With tens of thousands of interest groups and firms joining the AMA in its opposition to national health insurance, it would have been impossible for Congress to establish the program without alienating large numbers of important constituencies, in addition to the medical profession.

PROSPECTS FOR A PHYSICIAN BOYCOTT OF COMPULSORY HEALTH INSURANCE

Perhaps the most important political resource the AMA had to defeat national health insurance is the economic power of the medical profession, based upon the critical lifesaving and life-enhancing functions doctors perform. By withholding their services, they can inflict enormous damage upon society. The fact that doctors are well organized gave the AMA the ability to launch a boycott of any national health insurance program that might have been established.

Prospects of a physician boycott of national health insurance were very real. Consider the American Association of Physicians and Surgeons (AAPS), an interest group representing a substantial segment of the medical profession. In 1946, AAPS representatives sent Truman a letter informing him that the constitution and bylaws of the interest group made it "impossible for its members to service any compulsory local, State, or Federal health insurance program."[39]

Surgeon General Thomas Parran interpreted the AAPS letter as a "notice of noncooperation—indeed of boycott—on the people of the United States in the event they should decide to adopt any compulsory [health insurance] plan through governments by the processes of democracy."[40]

In 1965 organized medicine renewed its threat to boycott any compulsory health insurance program that might be established during Congress's consideration of Medicare. In May 1965 the Ohio State Medical Association passed a resolution urging its 10,000 members to boycott the program. The Ohio action was followed by an effort to launch a nationwide physician boycott of the program, undertaken by the AAPS. It sent a letter to each doctor in the United States declaring that "now is the time for you and every other ethical physician in the United States to individually and voluntarily pledge nonparticipation in . . . the socialized hospitalization and medical care program for the aged."[41] The AAPS urged doctors to refuse to treat Medicare patients.[42]

The AAPS's support for a physician boycott of Medicare could not be ignored. In 1965 the AAPS had 50,000 members, a quarter of the 200,000 doctors who belonged to the AMA that year.[43] Since many, if not most, AAPS members were also AMA members, the AAPS could exert pressure on the AMA to follow its lead in calling for a boycott.

At the AMA's annual session in Chicago on July 4, 1965, nine state delegations introduced resolutions calling for a physician boycott of Medicare. The 1965 race for the AMA presidency pitted Charles L. Hudson, who opposed a boycott, against Representative Durward G. Hall of Missouri, who favored it. Fearing that a boycott would tarnish the public image of the medical profession, the AMA's board of trustees gathered enough votes to elect Hudson.[44] He proceeded to urge "doctors to make the most of the new program," ending threats of a boycott.[45]

CONCLUSION

During the 1940s, the United States experienced a serious and extensive debate on national health insurance. No one group did more to influence the outcome of that debate than the AMA. It had the good fortune of being at the peak of its political power. Over two-thirds of all doctors were AMA members, allowing the interest group to represent itself as the true and authentic "voice of American medicine." The newfound affluence of the medical profession allowed the AMA to secure the financial resources to effectively get its message against national health insurance across to the public.

The AMA tailored its arguments against national health insurance to secure the widest possible outside support. To secure public support for its position, it charged that the program would reduce the quality of health care—a claim, however dubious, that no individual could ignore. To obtain backing for its position from business and other conservative interest groups, it warned that the program represented the opening wedge for the eventual nationalization of other industries—a possibility, however remote, that no business or other conservative group could dismiss.

In the end, the AMA succeeded in preventing the establishment of national health insurance by winning support for its position from a majority of the public and tens of thousands of interest groups and firms. Support for national health insurance among the informed public—those who were aware of both Truman's program and the AMA's opposition to it—declined substantially during the late 1940s. During the National Education Campaign, the AMA's opposition to the program won the support of perhaps the most extensive network of organized constituencies assembled in the history of interest-group politics. The debate on national health insurance during the 1940s shows that an interest group with substantial financial resources, strong public support, and a powerful network of organizational alliances can prevail in its opposition to the president on a domestic policy issue of vital concern to the group's members.

CHAPTER 3

The Development of Private Health Insurance, 1945–1950

The defeat of national health insurance meant that health insurance in America would be predominantly private.[1]

Paul Starr, sociologist, Princeton University

AMA opposition alone cannot explain the defeat of national health insurance during the 1940s. Rather, the most important reason why Congress did not establish national health insurance was the development of private plans, which experienced rapid growth during the decade. With a rapidly rising share of the public enrolling in private plans, practically all members of Congress saw no urgent and compelling public need for a government program. As a result, congressional support for national health insurance was almost nonexistent. The Wagner-Murray-Dingell bill was cosponsored by only eight senators and three representatives in the Eighty-first Congress.[2]

The extensive development of private health insurance remains the major reason why the United States has no government program. With 65 percent of the population privately insured as of March 1991, a majority of both the public and members of Congress have seen no immediate and overriding need for a government program.[3] As late as 1990, only a small fraction of the public considered health care to be an important issue, as we will see in Chapter 6. Public and congressional interest in the need for national health insurance did not begin to take hold until 1991, for reasons that will be discussed in that chapter.

THE AMA PROMOTES THE DEVELOPMENT OF PRIVATE HEALTH INSURANCE

On November 19, 1945, the AMA confronted a serious challenge to its power as a result of two developments. First, President Truman sent a message to Congress that recommended national health insurance.[4] Second, Senators Robert Wagner of New York and James Murray of Montana and Representative John Dingell of Michigan jointly introduced a bill to implement Truman's proposal.[5]

Truman's decision to place the power and prestige of his presidency behind congressional efforts to establish national health insurance created new opportunities for its adoption. Accordingly, the AMA acted quickly to deprive Congress of an urgent and compelling public need to institute the program. It did so by actively promoting the development of private insurance.

The distinct advantage the AMA had in its campaign to prevent national health insurance was the softness of public support for the program, revealed in polling data taken during the 1940s. They showed the public evenly divided in their preference between public and private insurance.

In 1945 the Opinion Research Corporation asked a representative sample of the public whether they preferred to receive their health insurance through Social Security or employers. Thirty-five percent chose Social Security, 31 percent employers, 17 percent did not care, and 17 percent had no opinion.[6] The softness of public support for national health insurance gave the AMA an opening to act. Two-thirds of the public either favored private over public insurance or did not care which alternative was developed. As a result, private insurance could be used to preempt a government program. If most of the public was covered by private insurance, then popular support for a government program, soft as it was, would dissipate, if not vanish. Congress would no longer see any immediate and persuasive public need for national health insurance.

The AMA wasted no time in responding to Truman's recommendation that Congress establish a national health insurance program. At its session in December 1945, the AMA's House of Delegates unveiled its strategy of using private health insurance as a means to defuse public and congressional support for a government program.[7] It ordered the board of trustees and the Council on Medical Service to "proceed as promptly as possible with the development of a national health program with emphasis on the nationwide organization of locally administered prepayment medical plans sponsored by medical societies."[8] It also urged Congress to withhold any action on the Wagner-Murray-Dingell bill, since national health insurance was no longer necessary now that the AMA was committed to promoting the development of private plans. "Voluntary prepayment medical plans now in operation in many parts of the United States and which are rapidly increasing in number will accomplish all the objects of this bill with far less expense to the people and under these plans the public will receive the highest type of service."[9]

Pursuant to the AMA's House of Delegates' order, on February 14, 1946, the board of trustees approved a ten-point national health program.[10] The most important principle was the sixth point, which committed the AMA to approve all private health insurance plans "acceptable" to the Council on Medical Service and the state medical societies where the plans operate. The council was assigned the responsibility to formulate standards that would govern the development of physician service insurance plans, known as Blue Shield.[11] Blue Shield served as a supplement to the hospital insurance plans, known as Blue Cross, that developed during the 1930s and 1940s under the organization and sponsorship of the AHA.[12]

By committing itself to support all "acceptable" private health insurance plans and adopting standards governing the operation of Blue Shield, the AMA pledged to back the plans' full development. This paved the way for the expansion of private insurance, depriving Congress of an urgent and compelling public need to establish a government program. Individuals were now assured that they could enroll in private plans, especially for physician services, with the certainty that their doctors would accept reimbursement from voluntary insurance. This provided individuals the incentive they needed to join private plans.

From 1945 to 1948, the share of the public covered for hospital care rose from 24 to 40 percent; for surgical care, from 9 to 23 percent; and for physician services performed in the hospital, from 3 to 9 percent.[13] The expansion in private health insurance was largely the result of a rise in Blue Cross and Blue Shield enrollments. From 1944 to 1948, Blue Cross enrollments increased from 15,748,000 to 30,448,000 and Blue Shield enrollments from 1,768,000 to 8,399,000.[14]

THE NATIONAL EDUCATION CAMPAIGN AND PRIVATE HEALTH INSURANCE

The AMA's support for private health insurance did not end with its decision in 1945–1946 to approve all "acceptable" private plans and promote the development of Blue Shield. Following Truman's stunning upset victory in the 1948 presidential election, the AMA stepped up its support for private insurance through its National Education Campaign. The primary objective of the campaign was to take the AMA's case against national health insurance directly to the public.

However, Whitaker and Baxter recognized that the AMA could not win public support for its case simply on the merits of its arguments. Rather, it had to offer the public an alternative to national health insurance, which remained private plans. As Clem Whitaker, a partner in Whitaker and Baxter, stressed at the outset of the National Education Campaign, "We will offer a positive program because we realize that you can't beat something with nothing."[15]

Whitaker and Baxter devoted a large part of the National Education Campaign to extolling the virtues of private health insurance as a preferable alternative to a government program. A major objective of the campaign was to urge the majority of the population who remained uninsured in 1948 to enroll in private plans. The AMA knew that if more individuals did so, Truman's hopes of securing the establishment of national health insurance would be dashed.

One of the key arguments made by the AMA in urging more individuals to insure themselves was that private plans were affordable, especially in relation to a government program. This was a major theme of "The Voluntary Way Is the American Way."

If a family can afford a daily pack of cigarettes or a Saturday night movie, that family can afford to buy voluntary health insurance. The monthly cost is about the same. If the family cannot afford this protection it certainly cannot afford to have another tax—at least twice as high as a voluntary health insurance premium—deducted from its income.[16]

The AMA left no stone unturned. The caption placed underneath its reproduction of "The Doctor"—the poster prominently displayed in the waiting rooms of doctors during the National Education Campaign—closed with the following message: "You have a right to prepaid medical care—of your own choice. Ask your Doctor, or your insurance man, about budget-basis health protection."[17]

The AMA spent substantial sums to finance the National Education Campaign. By making the promotion of private health insurance a major element of the campaign, the AMA contributed significantly to stimulating the expansion of private insurance enrollments during the late 1940s and early 1950s. From 1948 to 1950, the share of the public covered for hospital care rose from 40 to 51 percent; for surgical care, from 23 to 36 percent; and for physician services performed in the hospital, from 9 to 14 percent.[18]

As in the past, the expansion of private health insurance was led by a rise in Blue Cross and Blue Shield enrollments. From 1948 to 1950, Blue Cross enrollments increased from 30,448,000 to 37,435,000 and Blue Shield enrollments from 8,399,000 to 16,054,000.[19] The expansion of private insurance during the late 1940s and early 1950s ended any chances that Truman might establish a government program.

By 1950, the bitter and contentious national debate over what kind of health insurance system should be developed came to an end. The United States would forgo national health insurance in favor of private plans. This decision came in October 1950, as the AMA mounted its final drive to defeat national health insurance by undertaking its massive, multimillion dollar, corporate-sponsored advertising campaign against the program. The use of private insurance as a politically acceptable alternative to a government program has been the defining element of health care policy since 1950.

THE AMA AND HEALTH INSURANCE

The defining element of the AMA's policy toward health insurance during the 1940s was its strong opposition to a government program and its equally staunch support for private plans. The AMA had good reason for this position.

National health insurance reduces financial barriers impeding public access to health care, resulting in an increase in patient utilization of medical services and driving up their costs. As a result, the government must rigidly contain health care costs, including physician expenses. To do this, the government must control the fees and incomes of health care providers, including doctors.

True, health care providers may choose to boycott national health insurance by refusing to accept reimbursement from the government. However, most, if not practically all, individuals would be publicly insured under national health insurance. Those individuals will not see any health care provider who refuses to accept government reimbursement. Few individuals have the financial means either to purchase private insurance or to pay for their health care out of pocket. As a result, individuals will go only to health care providers who accept reimbursement from the government under national health insurance. Accordingly, health care providers who refuse such payments would lose practically all their patients and income. They would have no choice but to accept government reimbursements, regardless of how inadequate they might be.

By contrast, the private health insurance system consists of a diverse and fragmented maze of competing voluntary plans. To remain competitive in the private insurance market, voluntary plans must guarantee their subscribers the widest possible choice of health care providers and access to all needed medical services. Health care providers are unlikely to accept reimbursement under any private plan which rigidly contains medical costs, since such action would result in restrictions on the delivery of medical services and a reduction in provider rates, fees, and income.

As a result, private plans which stringently contain health care costs will deprive their subscribers of access to the health care providers and medical services they will want. Few individuals would be willing to enroll in such private plans, which would force them out of business. To remain competitive in the private insurance market, voluntary plans must attract a large number of subscribers. To do so, they must be willing to give those subscribers the widest possible choice of health care providers by agreeing to reimburse them generously without restricting their services.

As a result, doctors stand to lose financially under national health insurance, due to the stringent controls on health care costs the government would impose under the program. By contrast, doctors stand to gain financially under private insurance, since voluntary plans are willing to reimburse physicians whatever the market will bear. The international comparative data presented in Chapter 2 show that doctors have fared better financially under America's mostly private insurance system than they have under the government-sponsored insurance plans in Western Europe, Canada, and Japan. Accordingly, the AMA remained adamantly opposed to national health insurance during the 1940s, insisting on the development of private plans as an alternative.

THE DEVELOPMENT OF GROUP HEALTH INSURANCE

AMA support was not the only reason why private health insurance experienced rapid growth during the 1940s. Perhaps an even more important reason for this was the backing that group insurance—employment-based private plans—received from employers and the federal government. Group plans represent the foundation of the insurance system. In March 1991, 57.1 percent of all individuals were covered by group insurance.[20]

Group health insurance originated during World War II. From 1942 to 1946, the federal government strictly enforced wage and price controls. While imposing a freeze on wage increases, it allowed a growth in fringe benefits equal to 5 percent of wages. To compensate for their inability to raise wages, employers provided working families with group insurance, which quickly became an employee's most valuable fringe benefit.[21]

In 1943 the Internal Revenue Service ruled that all employer contributions to group health insurance plans are fully deductible as business expenses from the taxable income of corporations. This ruling was formally codified into law in the Internal Revenue Code of 1954.[22] By promising that the federal government would provide tax subsidies for employer contributions to group insurance, the IRS gave firms a financial incentive to provide their working families with group coverage. Many did so, which resulted in an expansion of group insurance.

From 1940 to 1950, the number of individuals enrolled in group plans who were covered for hospital care rose from 2.5 million to 22,305,000, and for surgical care from 1,430,000 to 21,219,000.[23] By 1950, 48.7 percent of all salaried workers were covered for hospital care. In addition to hospital insurance, 35.5 percent of all salaried workers were covered for surgical care and 16.4 percent for physician services performed in the hospital that year.[24]

THE BENEFITS AND INEQUITIES OF GROUP HEALTH INSURANCE

Group health insurance has both benefits and inequities. The major benefit of group insurance is that most of its cost is financed by employers. In 1989, 69 percent of the cost of group insurance was funded by employers.[25]

Because of substantial employer financing, group health insurance is a relatively inexpensive means for working families to secure coverage. Only affluent working families can afford to purchase their own private insurance. By providing working families access to employer-financed insurance, group plans have permitted the widespread diffusion of coverage throughout the population. In the

Table 3.1
**Percentage of Firms Providing and Working Families Receiving Group Health
Insurance in 1989**

Number of Employees in Firms	Percentage of Firms Providing Group Health Health Insurance	Percentage of Working Families Receiving Group Health Insurance
Less Than 10	33	42
10 to 24	72	70
25 to 99	94	94
100 to 499	99	97
500 to 999	100	100
1,000 or Over	100	100
Total	43	77

Source: Louis Uchitelle, "Insurance Linked to Jobs:
System Showing Its Age," The New York Times, May 1,
1991, p. A14.

absence of group plans, the number of uninsured individuals would probably be
very high—far more than it currently is.

The major inequity of group insurance is that its provision is purely voluntary.
An employer is free not to provide group insurance, and many choose not to.

Table 3.1 shows that practically all medium-size companies and virtually all
large corporations provide their working families with group health insurance.
As a result, nearly all working families employed in medium-sized companies
and every employed household working in big business have group insurance.
By contrast, a substantial share of small businesses do not provide their working
families with group insurance. Accordingly, a significant share of working families with no group insurance are employed in small business.

Practically all firms are small; 87 percent employed fewer than twenty workers
in 1989.[26] As a result, because many, if not most, working families employed
in small business do not have group insurance, only 77 percent of all employed
households are covered by group plans, as Table 3.1 shows.

Why do most small businesses fail to provide group health insurance to their
working families, while virtually every large corporation and practically all
medium-size companies do so? There are two reasons. First, it is much more
expensive to insure small groups than large ones. A 1991 study by the Urban
institute found that firms employing fewer than twenty-five workers must pay
16.7 percent more for comparable group insurance than corporations employing
1,000 or more workers.

Small businesses must pay more for health insurance than large and medium-
size companies do because of the way health care costs are distributed within
groups. They are spread among all members of each group and are financed by
the members' contributions.

Because they have a large number of members, large groups have significant resources to finance their health care costs, including catastrophic medical expenses. Given the availability of substantial financial resources, the rise in insurance premiums of large groups can be constrained, regardless of how many of its members suffer catastrophic illnesses or injuries. As a result, virtually every large corporation and practically all medium-size businesses can afford to provide their working families with group plans.

By contrast, because they have relatively few members, small groups lack adequate financing for their health care costs, especially catastrophic medical expenses. Given the limited availability of resources, small groups have difficulty paying for the cost of treatment of a catastrophic illness or injury suffered by even one member. Every time a catastrophic illness or injury strikes a member of a small group, its insurance premium must be raised substantially in order to fund the costs of treatment. Unable to afford the high cost of insurance, most small businesses find themselves incapable of providing their working families with group plans.

A second reason why small business must pay more for group health insurance than large and medium-size companies results from the existence of substantial wage differences between the two groups. Firms often finance group insurance by reducing the wages of their workers. Wages in small businesses are substantially lower than in large and medium-size companies. The Urban Institute study cited earlier found that firms employing fewer than twenty-five workers paid them 41.9 percent less than corporations employing 1,000 or more workers. High wages provide large and medium-size companies substantial discretionary income they use to provide their working families group insurance.[27] Low wages deprive many small businesses of the discretionary income to do the same. As a result, many, if not most, working families employed in small business must go without group insurance.

Another serious inequity of group health insurance coverage is that its benefits are directed mostly to affluent, rather than middle- and low-income, families. In 1987, 66 percent of working families earning weekly incomes under $250 and 26.6 percent making from $250 to $499 were not covered by group health insurance, compared with only 7.3 percent earning $600 or more.[28]

Because they generally have low incomes, most working families not covered by group health insurance cannot afford to purchase private health insurance. They have no alternative but to be uninsured. In 1987, 61.2 percent of working families without group coverage were uninsured.[29]

CONCLUSION

The development of private health insurance occurred as a result of two major factors: the provision of federal tax subsidies for employer contributions to group plans and the extension of coverage to most working families by employers. In addition, the expansion of private insurance was accelerated by the AMA, which promoted the enlargement of voluntary plans in general, and of Blue Shield in particular, in a successful effort to defuse public and congressional support for Truman's efforts to establish a government program.

Private health insurance has had the political and financial support of virtually every major organization involved in the provision and financing of health care: the AMA, AHA, hospitals, state and county medical societies, employers, and the federal government. Moreover, it has had substantial public support. An overwhelming majority of the public is satisfied with the capacity of the insurance system to meet their health care needs. A 1982 poll conducted by Yankelovich and White found that 88 percent of the respondents were satisfied with the quality of the services they received from their doctors, 81 percent with the quality of care from their hospitals, and another 81 percent with their access to health care. An additional 81 percent were either very or somewhat satisfied with their coverage.[30] Public satisfaction with coverage has continued since the 1980s. A 1991 Roper poll found that 81 percent of the respondents remained satisfied with their coverage.[31]

Since its development during the 1940s, private health insurance has assumed an increasingly dominant role in the financing of health care. The share of the cost of health care funded by private insurance rose from 8.5 percent in 1950 to 32.5 percent in 1990.[32] This reflects the fact that employers have greatly expanded group coverage over the years to take advantage of the federal tax subsidies available. Employer/employee contributions to group insurance rose from 0.61 percent of payroll in 1950 to 13.6 percent in 1990.[33] As employer contributions to group insurance have risen, so has the amount of federal tax subsidies for group plans, which increased from $2.4 billion in 1970 to $39 billion in 1992.[34]

True, private, and especially group, health insurance is plagued by major inequities. Coverage goes mainly to affluent families employed by either government or big business. Low-income families employed by small business usually receive no coverage. Nevertheless, most upper- and middle-class, and many low-income working, families receive group health insurance coverage. As long as this remains the case, the public is likely to be satisfied with performance of the insurance system in meeting their personal health care needs.

However, while the public may be satisfied with the performance of the health insurance system in meeting their own personal needs, they cannot completely depend upon their coverage. Since most of the insured public receive their benefits through their employers, they are almost certain to lose their coverage if they lose their jobs. This is of special concern, given the high unemployment rate and loss of job security which has characterized the economy of the 1990s. As a result, public support for health care reform has risen to an all-time high, while popular backing for the medical system in the United States is lower than that for practically every other advanced industrial democracy.

PART II

The Politics of National Health Insurance during the 1970s

CHAPTER 4

The Battle over the Hospital Cost Containment Act, 1977–1979

> The hospital lobby defeated hospital cost containment legislation last year.
> . . . That lobby opposing this legislation is even more determined this year,
> and it's equally well financed. But this year, we have a new Congress and
> a new opportunity to bring the outrageous increases in hospital costs under
> control.
>
> The patience of the American people is wearing thin, and rightly so. It's
> time for the public interest to prevail. It's time for the Congress to dem-
> onstrate its commitment to the battle against inflation by promptly enacting
> the hospital cost containment [Act] of 1979.[1]
>
> President Jimmy Carter, March 6, 1979

During the 1970s, national health insurance returned to a prominent place on
the political agenda. From 1970 to 1979, national health insurance bills were
sponsored by a number of political leaders and interest groups, including Kennedy, Nixon, Carter, House Ways and Means Committee Chairman Wilbur
Mills, the AHA, the Health Insurance Association of American (HIAA), and
Chamber of Commerce.[2] Even the AMA had reversed its longstanding opposition
to national health insurance and sponsored a bill of its own. However, the AMA
was adamantly opposed to the imposition of health care cost-containment measures, required to assure the economic and fiscal viability of national health
insurance, as we will see.

National health insurance enjoyed widespread congressional support during
the 1970s, with the introduction of national health insurance bills in Congress.
By May 1971, thirteen bills had been presented in the Ninety-second Congress.
By July 1974, twenty-two bills had been submitted in the Ninety-third Congress.[3]
In 1976 there were 125 congressional cosponsors of twenty-one national health
insurance bills.[4]

However, despite widespread support in the White House, Congress, and among major interest groups, lawmakers took no action on national health insurance during the 1970s. A major reason why was the development of the insurance system, which was fully completed in 1965. The system consisted of three programs: private insurance for full-time working families, Medicare for the elderly and (since 1972) the disabled, and Medicaid for the poor. As a result, 87 percent of the public was insured by 1979.[5] Given the fact that the overwhelming majority of the public was insured during the 1970s, the population, on the whole, saw no urgent and compelling need for a government program. As a result, public support for national health insurance remained weak.

Polling data show that public support for national health insurance remained essentially unchanged between the 1940s and 1970s—the two decades in which the program assumed a prominent place on the political agenda. The average share of respondents backing public insurance rose from 40 percent during 1944–1949 to 44 percent during 1972–1976. The share supporting private insurance remained 42 percent.[6]

However, the failure of Congress to take any action on national health insurance during the 1970s cannot be attributed solely to the development of the insurance system and the lack of strong support for the program. An even more important reason why national health insurance went nowhere was the cost of health care, which has soared since the establishment of Medicare and Medicaid, rising from 5.9 percent of GNP in 1965 to 14 percent in 1992.[7] Per capita health care spending increased from $205 in 1965 to $3,160 during the same period.[8]

The health care cost crisis complicated efforts to establish national health insurance during the 1970s for two reasons. First, by raising patient utilization of health care, especially among the poor and uninsured, the program threatened to drive up health care costs even further, adding to inflation. Second, to the extent that public insurance coverage would have been expanded, the program promised to boost the federal deficit.

The political, economic, and fiscal viability of national health insurance during the 1970s required health care cost containment measures. This was necessary to assure that the program would not substantially add to inflation and the deficit. However, despite the best efforts of some sponsors of national health insurance, none succeeded in securing the establishment of health care cost-containment measures. In the absence of such measures, no national health insurance program was possible, since it would be too costly and inflationary to implement.

REASONS FOR THE HEALTH CARE COST CRISIS

The health care cost crisis is largely due to three factors: the existence of a health insurance system that provides an overwhelming majority of the public coverage, the proliferation of advanced and expensive medical technology, and the aging of the population. The existence of an insurance system has largely insulated the public from the soaring cost of health care, 75 percent of which was financed by third-party payers in 1990.[9] This has allowed the majority of the public who are well insured to secure access to all needed health care, regardless of how costly or of how marginal the value. This has resulted in a substantial patient utilization of health care, driving up its cost.[10]

The proliferation of advanced and expensive medical technology has also been a major factor driving up health care costs.[11] The per capita amount more the United States spent on hospital care than Britain rose from $67.02 in 1960 (in 1978 dollars) to $153.57 in 1978. Henry J. Aaron and William B. Schwartz calculate that 49 percent of this difference was due to higher American utilization of eight medical technologies.[12] As the rapid development of medical technology continues, and even accelerates, the health care cost crisis is certain to worsen.[13]

The aging of the population is perhaps the most important reason for the health care cost crisis.[14] The elderly utilize a substantially larger amount of health care than the nonelderly do. As a result, their health care costs are significantly higher than they are for the nonelderly. In 1987 per capita health care spending was $5,360 for individuals aged sixty-five years or more, compared with $1,535 for persons from nineteen to sixty-four years old.[15] In 1980–1981, the elderly represented 11 percent of the population but accounted for 33 percent of all health care spending.[16]

The population will age rapidly during the first quarter of the twenty-first century when the baby-boom generation becomes elderly. It is estimated that the elderly will represent 19 percent of the population in 2030, when all surviving baby-boomers will be senior citizens.[17] As the aging of the population continues into the first quarter of the next century, the health care cost crisis is sure to become more severe.[18]

JIMMY CARTER AND HEALTH CARE COST CONTAINMENT

During the 1976 presidential campaign, Carter had promised to secure the establishment of national health insurance, if elected—but only on an economically and fiscally viable basis.[19] Consistent with his promise, Carter believed that it was necessary to contain health care costs before any national health insurance program could be established. Carter delayed recommendation of a national health insurance program until June 12, 1979—nearly two and a half years into his presidency.

The delay was intentional. Carter wanted to impose health care cost-containment measures before proceeding with the establishment of a national health insurance program. His efforts to institute such measures came through his recommendation of the Hospital Cost Containment Act, which was introduced in each Congress during his presidency. However, his efforts went nowhere. His two-and-a-half-year battle to secure passage of the Hospital Cost Containment Act ended in defeat when the House rejected the bill at the close of 1979.

The most urgent priority on Carter's health care policy agenda was not national health insurance but medical cost containment. His determination to withhold recommendation of national health insurance until the imposition of health care cost-containment measures was supported by members of his administration. As one of Carter's domestic policy advisers explained,

Most of us recognized that health insurance wouldn't make it. The money just wasn't available; the costs were astronomical. Hell, we couldn't even get a fix on the exact dollar estimates. Instead of going ahead with national health insurance, we decided to opt for cost containment. We felt that cost containment had to come first—the government couldn't undertake financing for health insurance if the costs continued to rise at 14 percent per year.[20]

Carter intended to use health care cost containment as a means to establish a fiscally and economically viable basis for instituting national health insurance. As one of Carter's health care policy advisers remarked, "We kept looking at the plans and calculating the costs. The costs kept rising, but the potential revenues kept falling. We felt we had to get some ceiling on health costs before we could go ahead with the health plan."[21]

CARTER RECOMMENDS PASSAGE OF THE HOSPITAL COST CONTAINMENT ACT

Upon entering the White House, Carter took quick action on health care cost containment. On April 25, 1977, he sent a message to Congress recommending passage of the Hospital Cost Containment Act, which would have imposed mandatory controls limiting hospital cost increases to 9 percent of revenues in fiscal 1978. Hospital cost increases would be reduced during subsequent years. In fiscal 1978 a ceiling of $2.5 billion would have been imposed on hospital capital spending.[22] Hospitals exempted from cost and capital spending controls included those owned by the federal government, those receiving at least 75 percent of their revenues from treating health maintenance organization (HMO) patients, those less than two years old, and those providing long-term care.[23]

The Hospital Cost Containment Act imposed stringent penalties upon hospitals that violated the cost ceilings set by the bill. Any hospital that raised its costs above the 9 percent annual ceiling would have been required to place its excess revenues in escrow and to reduce hospital costs during the following fiscal year by the same amount that it had raised costs above the 9 percent ceiling during the previous year. Any hospital that failed to do so would have been fined 150 percent of the amount it had earned by raising its costs above the 9 percent ceiling.[24]

Carter's decision to propose hospital cost containment through regulatory controls was largely based upon the fact that market forces are absent from the hospital industry. In a market system consumers pay for the goods and services they purchase. To receive value for their hard-earned income, consumers demand the highest-quality goods and services for the lowest possible prices. Producers have financial incentives to provide high-quality and low-priced goods and services. Those who do will expand their market shares and thrive. Those who do not will go out of business.

Market forces are absent from the hospital industry for three reasons. First, over 90 percent of the cost of hospital care is financed by third-party payers rather than patients. As a result, patients are insulated from the costs of hospital care, allowing them to utilize substantially more hospital services than they otherwise would and thereby driving up their cost.

Second, hospitals are mostly reimbursed on the basis of their costs. The greater the costs, the more income they earn. As a result, hospitals have financial incentives to inflate rather than reduce, their costs.

Finally, demand for hospital care is controlled by doctors rather than patients. They determine the diagnostic, therapeutic, and surgical care their patients receive in the hospital. Most, if not practically all, doctors have no idea of the cost of the hospital care their patients receive since nearly all hospital expenses are financed by third-party payers. As a result, doctors will provide substantially more hospital care to their patients than would be the case if their patients paid for their hospital services, again driving up their costs. While market forces serve to restrain the growth of costs in other sectors of the economy, the absence of market forces serves to drive up costs in the hospital industry. Given this fact, Carter believed that the only means to reduce the rise in hospital costs was through federal regulation.[25]

Carter's decision to recommend regulatory controls over hospital costs was largely based upon the fact that they had already been successfully applied in a number of states. During 1977–1978, nine states had mandatory hospital cost-containment measures. In 1977 and 1978 the increase in hospital costs for those states was 12 and 9.9 percent, respectively, compared with 14.2 and 13.3 percent for the United States as a whole during the same years.[26]

The success of mandatory hospital cost-containment measures in the nine states maintaining such controls was a major reason why Carter decided to press for national regulations. In his 1979 message to Congress urging passage of the Hospital Cost Containment Act, he noted that "Hospitals in these states, which include many of the most renowned medical institutions in the world, have reduced cost increases substantially while continuing to provide care of high quality."[27]

Carter could not have been more correct in making hospital cost containment the centerpiece of his health care policy agenda. The rising cost of health care since 1950 has been largely fueled by hospital care. The share of the cost of health care attributable to hospital care rose from 31 percent in 1950 to 43.9 percent in 1989.[28] On the day Carter recommended the Hospital Cost Containment Act, the Department of Health, Education and Welfare (HEW) released figures showing that the average daily cost of a stay in the hospital, measured in current dollars, increased from $15.62 in 1950 to $175.08 in 1976. While the consumer price index (CPI) grew by 125 percent during the same period, the cost of hospital care climbed over 1,000 percent.[29]

The soaring cost of hospital care is a result of the same factors that have driven up the overall cost of health care: the existence of a health insurance system, the proliferation of medical technology, and the aging of the population. The overwhelming majority of the public has insulated itself from rising hospital costs by securing comprehensive insurance coverage. In 1989, 94.6 percent of the cost of hospital care was financed by third-party payers.[30] With the overwhelming majority of the public well insured for hospital care, they have access to all needed hospital services. This has resulted in a substantial patient utilization of hospital care, driving up its cost. The soaring cost of hospital care has been sustained by the continued proliferation of advanced and expensive medical technology.[31]

The aging of the population is perhaps the most important reason for the soaring cost of hospital care. The elderly utilize a substantially larger amount of hospital care than the nonelderly do. In 1989 an average of 311 individuals per 1,000 persons aged 75 years or more were discharged from the hospital, compared with only 67 individuals in an identically sized group from 15 to 44 years old. The average hospital stay was 9.4 days for the older group, compared with 5.5 days for the younger one.[32] Because the elderly utilize a substantially larger amount of hospital care than the nonelderly do, hospital costs for senior citizens are significantly higher than for their younger counterparts. In 1981 per capita spending on hospital care was $1,381 for the elderly, compared with only $392 for the nonelderly.[33]

CONGRESS BEGINS CONSIDERATION OF THE HOSPITAL COST CONTAINMENT ACT

Before it could receive consideration on the floor of either house of Congress, the Hospital Cost Containment Act had to be reviewed by no fewer than seven committees and subcommittees with jurisdiction over the bill: the Senate Finance Committee, the Senate Labor and Human Resources Committee and its Subcommittee on Health and Scientific Research, the House Ways and Means Committee and its Subcommittee on Health, and the House Energy and Commerce Committee and its Subcommittee on Health and the Environment. The fact that the Hospital Cost Containment Act fell under the jurisdiction of seven committees and subcommittees, each of which had some measure of veto power over the bill, created a legislative obstacle course that made passage of the measure difficult, if not impossible. This was all the more true given the fact that members of at least the two House committees enjoyed a close financial relationship with interest groups opposed to the measure.

The Senate Labor and Human Resources Committee was the first congressional body to take action on the Hospital Cost Containment Act. On August 2, 1977, it approved a revised version of the bill that made two major changes in the original version. First, it tightened controls on hospital capital spending by imposing a moratorium on such outlays through fiscal 1978. Second, it expanded the number of hospitals exempted from the provisions of the bill. In addition to federal hospitals, the subcommittee excluded from cost and capital spending controls hospitals with annual admissions of fewer than 2,000 and those with admissions of from 2,000 to 4,000 that were the only hospitals in their communities.[34]

However, despite the Senate Labor and Human Resources Committee's approval, the Hospital Cost Containment Act soon ran into powerful opposition from the hospital industry, which was committed to defeating the measure—with good reason. The bill would have imposed financial losses upon hospitals. The annual limit of 9 percent on hospital cost increases would have cut deeply into revenues, given the fact that hospital costs have risen at double-digit levels since the late 1970s. The financial losses hospitals would have incurred under the Hospital Cost Containment Act made it unacceptable not just to the hospital industry but to the medical profession as well.

All patients who receive hospital care do so upon the recommendations of their doctors. The hospital industry is dependent upon the medical profession for its financial survival. Hospitals in turn provide doctors with access to needed technology to perform their surgical, therapeutic, and diagnostic procedures. Much, if not most, of the income doctors earn is derived from the work they perform in hospitals. As a result, the AMA felt obliged to stand with the hospital industry in opposing legislation that undermined the financial interests of hospitals.

NEGOTIATING AN AGREEMENT ON A COMPROMISE HOSPITAL COST CONTAINMENT BILL

Because the Hospital Cost Containment Act promised to impose financial losses upon hospitals, the hospital industry mounted an intensive campaign to defeat the bill in Congress.[35] However, the Carter administration refused to budge from its support for the Hospital Cost Containment Act, urging Congress to pass the bill. In a bid to settle the dispute between the administration and the hospital industry, Representative Daniel Rostenkowski of Illinois recommended a compromise plan. In a speech on the House floor on November 2, 1977, he proposed that hospitals be given an opportunity to contain their costs by voluntary means. Only if this failed should Congress consider the imposition of mandatory ceilings on hospital costs.

Rostenkowski recommended his compromise hospital cost-containment plan in response to the pleas of hospital industry representatives, who assured him that the industry could contain its costs on a voluntary basis, without the need for mandatory ceilings. To give them a chance to prove this, he suggested that the industry be provided the opportunity to establish a voluntary cost-containment plan between November 1977 and January 1978, when Congress would be in recess. "If the industry is as confident as their representatives have indicated to me that they can solve the hospital cost problem on a voluntary basis, they should be in a position to develop and to begin to implement a responsible alternative before Congressional debate on this issue resumes in February," Rostenkowski declared.[36]

Organized medicine responded immediately and favorably to Rostenkowski's compromise hospital cost-containment plan, determined to meet his deadline of establishing a voluntary program by January 1978. In November 1977 the AHA, FAHS, and AMA jointly established the National Steering Committee for the Voluntary Effort.[37] By 1980, its membership had been expanded to include a number of other key members of the health care industry, including the Blue Cross and Blue Shield Associations, the HIAA, and the Health Industry Manufacturers Association.[38]

In December 1977 members of the National Steering Committee for the Voluntary Effort met and agreed on a goal to reduce hospital cost increases by 2 percent in 1978 and in 1979. The following month the committee sent letters to all chairpersons, executive officers of the boards of directors, and chiefs of medical staffs in the hospital industry, informing them of its cost-containment goal.[39] To guarantee enforcement of this goal, health care cost-containment committees were organized in each state and the District of Columbia.

On December 19, 1979, the National Steering Committee for the Voluntary Effort issued a report on its two-year hospital cost-containment program. It showed that the annual rate of growth in hospital costs declined from 15.6 percent in 1977 to 12.8 percent in 1978, then rose to 13.4 percent in 1979. By comparison, the Consumer Price Index (CPI) rose from 6.8 percent to 9 percent to 12.6 percent during the same three years.[40]

The data show that the Voluntary Effort succeeded in reducing hospital costs from 1977 to 1979. Moreover, the ratio between the hospital inflation rate and the CPI was cut substantially during this period. However, the decline in hospital costs was still so marginal that it fell short of the Voluntary Effort's own goals, which were to cut the rate of growth in costs to 13.6 percent in 1978 and 11.6 percent the following year. The Voluntary Effort more than met its 1978 target but failed to do so the following year.

The Voluntary Effort did not represent a genuine attempt to contain hospital costs, since it would have allowed hospital cost increases to run at 11.6 percent by 1979, well above the 9 percent permitted under the Hospital Cost Containment Act. Rather, the Voluntary Effort was a political ploy designed to give the hospital industry's congressional allies a credible basis to oppose the bill. With the industry taking voluntary action to contain hospital costs, its congressional allies could legitimately claim that the bill was unnecessary.

When Congress reconvened to take up the Hospital Cost Containment Act, Rostenkowski relying on the goals of the Voluntary Effort, introduced a new, watered-down version of the bill. Consistent with the goals of the Voluntary Effort, the Rostenkowski plan required that hospitals voluntarily reduce their costs by 2 percent in 1978 and in 1979. After 1979, hospitals would be required to hold their cost increases to an annual rate of 12 percent.

The federal government would be granted standby authority to impose a ceiling on cost increases if hospitals failed to meet the annual voluntary cost-containment limit provided for in the Rostenkowski plan. The ceiling would limit hospital cost increases to 12 percent of revenues, effective the year following the one in which hospitals had failed to meet the limit. Mandatory hospital cost controls would expire four years after they took effect. Hospitals exempted from cost controls included those that treated primarily HMO enrollees, were less than three years old, were mental institutions, and were small rural hospitals that were the sole providers of care in their communities. Any hospital that raised its costs above the cost-containment limit would have to pay a tax equal to the amount of revenue it earned by violating the cost ceilings.

The hospital industry lobbied intensively against the Rostenkowski plan—with good reason. If the industry fell short of its cost-containment target under the Voluntary Effort, mandatory cost-containment measures would have gone into effect, had the bill been passed. Nevertheless, on February 28, 1978, the Subcommittee on Health of the House Ways and Means Committee defied the industry and passed the bill by the narrowest of margins—seven to six.[41]

The outcome of the vote on the Hospital Cost Containment Act in the Health Subcommittee was influenced by campaign contributions from the health care industry. During the 1974 and 1976 congressional campaigns, the industry contributed $73,462 to subcommittee members. Most of those contributions came from a single source, the American Medical Political Action Committee (AMPAC). It was formed by the AMA during the spring of 1961, originally to assist the interest group in its unsuccessful campaign to defeat Medicare.[42] Since 1968, AMPAC has been among the top two contributors to congressional campaigns among all PACs with the exception of 1980 when it slipped to third place.[43]

The Subcommittee on Health of the House Ways and Means Committee was a major beneficiary of AMPAC contributions. During the 1974 and 1976 congressional campaigns, AMPAC contributed over $63,000 to the campaigns of subcommittee members.[44] One reason why the hospital industry came within an eyelash of securing the subcommittee's rejection of the Hospital Cost Containment Act was the substantial contributions its members received from AMPAC.

Prospects for approval of the Hospital Cost Containment Act appeared to be better in the Energy and Commerce Committee, which shared jurisdiction over the bill with the Ways and Means Committee in the House. Unlike Rostenkowski, the Chairman of Energy and Commerce's Subcommittee on Health and the Environment, Paul G. Rogers of Florida, supported the bill unequivocally. The committee's vote on the bill came on July 18, 1978. It took up an amendment to the Hospital Cost Containment Act, introduced by Representative James T. Broyhill of North Carolina, that struck out provisions in the bill granting the federal government standby authority to impose cost ceilings if hospitals failed to reduce their costs by 2 percent in 1978 and in 1979. Instead, the amendment endorsed the Voluntary Effort. The committee passed the Broyhill Amendment, by the narrowest of margins—twenty-two to twenty-one.[45] By prohibiting the federal government from imposing mandatory hospital cost ceilings, the amendment effectively killed the Hospital Cost Containment Act.

The one-vote margin of defeat in the House Energy and Commerce Committee occurred because a committee supporter of the bill, Marty Russo of Illinois, changed his mind and voted for the Broyhill Amendment after being intensively lobbied by the hospital industry during the weekend before the vote.[46] Organized medicine's pressure tactics against Russo were part of its overall campaign to influence the House Energy and Commerce Committee's rejection of the bill. As the committee readied itself to vote on the Hospital Cost Containment Act, AMPAC and the hospital industry poured large amounts of money into the campaign coffers of committee members. A committee member, Toby Moffett of Connecticut, recalls, "I remember during the Carter years, right in the middle of the hospital cost-control vote—the hospitals and the AMA were just throwing money at the [House Commerce] Committee [which was handling the bill] as fast as they could. It was coming in wheelbarrows."[47]

As Moffett has noted, AMPAC attempted to use its financial power to defeat the Hospital Cost-Containment Act in the House Energy and Commerce Committee. During the 1976 congressional campaign and the 1978 campaign prior to the vote on the bill, committee members who opposed the bill received $85,150 in AMPAC contributions. By contrast, committee members who supported the bill secured only $16,109.[48]

Following the House Energy and Commerce Committee's rejection of the Hospital Cost Containment Act, the Carter administration joined Senator Gaylord Nelson of Wisconsin in a last-ditch effort to salvage the bill. The administration introduced a hospital cost containment bill sponsored by Nelson that essentially included the same measures as those in the legislation presented by Rostenkowski.[49] Like the Rostenkowski bill, the Nelson plan would have granted the federal government standby authority to impose mandatory cost controls if hospitals failed to voluntarily reduce their costs by 2 percent in 1978 and in 1979 and to hold their annual cost increases to 12 percent thereafter.[50] This stood in sharp contrast to Carter's original version of the bill, which would have imposed mandatory hospital cost controls, depriving hospitals of the opportunity to voluntarily reduce their own costs.

Because it represented a watered-down version of the Hospital Cost Containment Act, the Carter administration hoped that the Nelson plan would gain support among members of Congress who were willing to accept modest hospital cost controls. However, despite the compromises in the Nelson plan, on August 3, 1978, the Senate Finance Committee rejected the measure by a decisive margin of eleven to seven. On August 11 the committee approved a more limited health care cost-containment bill sponsored by Senator Herman Talmadge of Georgia. The bill would have established a prospective payment system to reduce hospital costs—but only under Medicare and Medicaid.

Nevertheless, refusing to accept defeat, on October 12 Nelson attached his plan as an amendment to the Talmadge bill, which he introduced on the Senate floor for a vote. The Senate passed the amendment by a margin of forty-seven to forty-two.[51] Senate passage of the Nelson Amendment represented a major victory for the Carter administration in its eighteen-month fight to secure passage of the Hospital Cost Containment Act. However, the victory proved to be short-lived. Three days after the Senate's passage of the Nelson Amendment, the Ninety-fifth Congress adjourned before the House had time to take action on the measure.[52]

CARTER CONTINUES HIS CAMPAIGN TO PASS THE HOSPITAL COST CONTAINMENT ACT

Despite the failure of the Ninety-fifth Congress to pass the Hospital Cost Containment Act, Carter refused to concede defeat. He continued his campaign to secure passage of the bill when the Ninety-sixth Congress convened in 1979. Carter was even more determined to obtain approval of the bill in 1979 than he had been during the previous two years. This was due to the dramatic rise in the inflation rate in 1979, which soared to double-digit levels. Carter no longer saw the bill only as a means to reduce health care costs. Rather, he viewed it as indispensable to the fight against inflation. This was consistent with Carter's belief that soaring hospital costs were a major source of inflation, and that rising prices could be reduced only after hospital costs were contained. In a message to Congress on March 6, 1979, that urged passage of the Hospital Cost Containment Act, Carter made clear the importance he attached to the bill as a weapon in the fight against inflation.

Inflation is America's most serious domestic problem. . . .
One of the most important components of inflation is the soaring cost of hospital care, which continues to outpace inflation in the rest of the economy. . . .
The Hospital Cost Containment Act of 1979 will be one of the clearest tests of Congress's seriousness in dealing with the problem of inflation. Through this one piece of legislation, we can, at a stroke, reduce inflation, cut the Federal budget, and save billions of dollars of unnecessary public and private spending. . . .
I call upon the Congress to demonstrate its commitment to the fight against inflation by promptly enacting the Hospital Cost Containment Act of 1979.[53]

In his March 6, 1979, message to Congress, Carter recommended a substantially watered-down version of the Hospital Cost Containment Act. Instead of imposing a rigid ceiling on hospital costs, the new version required that hospitals voluntarily reduce their cost increases according to a flexible formula based upon three factors: a "market basket" reflecting the increase in the cost of goods and services purchased by hospitals, an allowance for population growth, and another allowance for net new services (the cost of additional services subtracted from savings achieved by increased productivity and efficiency). Based upon this formula, the federal government would impose a national voluntary limit on hospital cost increases of 9.7 percent of revenues for 1979. The federal government would be granted standby authority to reduce hospital cost increases to 9.7 percent in 1980 if hospitals failed to do so voluntarily in 1979.[54]

However, Carter diluted the effectiveness of the cost controls provided for in the Hospital Cost Containment Act by expanding the number of hospitals exempted from the provisions of the bill. Fully 57 percent of hospitals would receive exemptions.[55] They included hospitals in states that met the national voluntary hospital cost-containment limit, those in states with their own mandatory cost-containment plans that restrained the rise in hospital costs to no more than 1 percent of the national limit, nonmetropolitan hospitals with less than 4,000 admissions, those less than three years old, and those with at least 75 percent of their patients HMO enrollees.[56] By adopting a flexible formula for reducing hospital cost increases and enlarging the number of hospitals exempted from the provisions of the Hospital Cost Containment Act, Carter hoped to gain support for the bill among members of Congress who backed federal hospital cost controls, as long as they were enforced on a nonrestrictive basis.

Despite the fact that Carter substantially weakened the Hospital Cost Containment Act in 1979 to make it more acceptable to Congress, the bill would have imposed substantial reductions in hospital costs. In 1979 the Congressional Budget Office (CBO) estimated that Carter's latest version of the bill would have reduced hospital costs by $32 billion from 1980 to 1984.[57] In testimony before a congressional subcommittee on March 9, 1979, HEW Secretary Joseph A. Califano, Jr., estimated that passage of the bill would reduce the rise in hospital costs to $126.5 billion in 1984.[58] This was well below the $158.8 billion that they actually amounted to that year. The bill promised to reduce hospital costs by 20 percent by 1984.[59]

The Ninety-sixth Congress took rapid action on the Hospital Cost Containment Act, sending it through the legislative maze of committees and subcommittees for consideration before it came to the House floor for a vote. The first body of the Ninety-sixth Congress to consider it was the Subcommittee on Health of the House Ways and Means Committee. On April 25 the subcommittee approved the bill on a party-line vote. Six Democrats supported the bill and three Republicans opposed it. On June 13 the Senate Labor and Human Resources Committee approved the bill by a margin of eleven to four.

However, on July 12 the Hospital Cost Containment Act received a serious setback when the Senate Finance Committee rejected the bill by a narrow margin of eleven to nine. Nevertheless, the setback proved to be short-lived. On July 17 the House Ways and Means Committee approved the bill by an overwhelming margin of twenty-one to fourteen.[60]

However, the Ways and Means Committee approved a revised version of the Hospital Cost Containment Act that was substantially weaker than the version recommended by Carter. The committee raised the national voluntary limit on hospital cost increases to 11.6 percent of revenues for 1979. The federal government was granted standby authority to reduce hospital cost increases to 11.6 percent in 1980 if hospitals failed to do so voluntarily in 1979. Federal power to impose hospital cost controls would expire at the end of 1983.

In addition to the exemptions recommended by Carter, the House Ways and Means Committee excluded from cost controls hospitals providing long-term care (with an average length of stay of thirty days), federal hospitals, charitable hospitals, and mental and children's institutions.[61] As a result of those exemptions, HEW estimated that only 35–40 percent of hospitals would be subject to federal cost controls under the committee's version of the bill.

In addition to diluting key provisions of the Hospital Cost Containment Act, the House Ways and Means Committee placed a gaping loophole in the bill that would have allowed hospitals to escape cost controls altogether, even if they raised their costs above the national voluntary limit. The committee's version of the bill required that the HEW secretary determine by July 1 of each year, beginning in 1980, whether hospitals had contained their costs within the national voluntary limit during the previous year. The HEW secretary would impose mandatory hospital cost controls if cost increases had exceeded the limit. However, either house of Congress could block the implementation of those controls by passing a resolution of disapproval within thirty days after the HEW Secretary had announced that hospital cost increases had exceeded the limit. By granting this power to block the implementation of mandatory hospital cost controls, the committee rendered the bill ineffective. The hospital industry could have used its substantial political clout and financial influence with Congress to pressure its members in either house to block implementation of any mandatory hospital cost controls the HEW secretary might impose.

Nevertheless, despite weakening key provisions of the Hospital Cost Containment Act, the House Ways and Means Committee strengthened it in one important respect: It toughened the enforcement mechanisms of the bill by imposing stringent penalties on hospitals that violated the bill. Hospitals that raised their costs above the national voluntary limit would be required either to deposit all excess revenues in an escrow account or pay a fine equal to 150 percent of those additional revenues. Hospitals could draw upon their escrow accounts when their revenues fell below the national voluntary limit.[62]

Despite undermining important provisions of the Hospital Cost Containment Act, the House Ways and Means Committee's version of the measure still would have imposed substantial reductions in hospital costs. In 1979 the CBO estimated that the committee's version of the bill would have reduced hospital costs by $23.5 billion from 1980 to 1983.[63]

On September 6 the Hospital Cost Containment Act received another setback when the Subcommittee on Health and the Environment of the House Energy and Commerce Committee rejected the bill by a margin of eight to four. Once again, however, the setback proved to be short-lived. Subcommittee Chairman Henry A. Waxman, a strong supporter of the bill, took it to the full committee for a vote. On September 26 Energy and Commerce approved, by the decisive margin of twenty-three to nineteen, essentially the same version of the bill as that passed by Ways and Means.[64]

The Energy and Commerce Committee's approval of the Hospital Cost Containment Act cleared the way for the bill to be voted upon by the House. On November 13, as the House readied itself to vote on the bill, Carter sent a letter to House members, appealing to them to pass the bill. In his letter, Carter reiterated his argument that passage of the bill was vital to the successful fight against inflation.

You will have an opportunity this week to help our fight against inflation by passing Hospital Cost Containment legislation that can save Americans more than $40 billion over the next five years. I urge you to join this effort. . . .

No other bill before the Congress will have such a direct effect on reducing the cost of living for all Americans. A vote for this bill will clearly and properly be seen by the public as a vote to reduce inflation. It will also be seen as a measure of Congress's commitment in working to fight inflation. . . .

The time for positive action against inflation is now. I urge you to take that action by voting for Hospital Cost Containment legislation.[65]

THE HOUSE REJECTS THE HOSPITAL COST CONTAINMENT ACT

However, despite its approval by both the Ways and Means and the Energy and Commerce committees and the strong support of President Carter, the full House rejected the Hospital Cost Containment Act on November 15. Leading the opposition to the bill was Richard Gephardt of Missouri. He introduced an amendment to the bill that struck out provisions granting the federal government standby authority to impose a mandatory ceiling on hospital costs if they exceeded the national voluntary limit. Instead, the amendment established a fifteen-member national commission, which the president would appoint, to study the hospital cost crisis. The commission would report its findings to Congress within a year. The amendment also provided $10 million in federal aid to the states in fiscal 1980, and whatever additional assistance needed through fiscal 1982, to support them in developing their own hospital cost-containment plans. The House approved the amendment by an overwhelming margin of 234 to 166.[66] By prohibiting the federal government from imposing a mandatory ceiling on hospital costs, the amendment effectively killed the bill.

Carter responded angrily to the defeat of the Hospital Cost Containment Act. Following the House's rejection of the bill, he issued a statement declaring "that the action of the House of Representatives is a blow to the fight against inflation." Blaming the hospital industry for the death of the bill, he asserted "that the action in the House was a victory for a highly financed, special-interest lobby, and a defeat for the common good." He concluded by warning "that the action of the House today will add literally tens of billions of dollars to the Federal

Table 4.1
The House Energy and Commerce Committee's Vote on the Broyhill Amendment

	Percentage of Committee Members Supporting the Broyhill Amendment	Percentage of Committee Members Opposing the Broyhill Amendment
Republicans	30	2
Northern Democrats	14	35
Southern Democrats	7	12
Total	51	49

Source: Congressional Quarterly Alamanac 1978, p. 623.

deficit in the coming years, and tens of billions of dollars to the cost of living for Americans who are already having difficulty making ends meet."[67]

Carter was correct in his argument that the defeat of the Hospital Cost Containment Act would result in a continuation of the soaring rise in hospital costs. By rejecting the bill, the House deprived business, workers, and consumers of comprehensive federal protection from the skyrocketing cost of hospital care. This has resulted in a continuation in the upward spiral in hospital costs. The average daily cost of a stay in the hospital rose from $175 in 1976 to $432 in 1984.[68]

CONGRESSIONAL VOTES ON THE HOSPITAL COST CONTAINMENT ACT

As we have seen, members of Congress cast a number of votes on the Hospital Cost Containment Act on both the House and the Senate floors as well as in committee during 1977–1979. In addition to the full House and Senate votes, votes on the bill were cast by the Senate Labor and Human Resources Committee and its Subcommittee on Health and Scientific Research, the Senate Finance Committee, the House Ways and Means Committee and its Subcommittee on Health, and the House Energy and Commerce Committee and its Subcommittee on Health and the Environment. Tables 4.1 through 4.5 show the key congressional votes on the bill.

Tables 4.1, 4.2, and 4.3 show that the House Energy and Commerce, and Ways and Means Committees' votes on the Hospital Cost Containment Act were made largely on a party-line basis. An overwhelming majority of Democrats supported the bill; practically all Republicans opposed it. Backing for the bill within the two committees transcended sectional divisions within the Democratic Party. The overwhelming majority of both Northern and Southern Democrats favored the bill.

Table 4.2
The House Ways and Means Committee's Vote on the Hospital Cost Containment Act

	Percentage of Committee Members Supporting the Hospital Cost Containment Act	Percentage of Committee Members Opposing the Hospital Cost Containment Act
Northern Democrats	42	3
Southern Democrats	19	3
Republicans	0	33
Total	61	39

Source: Congressional Quarterly Almanac 1979, p. 515.

Table 4.3
The House Energy and Commerce Committee's Vote on the Hospital Cost Containment Act

	Percentage of Committee Members Supporting the Hospital Cost Containment Act	Percentage of Committee Members Opposing the Hospital Cost Containment Act
Northern Democrats	36	9
Southern Democrats	12	7
Republicans	7	29
Total	55	45

Source: Congressional Quarterly Almanac 1979, p. 516.

However, the partisan and regional distribution of votes for the Hospital Cost Containment Act changed when it went to the House floor for a vote. Table 4.4 reveals that the bill was defeated in the House by a formidable coalition of Republicans and Southern Democrats, practically of whom opposed the bill. Support for the bill was largely limited to Northern Democrats, the overwhelming majority of whom supported the bill.

The data contained in Tables 4.1 through 4.4 show that House members divided along party and regional lines in their vote on the Hospital Cost Containment Act. Republicans were solidly opposed to the bill both in the House and in its

Table 4.4
The House Vote on the Gephardt Amendment

	Percentage of House Members Supporting the Gephardt Amendment	Percentage of House Members Opposing the Gephardt Amendment
Republicans	31	2
Northern Democrats	9	31
Southern Democrats	14	5
Total	54	38

Source: Congressional Alamanac 1979, pp. 176-77-H.
Note: Eight percent of House members did not vote on the Gephardt amendment.

Ways and Means and Energy and Commerce committees. Northern Democrats almost as solidly supported the bill, both on the floor and in the two committees.

With Republicans and Northern Democrats divided over the Hospital Cost Containment Act, Southern Democrats cast the swing votes that determined the fate of the bill in the House. Southern Democrats were divided between those who served on the House Ways and Means and Energy and Commerce committees and members of the House as a whole. The two committees approved the bill because the overwhelming majority of Southern Democratic members supported the measure. By contrast, the bill was defeated on the House floor because an equally overwhelming majority of Southern Democratic members of the House as whole opposed the bill.

As Tables 4.5 and 4.6 reveal, the coalition of Republicans and Southern Democrats opposing the Hospital Cost Containment Act was much stronger in the Senate than it was in the House. As in the House, the Senate vote on the bill divided along partisan and regional lines. The overwhelming majority of Republicans opposed the bill both in the Senate and on its Finance Committee. An equally overwhelming majority of Northern Democrats supported the bill in both the Senate and the committee.

Southern Democrats generally joined Republicans in their opposition to the bill. True, Southern Democratic members of the Senate Finance Committee were equally divided between those supporting and those opposing the bill. However, the overwhelming majority of Southern Democratic members of the Senate as a whole opposed the bill.

Given the fact that Republicans and Southern Democrats, who jointly controlled the Senate, opposed the Hospital Cost Containment Act, how is it that the Senate approved the bill when it passed the Nelson Amendment? The answer

Table 4.5
The Senate Vote on the Nelson Amendment

	Percentage of Senators Supporting the Nelson Amendment	Percentage of Senators Opposing the Nelson Amendment
Northern Democrats	33	5
Southern Democrats	8	12
Republicans	6	24
Total	47	41

Source: Congressional Quarterly Alamanac 1978, p. 70-S.
Note: Eleven percent of the Senate did not vote on the Nelson amendment. The only independent member of the Senate voted against the amendment.

Table 4.6
The Senate Finance Committee's Vote on the Hospital Cost Containment Act

	Percentage of Committee Members Opposing the Hospital Cost Containment Act	Percentage of Committee Members Supporting the Hospital Cost Containment Act
Republicans	35	5
Northern Democrats	5	30
Southern Democrats	10	10
Total	50	45

Source: Congressional Quarterly Almanac 1979, p. 514.
Note: The only independent member of the Senate, who served on the twenty-member committee, also voted against against the Hospital Cost Containment Act.

lies in the fact that a substantial group of Northeastern Republicans broke ranks with their party to vote for the bill, providing the crucial swing votes. Of the six Republican Senators supporting the bill, five represented the Northeast.

Although numerous national health insurance bills were introduced in Congress, no legislative vote on the program was taken during the 1970s. Nevertheless, the Hospital Cost Containment Act gave members of Congress an indirect opportunity to register their feelings on the program. Passage of the bill was essential to the establishment of national health insurance. Without a means of controlling hospital costs, national health insurance could not be instituted on a fiscally and economically viable basis, and therefore stood no chance of adoption. Accordingly, a vote for the bill was a vote in support of national health insurance; a vote against the measure was a vote against national health insurance. The fact that the overwhelming majority of members of Congress, especially in the House, opposed the bill suggests the existence of widespread legislative opposition to national health insurance. The program stood virtually no chance of passage during the 1970s.

WHY WAS THE HOSPITAL COST CONTAINMENT ACT DEFEATED?

The defeat of the Hospital Cost Containment Act was due to seven factors: (1) Congress was fearful that the bill would result in health care rationing; (2) the public was unconcerned about hospital cost containment; (3) the hospital industry was well organized to lobby against the bill; (4) the Voluntary Effort gave opponents of the bill a reason to vote against it; (5) substantial political and academic opposition to federal regulation existed, both in Congress and among health care policy experts, which made lawmakers reluctant to pass the bill; (6) Congress pursued hospital cost-containment measures which served as an alternative to those specified in the bill; and (7) AMPAC was well positioned to use its financial influence to defeat the bill.

Rationing Health Care

A key argument against the Hospital Cost Containment Act made by the hospital industry was that the bill would have resulted in health care rationing. This would have been the only way hospitals could meet the cost ceilings imposed under the bill, since much of the soaring cost of hospital care has been driven by the development of advanced and costly medical technology. Rationing would be essential because the cost ceilings would have been sufficiently stringent to reduce hospital costs by 20 percent by 1984.

The argument that passage of the Hospital Cost Containment Act would lead to health care rationing was perhaps most explicitly made by FAHS President Michael D. Bromberg. On May 26, 1977, he issued a statement to a Senate subcommittee holding hearings on the Hospital Cost Containment Act:

If Congress votes to place a ceiling on hospital revenues and on hospital based technology, then Congress will be voting to establish itself as the moral judge of the dollar value of increased life spans, fewer fatal heart attacks, reduced infant mortality, significant survival rates for cancer patients, and every life saving device or technique. . . .

Rationing can be forced through that approach, but if Congress adopts that approach to resource allocation, it will be telling the American people that our values have changed from assuring that community health needs are met to reducing medical advances to a level set by the federal government based on the advice of economists instead of community representatives, consumers, or health professionals.[69]

The hospital industry's warning that passage of the Hospital Cost Containment Act would lead to health care rationing had a powerful effect on Congress. To meet the cost ceilings provided for in the bill, hospitals would have had to deny access to lifesaving and costly medical technology to a substantial number of terminally ill and elderly patients. Angry relatives of those patients could be expected to complain to their senators and representatives about this. They would have pointed out that the health, and perhaps the lives, of their relatives were being needlessly and recklessly threatened by the existence of arbitrary ceilings on hospital costs that had prevented their relatives from securing access to needed lifesaving medical technology.

Members of Congress would have had to take political responsibility for the premature deaths of many terminally ill and elderly individuals who would have been denied access to lifesaving medical technology. This would have given members the public image of being cruel and heartless, damaging their credibility with constituents. This is not an image that any member wants to have when campaigning for reelection. To avoid confronting the negative political fallout from health care rationing, House members had a rational interest in opposing the Hospital Cost Containment Act.

A major argument used by opponents of the Hospital Cost Containment Act to defeat it in the House was that it would result in health care rationing. As one leading opponent of the bill, Bill Gradison of Ohio, declared on the House floor, "Had this legislation been in effect over the years it is doubtful that the hospitals of America would have available for the treatment of patients such facilities as we take for granted today, including intensive care units, recovery rooms, and coronary care, all of which are extremely valuable, save lives, but are also very expensive."[70]

The Lack of Public Interest in Hospital Cost Containment

A major problem the Carter administration confronted in pressing its case for the Hospital Cost Containment Act was that it failed to garner any active public interest, let alone support. In his memoirs, Joseph Califano says that prospects for passage of the bill were crippled by "the problem of getting the American people to appreciate the financial significance of hospital cost-containment to them personally." He attributes this problem to the fact that most of the cost of hospital care is financed by third parties. "Most Americans do not think they are paying their hospital bills since less than 10 percent of the money that goes to hospitals is paid directly by individual patients."[71]

As Califano points out, because practically the entire cost of hospital care is financed by third parties, public clamor for relief from soaring hospital costs is virtually nonexistent. The insured public is assured that they will have access to all needed hospital care, regardless of its cost. They have little need to be concerned about soaring hospital costs.

In waging its fight for the Hospital Cost Containment Act, the Carter administration was left standing alone. It was seeking to provide the public relief from soaring hospital costs, without the benefit of any discernible popular support. An organized constituency in support of the bill was nonexistent. The only organized voices heard in Washington on the bill came from its chief opponent—organized medicine.

The Power of the Hospital Industry

The hospital industry waged its fight against the Hospital Cost Containment Act primarily through two means: lobbying and the launching of the Voluntary Effort. Hospitals are well organized for lobbying purposes. As of 1990, there were 5,455 hospitals, operating in virtually every congressional district.[72]

Members of the board of trustees of each hospital are distinguished and respected members of the community. They have easy access to their representatives in Congress. They needed only to call or meet their representatives to register their opposition to the Hospital Cost Containment Act, which they did. One member of Carter's congressional liaison staff described how this occurred.

Hospital administrators were a force who were hard to deal with. If you just think about your own home towns and your hospital board, think about who's on the board. It's usually the blue ribbon committees; usually a philanthropist who they put on. . . .

The hospital administrators have some damn good people in Washington who understood hospital and community politics. They mobilized the trustees and the boards of the hospital to call the congressman. You're getting ready to vote on this thing, the administration presented their views and it makes sense. Suddenly you get a call. Maybe you've got four or five towns of any size in your district, and in three days you get calls from fifteen people who are the wealthiest, most powerful people in those towns. In addition, they're people who said, "I've never called you before. You've been my congressman for six years or eight years and I'm asking you this one thing for me. Vote against that. We can't run our hospital if we're constrained. We'll have to go to the county commissioners if it's a public hospital, raise additional money." If it's a university hospital, you know, "I'm the President of the university and a powerful, powerful force, and one that you can't combat on a one to one." We couldn't go into that town and pick someone that's equally influential and get them to call their congressman and say "No, it's not true."[73]

Hospitals provide critical, life-enhancing and life-saving functions for the residents of the communities they serve. They are highly reputable organizations in their communities. This made it particularly difficult for the Carter administration to wage a legislative battle against the hospital industry. Members of Congress were very reluctant to defy the appeals of the industry and vote for the Hospital Cost Containment Act, given the favorable public image hospitals have. As one political observer remarked,

The whole hospital cost containment thing is a quagmire. I don't know how in the hell the administration got involved with it as their first move. Here you have thousands of hospitals in this country. More than half of them are community hospitals, and you know what that means. There's a lot of community pride wrapped up in them; they've been financed by bake sales. "It's our hospital." Others of them are proprietary hospitals, owned by politically powerful physicians. The rest of them have some religious affiliation and here they are doing the Lord's work. Why would you take them on? Dumb, dumb, dumb.[74]

The difficulty of challenging the power of the hospital industry, due to its favorable public image, was emphasized by a congressional staffer. He outlined the problems faced by the Carter administration in passing the Hospital Cost Containment Act.

The support for this kind of legislation is quite weak compared to the opposition by the interests that are directly affected by it and see a really large stake in it. Hospitals, providers, and those natural opponents of the bill have gone out and enlisted allies like suppliers. The opposition has not only been constant, but it has increased. And the hospitals are still among the good guys, you know, the community leaders. It's tough to go against them.[75]

In addition to lobbying effectively against the Hospital Cost Containment Act, the hospital industry succeeded in imposing voluntary cost-containment measures that undermined the Carter administration's case for the bill. The failure of the Ninety-fifth Congress to pass the bill gave hospitals breathing room in which to prove that the Voluntary Effort could meet its target of reducing costs by 2 percent in 1978. The fact that hospital costs had been reduced by over 2 percent in 1978 gave the AHA, FAHS, and AMA sufficient political credibility to defeat the bill in the House the following year. All three interest groups argued in congressional hearings that since hospitals had more than met their targets for reducing costs, the bill was unnecessary.[76] On March 9, 1979, the AHA issued a statement to a Senate subcommittee holding hearings on the Hospital Cost Containment Act that summarized the hospital industry's case against the bill.

Hospitals are sincerely committed to containing health cost increases and are actively participating in the only organized, industry-wide voluntary program to fight inflation. It is our strong conviction that such voluntary actions are the most effective ways of dealing with the containment of health care costs while maintaining quality. The Voluntary Effort is succeeding and should be allowed to develop without further governmental intervention which would undermine its continued success.[77]

AHA President John Alexander McMahon claimed that the success of the Voluntary Effort was the "single most important factor in winning Congress' support in the fight against" the Hospital Cost Containment Act. He reported that the Voluntary Effort had reduced hospital costs by $900 million in fiscal

1978 and would save an additional $4 billion by fiscal 1983.[78] However, this was less than a fifth of the $23.5 billion in lower hospital costs the CBO estimated would have been achieved under the House Ways and Means Committee's version of the Hospital Cost Containment Act from 1980 to 1983. The marginal savings arising from the Voluntary Effort were only a token concession to the public, designed more to defuse congressional support for the bill then to make genuine, meaningful reductions in hospital costs.

A major argument used by opponents to defeat the Hospital Cost Containment Act in the House was that the Voluntary Effort was working, and mandatory federal controls on hospital costs were therefore unnecessary. This was the most important claim Gephardt used to mobilize overwhelming House support for his amendment to kill the bill.

In 1977 . . . hospital costs were rising at the rate of 15.6 percent and the inflation rate was 6.6 percent. As a result of that problem, frankly, the hospital industry got interested, perhaps for the first time, in lowering hospital costs. They became sensitized to the problem and started a voluntary effort to do something about the problem.

I submit to the Members [of the House] that voluntary effort . . . has achieved substantial and tangible success. In 1978 the voluntary program reduced the rate of increase [in hospital costs] from 15.6 to 12.8 percent as inflation was rising from the rate of the year before.

The Voluntary goal for 1979 was to reduce the rate [of increase in hospital costs] to 11.6 percent. However, inflation for the first 7 months of this year, as the Members know, has been at the rate of 13.5 percent, but hospital costs for that period have increased by 13.3 percent. So indeed the original goal of hospital cost containment has been realized by the voluntary effort, because today for the first 7 months of this year hospital costs have risen at a rate lower than the rate of inflation.

So the voluntary program has worked well.[79]

As Gephardt noted, the Voluntary Effort did indeed succeed in reducing hospital costs in relation to inflation. In 1979 hospital costs were rising at roughly the same rate as the growth in the CPI. This was a substantial improvement from 1977, when hospital costs increased at more than double the rate of growth in the CPI. However, while the ratio between hospital cost increases and the CPI declined significantly, the fact remains that hospital costs rose at annual double-digit rates during the late 1970s—a development that was hardly encouraging. Nevertheless, the Voluntary Effort succeeded in reducing hospital costs to levels that allowed congressional opponents of the Hospital Cost Containment Act to justify their votes against the bill by arguing that it was unnecessary.

The Opposition to Federal Regulation

A major reason for the defeat of the Hospital Cost Containment Act relates to the political mood prevailing in Washington. The bill had the misfortune to be considered during the late 1970s, a time of substantial opposition to federal regulation. Rather than expanding federal regulatory powers over the market, Congress was looking for ways to deregulate the economy. During the 1970s and 1980s, the Carter and Reagan administrations joined Congress in deregulating substantial segments of the market, including energy, airlines, and trucking.[80] With deregulation in full swing, Congress was not about to impose new regulations on a major segment of the market, the hospital industry. The mood against federal regulation sweeping Washington made passage of the Hospital Cost Containment Act a political impossibility.

A major argument that opponents of the Hospital Cost Containment Act used to defeat the bill in the House was that it was inconsistent and contradictory to impose federal regulations on hospital costs when Washington was in the process of deregulating other sectors of the market. A leading opponent of the bill, Bill Frenzel of Minnesota, asserted on the House floor:

I wonder how many Members of this body actually believe that we reduce costs by more regulation. The same people [in the Carter administration] who are asking us to accept this bill are telling us that deregulation was the cure for airline costs. They are telling us that deregulation will give us a better cost situation in surface transportation. But they are also telling us that to give HEW a chance to regulate one of the most important services in this country will somehow decrease the costs. . . .

I find difficulty in following people who are wholly, and consistently, inconsistent in their logic.[81]

Consistent with the opposition to federal regulation, in 1980 leading members of Congress and health care policy experts published works attacking the Hospital Cost Containment Act. Two major opponents of the bill in the House were David A. Stockman of Michigan and W. Philip Gramm of Texas. They cited data provided by the Health Care Financing Administration showing that nearly 40 percent of the increase in hospital costs from 1969 to 1978 was due to improvements in the quality of care: increases in the quantity and quality of hospital personnel, diagnostic services, and specialized facilities. Costs were also driven up by an increase in the utilization of hospital care due to the aging of the population.[82]

Stockman and Gramm charged that the imposition of ceilings on hospital costs would require hospitals to reduce costs by cutting the provision of services to their communities, denying many sick individuals needed care. The quality of hospital care would decline drastically. "Blanket [hospital] revenue caps, because they fail to deal with the underlying problem of excessive demand for services, cannot possibly deliver on the promise of a quality product for fewer dollars," Stockman and Gramm concluded. "Such regulation can only ensure that expenditures keep rising while the product deteriorates."[83]

Joining Stockman and Gramm in their opposition to the Hospital Cost Containment Act were Jack A. Meyer and Rudolph G. Penner of the American Enterprise Institute. They charged that Carter's health care policy was confused and contradictory. On the one hand, Carter wanted to guarantee universal health insurance coverage, through his National Health Plan. This was sure to increase patient utilization of health care, especially among the poor and currently uninsured. However, Carter also wanted to contain hospital costs through passage of the Hospital Cost Containment Act. Meyer and Penner agreed with Stockman and Gramm that hospitals would be forced to respond to cost ceilings by reducing the availability of care.[84] They concluded that Carter's combination of universal insurance coverage and hospital cost containment would lead to "a combination of longer waiting times for treatments, a deterioration in the quality of services, and an explosion in costs when consumers ultimately insist on a restoration of the kind of services to which they have grown accustomed."[85]

A final major opponent of the Hospital Cost Containment Act was Alain C. Enthoven of Stanford University. He charged that the bill was inequitable because it would have "rewarded the fat and punished the lean."[86] It would have allowed each hospital to raise its costs by a certain share of total revenues. The inefficient hospitals—those with the highest revenues—would have been permitted the greatest cost increases. The most efficient hospitals—those with the lowest revenues—would have been allowed the smallest cost increases.[87] This was another major argument that opponents of the measure used to defeat it in the House. As Gradison put it on the House floor,

This bill promotes the survival of the least efficient hospitals, what I call the "survival of the fattest," and penalizes the efficient hospitals. Basically, this is because a percentage increase applied to a high-cost hospital permits them to increase their expenditures at a higher dollar amount than the same percentage applied to the revenues of the hospital which is already more efficient.[88]

To Carter's credit, the 1979 version of the Hospital Cost Containment Act would have rewarded efficient hospitals by allowing them to raise their costs by up to 1 percent above the ceilings provided for in the bill. The 1979 version would have also penalized inefficient hospitals by reducing their costs by up to 2 percent below those ceilings.[89] However, Enthoven did not believe that this was sufficient.

Enthoven argued that the underlying cause of the hospital cost crisis is the fact that hospitals are usually reimbursed according to their costs. The higher their costs, the greater the revenues they earn.[90] Cost reimbursement gives hospitals a financial incentive to inflate their costs, which they have done. Because the Hospital Cost Containment Act did nothing to reduce the incentives to raise hospital costs, it failed to address the hospital cost crisis. Enthoven concluded,

The main thing wrong with the proposed Hospital Cost Containment Act is that it contained nothing to correct the perverse incentives in our dominant financing and delivery system. It contained nothing to help basic reform of the financing and delivery system. It was pure spending restraint that reflected no concern for health care quality, efficiency, or equity.[91]

The defeat of the Hospital Cost Containment Act was due in part to the existence of substantial congressional opposition to federal regulation. As Paul Starr puts it, "To its opponents, led by Representative David Stockman of Michigan, the bill was a symbol of overregulation, a blind intrusion by government into the private sector which would penalize hospitals that had been efficient and could only reduce the quality of hospital services."[92]

Alternatives to the Hospital Cost Containment Act

Another important reason for the defeat of the Hospital Cost Containment Act was that Congress imposed health care cost-containment measures which served as an alternative to those provided for in the bill. They included both pro-competitive and regulatory reforms. During the 1970s, Congress acted to stimulate the development of a competitive health care market by providing $520 million in aid to promote the expansion of HMOs.[93] HMOs provide consumers an attractive alternative to conventional health insurance plans operated by third-party payers. Third-party payers are limited to financing the provision of health care for their subscribers. The actual delivery of health care is performed by doctors in private practice. Third-party payers are primarily interested in limiting their financial liabilities to subscribers rather than in providing them full access to health care. To minimize their costs, third-party payers usually impose substantial patient cost-sharing requirements on their subscribers, in the form of deductibles, coinsurance charges, and copayments.

By contrast, HMOs are responsible for organizing both financing and delivery of health care. They are mainly interested in providing their enrollees primary care to assure the treatment of illnesses in early stages, before complications begin, if not prevent ailments altogether. Accordingly, HMOs usually provide their enrollees full access to health care, especially primary care, by extending comprehensive insurance coverage, generally with minimal patient cost-sharing requirements, including no deductibles and, at most, minimal coinsurance charges and copayments. Because they impose only modest patient cost-sharing requirements, HMOs are a highly attractive alternative to traditional third-party payment plans. As a result, the share of the public enrolled in HMOs has soared, from 1.4 percent of the population in 1970 to 15.6 percent in 1993. The number of HMOs increased from 26 to 600 during the same period.[94]

By usually providing their enrollees full access to health care, HMOs run the risk that their patients may utilize substantial amounts of medical services, driving up their cost, raising HMO premiums, and rendering HMOs uncompetitive in the health care market. To prevent this, HMOs use their control over the delivery of health care to their enrollees to ration health care, especially hospital services. Harold S. Luft found that HMO enrollees spend an average of 20 to 30 percent fewer days in the hospital than those insured by third-party payers. As a result, the cost of providing health care in one segment of the HMO industry, prepaid group practices, was 10 to 40 percent below costs incurred by third-party payers.[95]

In addition to HMOs, the 1980s were marked by the development of another kind of managed-care network, preferred provider organizations (PPOs). They contract with selected groups of health care providers who agree to deliver their services more efficiently and at reduced cost. PPO subscribers are free to see any doctor they wish; however, they receive more comprehensive coverage if they obtain their services from PPO doctors and hospitals. Private health insurance plans pay higher coinsurance rates for subscribers who receive their services from PPO doctors and hospitals. In addition, PPO doctors and hospitals agree to accept the third-party payers' approved charges as payment in full for all services rendered. They are prohibited from billing PPO subscribers for any additional charges.

By providing more comprehensive coverage while containing their health care costs, PPOs save their subscribers money in reduced out-of-pocket medical expenses. As a result, the share of the public enrolled in PPOs has skyrocketed, from 1 percent in 1984 to 20 percent in 1990.[96] In 1985 there were 334 PPOs.[97]

Because of their lower costs, HMO premiums tend to be less expensive than those of third-party payment plans, including PPOs. A survey found that premiums for each individual enrolled in HMOs averaged $2,683 in 1990, compared to $2,952 for PPOs, and $3,214 for traditional third-party payers.[98] By rationing hospital care, HMOs have served to reduce hospital costs. The growth of HMOs during the 1970s and 1980s has afforded the health care system a greater institutional capacity to contain hospital costs through market-oriented means.

In addition to stimulating procompetitive reforms, the government acted to reduce Medicare and Medicaid spending by cutting hospital and physician reimbursements under the two programs. The single most important measure to slash the cost of public health insurance was the Medicare Prospective Payment System (PPS), which Congress established on October 1, 1983. The Department of Health and Human Services (HHS) has defined 467 diagnosis-related groups (DRGs), which categorize Medicare patients into groups based upon their medical conditions. Hospitals receive a fixed sum for the treatment of a DRG. If the cost of care is less than the DRG rate, then the hospital pockets the difference. However, if the cost exceeds the rate, then the hospital absorbs the loss.[99]

PPS provides hospitals with financial incentives to reduce their costs by minimizing the amount of care provided to Medicare beneficiaries, since this is the only way that they can avoid financial losses under PPS. By using a system that provides hospitals financial incentives to ration care to the elderly, PPS has served to reduce hospital costs under Medicare by $18 billion during 1983 to 1990.[100]

The success of PPS in reducing hospital costs under Medicare provides irrefutable evidence that federal regulation can serve as an effective means to contain health care expenses, much as Carter argued in recommending the Hospital Cost Containment Act. However, since PPS applies only to services provided under Medicare, it gives the federal government much more limited authority to contain hospital costs through regulatory means than would have been the case under the Hospital Cost Containment Act, which would have applied to all hospital costs. Nevertheless, PPS remains the most important regulatory framework established thus far to contain hospital costs.

The establishment of PPS and the expansion of HMOs have served to substantially reduce the amount of hospital care provided to both Medicare and nonMedicare populations. During 1982 to 1988, the number of days spent in the hospital, adjusted for the historical trend from 1976 to 1982, declined by 41.1. percent for Medicare beneficiaries and 15.4 percent for their nonMedicare counterparts.[101] As a result of the substantial fall in hospitalization among Medicare beneficiaries, the average rise in hospital costs for them dropped from 9.2 percent during 1976 to 1981 to 4.7 percent during 1982 to 1988. By contrast, due to the more modest decline in hospitalization among the nonMedicare population, the average increase in hospital costs for them rose slightly, from 4.6 to 5.7 percent, during the same period.[102]

In addition to the action of the public sector to reduce Medicare and Medicaid spending, state and local governments also acted to cut reimbursements to charitable hospitals for the uncompensated care they provide to the uninsured. As a result, those hospitals were forced to absorb increased financial losses for providing uncompensated care. Financial losses sustained by hospitals due to uncompensated care rose from $2.8 billion in 1980 to $8.9 billion in 1989, increasing from 3.7 percent to 4.8 percent of total hospital costs during the same period.[103]

Despite reducing the rate of growth in hospital costs at least for Medicare beneficiaries and raising the cost of uncompensated care hospitals must absorb, the expansion of managed-care networks and the reductions in government hospital and physician reimbursements to provide health care for Medicare and Medicaid beneficiaries and the uninsured, failed to curtail soaring medical expenses during the 1970s and 1980s. Health care costs rose from 7.6 percent of the GNP in 1970 to 12.2 percent in 1990.[104] Per capita health care costs, measured in 1990 dollars, increased from $1,136 to $2,604 during the same period.[105]

Why did health care costs continue to soar, despite government action to reduce medical expenses during the 1970s and 1980s? The answer lies in cost-shifting. Doctors and hospitals recover their financial losses incurred through reductions in their reimbursements for treating Medicare and Medicaid beneficiaries and the uninsured by inflating their charges for services provided to privately-insured patients. As a result, privately-insured patients subsidize a portion of the costs of providing services to Medicare and Medicaid beneficiaries and the uninsured.

As Table 4.7 shows, in 1990 hospitals earned sufficient revenues from providing services to privately-insured patients to fully recover all their financial losses incurred from treating Medicare and Medicaid beneficiaries and the uninsured.

Doctors do the same. Private health insurance reimburses doctors 40 to 50 percent more than Medicare for the same services. Medicare in turn pays doctors 30 percent more than Medicaid for comparable services.[106] In 1987, 44.6 percent

Table 4.7
Hospital Reimbursements Made by Third-Party Payers in 1990

Third-Party Payer	Reimbursement as a Percentage of Cost	Gains or Losses Sustained in Dollars
Below-Cost Reimbursements		
Medicare	89.6	-8.2
Medicaid	80.1	-4.6
Uncompensated Care	21.0	-9.6
Total		-22.4
Above-Cost Reimbursements		
Private Health Insurance	127.6	+22.5
Other Government Payers	106.4	+0.2
Total		+22.7

Source: President Clinton's New Beginning: The Complete
Text, With Illustrations of the Historic Clinton-Gore
Economic Conference in Little Rock, Arkansas, December
14-15, 1992 (New York: Donald I.Fine, 1992), p. 58.

of the cost of physician services was financed by private insurance, compared
to 31.8 percent by the government.[107] Because they receive more reimbursements
from private insurance than the government, the income doctors earn from providing services to privately-insured patients is sufficient to offset most, if not
all, the financial losses they incur from treating Medicare and Medicaid beneficiaries.

Due to cost-shifting, government action to reduce health care costs during the
1970s and 1980s was ineffective. Nevertheless, this action served as an alternative to the Hospital Cost Containment Act in reducing health care costs,
allowing its congressional opponents to legitimately argue that passage of the
bill was politically unnecessary.

The Power of AMPAC

In waging its fight against the Hospital Cost Containment Act, the hospital
industry received valuable support from AMPAC. It was effective in using its
financial influence to mobilize opposition to the bill in the House. A correlation
exists between the campaign contributions a House member received from AM-

Table 4.8
AMPAC Campaign Contributions to House Members and Their Vote on the
Gephardt Amendment

```
------------------------------------------------------------
Amount Received From        Percentage of House
AMPAC During                Members Supporting
1977 Through 1980           Gephardt Amendment
------------------------------------------------------------
Over $15,000                         100
$10,000 to $15,000                    95
$5,000 to $10,000                     82
$2,500 to $5,000                      80
$1 to $2,500                          38
Zero                                  37
------------------------------------------------------------
```

Source: Philip M. Stern, The Best Congress Money Can
Buy (New York: Pantheon Books, 1988), 142.

PAC during the 1978 and 1980 congressional campaigns and his or her vote on
the Gephardt Amendment. Virtually every House member who received over
$15,000 in AMPAC contributions during those campaigns voted for the amend-
ment. By contrast, 63 percent of those who received no AMPAC contributions
voted against the amendment.[108]

Of the 234 members who voted for the Gephardt Amendment, 202 received
a total of $1,647,897 in AMPAC contributions during the 1976 and 1978 congres-
sional campaigns—a per capita average of $8,157. Of the 166 members who
voted against the amendment, 122 secured a per capita average of $2,287 from
AMPAC. Forty-four of those members received no AMPAC contributions. Forty-
eight of the top fifty House recipients of AMPAC contributions voted for the
amendment. The average per capita AMPAC contribution to the top fifty was
$17,300.[109] Table 4.8 shows the correlation between the amount of AMPAC
contributions a House member received and his or her vote on the Gephardt
Amendment.

Larry J. Sabato urges us not to make too much of the correlation between the
amount of campaign contributions a House member received from AMPAC and
his or her vote on the Gephardt Amendment. ''As conclusive as these statistics
seem on the surface, there is no 'smoking gun.' A correlation does not prove
causation.''[110]

Nevertheless, the data showing a correlation between the amount of campaign
contributions a House member received from AMPAC and his or her vote on
the Gephardt Amendment cannot be brushed aside. They suggest that AMPAC
contributions played a substantial, and perhaps decisive, role in influencing the
House to reject the Hospital Cost Containment Act. Following the House's defeat
of the bill, Common Cause, a public interest group, was quick to name AMPAC
contributions to House members as the major reason for the death of the bill.
''AMA campaign contributions helped kill the hospital cost containment bill,''

Common Cause declared in a press release on December 18, 1979. "The American Medical Association has played the central role in the determination of our nation's health policies, and political contributions are the primary source of its power."[111]

Carter and Califano agreed with this view in their memoirs. Califano charged that the House rejected the Hospital Cost Containment Act largely because of the financial power of AMPAC and the hospital industry. "[Hospital] profits provided resources for financial contributions to key committee members in the House," Califano noted. "When the American Medical Association funds were added, because it feared that cost controls on physicians could not be far behind such controls on hospitals, the combined economic interests of the industry were too powerful for the Carter administration."[112] Carter supported Califano's argument. "In the final showdown, Congress was flooded with money, in the form of campaign contributions from the health industry. They prevailed, and the American people lost."[113]

Carter, Califano, and Common Cause are correct to attribute the House's rejection of the Hospital Cost Containment Act to AMPAC campaign contributions. True, it is doubtful that House supporters of the Gephardt Amendment were motivated solely by their desire to secure AMPAC campaign contributions. Rather, as this chapter has attempted to show, Congress had a number of reasons for opposing the Hospital Cost Containment Act that relate to the absence of public support for the bill, the existence of congressional opposition to health care rationing and federal regulation, congressional deference to the power and prestige of the hospital industry, and the availability of alternative means to contain hospital costs. Those reasons were at least as important as the need to secure AMPAC contributions in determining the House's rejection of the Hospital Cost Containment Act—if not more so.

Nevertheless, the fact remains that AMPAC campaign contributions were an important, perhaps critical, factor in motivating the House to reject the Hospital Cost Containment Act. The role AMPAC played in the defeat of the bill is a disturbing indictment of the American political system. There were few, if any, pieces of legislation more important to the public during the 1970s than the Hospital Cost Containment Act. It would have reduced hospital costs by a fifth, saving the public hundreds of billions of dollars in unnecessary health care bills. Its passage would have created a viable fiscal and economic basis for the establishment of a national health insurance program, assuring tens of millions of uninsured individuals access to health care they did not have.

The fact that House members would reject such a vital piece of legislation at least in part in order to maintain access to AMPAC campaign contributions brings into question the credibility and integrity of the American political system. It suggests that Congress, under the current campaign finance system, is incapable of establishing health care cost-containment measures because they are sure to impose financial losses upon organized medicine and to jeopardize access to contributions that members of Congress receive from AMPAC and other medical interest groups. We will explore the link between health care reform and political money in greater detail in Chapter 7.

CONCLUSION

The House's rejection of the Hospital Cost Containment Act was a major reason why Congress did not establish national health insurance during the 1970s. Hospital cost-containment measures were necessary to assure that national health insurance would not add substantially to the deficit and inflation. Without those measures, there was no way that a national health insurance program could have been established on an economically and fiscally sound basis. Thus, the program stood no chance of adoption.

The Hospital Cost Containment Act fell victim to a complicated array of factors that made its passage politically impossible. They include fear that the act would result in health care rationing; the lack of public interest in, let alone support for, the bill; the lobbying power of the hospital industry; the token financial relief organized medicine provided the public through the Voluntary Effort; the existence of substantial congressional opposition to federal regulation; the availability of alternative means to reduce hospital costs; and the significant financial clout AMPAC wields on Capitol Hill. Given the political odds against passage of the Hospital Cost Containment Act, few members of Congress were enthusiastic supporters of the bill. As one congressional staffer explained,

This particular piece of legislation is not near and dear to the heart of anyone on Capitol Hill. The ones that favor it, favor it only out of a sense of obligation and duty, out of a sense that they must do something about cost inflation, and out of loyalty to the White House.[114]

Members of Carter's congressional liaison staff had no illusions concerning the insurmountable political obstacles impeding passage of the Hospital Cost Containment Act. As one staffer remarked, "It was one of those things where you just couldn't get the engine going." Another staffer agreed. "It's just one of those issues that had all of the trappings of a loss."[115]

CHAPTER 5

The Politics of National Health Insurance: Kennedy versus Carter

A universal, comprehensive national health insurance program is one of the major unfinished items on America's social agenda. The National Health Plan I am submitting today creates both the framework and momentum to reach that long-sought goal.[1]

President Jimmy Carter, June 12, 1979

National health insurance has been talked about for many years. Now, at last, serious proposals have been introduced by Members in both Houses of Congress. Soon the President's proposal will be introduced. I hope that now the debate can begin in earnest. This can be the national health insurance Congress.[2]

Senator Edward M. Kennedy of Massachusetts, address on the Senate floor, September 6, 1979

During 1978–1979, the political system made its most serious and sustained effort thus far to establish national health insurance. Having been elected to the presidency on a pledge to secure the adoption of the program, Jimmy Carter was determined to fulfill his campaign promise before the end of his first, and only, term. Carter had a responsibility to the United Auto Workers (UAW) to obtain the institution of the program. During the spring 1976 primaries, the UAW had endorsed Carter for the Democratic presidential nomination. Its support was largely based upon his backing of national health insurance.[3] As a chief sponsor of the Health Security Act, the UAW was a strong supporter of national health insurance.[4] As a result, Carter had a special obligation to secure the establishment of the program to repay the substantial political debt he owed the UAW for its early and enthusiastic support of his presidential campaign.[5]

Edward Kennedy was committed to assist Carter in securing the establishment of national health insurance. Together, they had the potential to combine their substantial political resources in launching a credible effort to obtain the adoption of the program. However, Kennedy and Carter were deeply divided over the kind of national health insurance plan they believed should be instituted. As a result, despite their best efforts, they failed to negotiate a compromise plan they could jointly support, thus dooming prospects for the establishment of the program.

True, national health insurance stood no chance of establishment once the House rejected the Hospital Cost Containment Act. In the absence of health care cost-containment measures, national health insurance promised to be too costly and inflationary to implement. The House's rejection of the bill gave the overwhelming majority of its members the opportunity to voice their opposition to national health insurance, making its establishment a political impossibility.

Nevertheless, had Kennedy and Carter agreed on a compromise national health insurance plan, they might have been able to join forces in mobilizing substantial public support for their program. They could have used this support to pressure Congress into reversing its opposition to the program. Their inability to agree on a compromise plan deprived supporters of national health insurance of the opportunity to mount an effective political challenge against congressional opponents of the program. As a result, the opponents were able to take the political offensive, sabotaging Carter's efforts to secure the establishment of national health insurance by blocking his plan to contain health care costs. This deprived the political system of the capacity to create a fiscally and economically viable basis to institute national health insurance. The division between Kennedy and Carter over national health insurance dealt a fatal blow to prospects for its adoption during the late 1970s.

THE DIFFERENCES BETWEEN KENNEDY AND CARTER

During 1977–1978, Kennedy and Carter held a series of White House meetings in an effort to negotiate a compromise national health insurance plan they could jointly support.[6] They entered negotiations with substantial differences over the kind of national health insurance program they believed should be established. The most important difference was the extent to which private plans should play a role in any national health insurance program.

Kennedy had long opposed private health insurance as inequitable, wasteful, and inefficient. As he argued on the Senate floor on January 15, 1975, "I believe that the private health insurance industry has failed us. It fails to control costs. It fails to control quality. It provides partial benefits, not comprehensive benefits; acute care, not preventive care. It ignores the poor and the medically indigent."[7]

Kennedy believed that only the federal government had the capacity to establish an equitable and efficient health insurance program. As a result, his original national health insurance bill, the Health Security Act, would have scrapped and replaced private plans with a federally financed and administered insurance program providing universal, comprehensive coverage. In his address on the Senate floor on January 15, 1975, in which he introduced the bill in the Ninety-fourth Congress, Kennedy argued that it was "essential" that the federal government serve as "the insurance agent for all Americans."

It is essential in order to assure that all Americans have the same comprehensive insurance coverage at a cost they could afford. It is essential also to bringing reform in our health care system, because this role as the insurance carrier is the lever we need to control costs and improve the way health care is organized and delivered in our Nation.[8]

However, Carter rejected Kennedy's insistence on scrapping and replacing private health insurance with a federally financed and administered universal, comprehensive program. Rather, as early as his 1976 campaign, Carter committed himself to giving private plans a major role in the national health insurance program he intended to introduce, if elected president. "I would like to reserve the right to include the private sector, say, Blue Cross and Blue Shield, as a copartner with the federal government in the administration of a national health insurance program," Carter declared on March 14, 1976.[9]

Carter also promised that his national health insurance program would limit comprehensive coverage to the very poor. It would be extended to the remainder of the public only when such an expansion could occur on a fiscally and economically sound basis. "As President, I would want to give our people the most rapid improvement in individual health care the nation can afford, accommodating first those who need it most, with the understanding that it will be a comprehensive program in the end," Carter declared in a speech to the Student National Medical Association on April 16, 1976. "National priorities of [financial] need and [fiscal and economic] feasibility should determine the stages of the system's implementation."[10]

Carter's opposition to scrapping and replacing private health insurance with a federally financed and administered universal, comprehensive plan was based upon fiscal and economic considerations. Requiring the government to provide the entire public with universal, comprehensive coverage would have resulted in a substantial increase in federal spending. In the absence of either tax increases or spending reductions in other programs, such a program would raise the budget deficit. By reducing financial barriers impeding public access to health care, such a program also would have resulted in a rise in patient utilization of health care, especially among the poor and uninsured, leading to a rise in medical costs and the overall inflation rate. As a result, Carter considered such a program to be fiscally and economically reckless.

Consistent with his opposition to a federally financed and administered universal, comprehensive insurance plan, Carter strongly opposed the Health Security Act. In a June 1, 1978, meeting with his cabinet, he made it clear that he considered the bill to be economically and fiscally reckless. "It is ridiculous to think about endorsing a bill like Kennedy's. I am not going to destroy my credibility on inflation and budgetary matters. I intend to be honest and responsible with the American people."[11]

In a White House meeting in December 1977, Carter informed Kennedy that he would oppose any national health insurance program that did not preserve the existing, mostly private insurance system. As a result, to placate Carter, Kennedy abandoned his insistence on a federally financed and administered insurance program, agreeing to accept the President's demand that universal coverage be achieved largely through private plans.[12] However, after a stormy and unsuccessful White House meeting on July 28, 1978, Kennedy and Carter broke off their efforts to negotiate a national health insurance plan.[13] They sharply disagreed over three issues: the amount of health insurance coverage each individual should be guaranteed; how national health insurance was to be financed; the extent to which the existing insurance system should be reformed.

Kennedy insisted that the federal government require private health insurance plans to provide all citizens and residents comprehensive coverage under a single federally mandated plan. It would be progressively financed through income-related premiums; the higher the income, the greater the premium each family would be required to pay. The existing insurance system would be thoroughly restructured, with the federal government imposing a sweeping and far-reaching reorganization and consolidation of the insurance industry and stringent cost-containment measures.

Carter disagreed with Kennedy, proposing instead that private health insurance plans be free to market their own policies, each with its own benefit package. Individuals' coverage would depend upon what either they or their employers were willing to pay for, as is currently the case. National health insurance would be regressively financed through flat, nonincome-related premiums, as is also presently the case. The federal government would be restricted to requiring private plans to provide a minimum package of health care benefits and to impose a stop-loss to limit the amount of annual out-of-pocket expenses for medical services consumers would have to pay. In addition, the federal government would extend limited coverage to families not protected by group insurance. The existing insurance system would be left essentially intact, with the federal government imposing only modest cost-containment measures.

Due to their failure to resolve their differences over national health insurance, Kennedy and Carter went their separate ways on the issue. During the spring of 1979, each introduced his own national health insurance plan. On May 14 Kennedy joined Henry Waxman in presenting a national health insurance bill. On June 12 Carter followed by unveiling his National Health Plan.[14]

The Kennedy-Waxman bill would have reorganized the health insurance industry into five consortia: Blue Cross/Blue Shield, commercial plans, prepaid group practices, independent practice associations, and self-insured groups.[15] All citizens and residents not covered by Medicare would have been required to enroll in one of the five consortia. Medicare coverage would have been expanded to include all elderly and disabled individuals, rather than just those who are Social Security beneficiaries, as is currently the case.

All privately and publicly insured individuals would have received a uniform and federally mandated comprehensive package of health care benefits, completely free of charge, with no patient cost-sharing requirements on all covered medical services. Health insurance coverage would have been financed through income-related and community-rated premiums. Employers would have been required to fund at least 65 percent of the cost of insurance for their working families. The government would have provided tax credits to finance employer contributions to the private plans of their working families that exceeded 3 percent of payroll. The federal government and states would have funded the full cost of insurance for Supplemental Security Income (SSI) and Aid to Families with Dependent Children (AFDC) recipients, respectively. The federal government and states also would have contained health care costs through the imposition of annual prospective budgets.[16]

By requiring that universal health insurance coverage be achieved through private plans, the Kennedy-Waxman bill was designed to meet Carter's insistence that the private sector continue to play a dominant role in the financing and administration of health care. Kennedy candidly admitted this in an interview with *Newsweek* in May 1979: "The President indicated to us a year and a half ago that he wanted a system built on the private sector, and wanted the money off the budget. We tried to conform and comply with that request."[17]

Unlike the Kennedy-Waxman bill, the National Health Plan promised no sweeping transformation of the existing health insurance system. Rather, it pledged only to build upon the current voluntary, employment-based health insurance system. Employers would have been required to provide their full-time working families with group insurance and to finance 75 percent of its cost. The federal government would have provided assistance to employers facing excessive group insurance costs in one of two ways. It either would have provided subsidies for employers whose contributions to their group insurance exceeded 5 percent of payroll, or it would have extended employers subsidies equal to 5 percent of their payrolls to finance contributions to their group insurance.

Medicare and Medicaid would have been scrapped and replaced by a new federally financed and administered health insurance program, HealthCare, which would have provided coverage for individuals not enrolled in a group plan. Low-income families would have received premium-free HealthCare coverage. The elderly and disabled would have paid the same premiums for their HealthCare coverage as under Medicare. The remainder of the public not covered by group insurance would purchase their HealthCare coverage by paying community-rated premiums.

Both private and public health insurance plans would have been permitted to impose substantial patient cost-sharing requirements by charging premiums, deductibles, coinsurance, and copayments. A stop-loss would have been imposed that limited the maximum annual out-of-pocket health care expenses families incurred before receiving full coverage. The stop-loss would have been $1,250 for the elderly and disabled and $2,500 for the remainder of the public on all covered health care services. However, AFDC and SSI recipients, as well as families with incomes at or below 55 percent of the poverty line, would have received comprehensive HealthCare coverage, completely free of charge, with no patient cost-sharing requirements. All other families would have been eligible to receive such coverage once their health care expenses had reduced their incomes to at or below 55 percent of the poverty line.[18]

NATIONAL HEALTH INSURANCE: KENNEDY VERSUS CARTER

Having introduced their sharply opposing national health insurance plans, Kennedy and Carter remained adamant in their refusal to resolve their differences by negotiating a compromise program they could jointly support. Rather, each insisted on passage of his own plan and denounced the program of the other. The Carter administration launched a blistering attack against the Kennedy-Waxman bill, opposing it for four reasons: it would have imposed a substantial increase in federal spending; it would have required excessive federal regulation of the health care system; it would have resulted in severe health care rationing; and it was politically unfeasible.

The Kennedy-Waxman bill would have required the federal government to provide Medicare, AFDC, and SSI beneficiaries with comprehensive health insurance coverage without any patient cost-sharing requirements. By contrast, the National Health Plan would have mandated the federal government to give low-income families, the elderly, and disabled more limited coverage. Members of the three groups would have had to assume substantial cost-sharing requirements. Only the very poor would have been exempt from cost sharing.

As a result, HEW estimated that in 1980 the Kennedy-Waxman bill would have raised federal spending by $30.7 billion, compared with $17.6 billion for the National Health Plan.[19] Carter considered the Kennedy-Waxman bill to be fiscally reckless and refused even to consider it. "What the Massachusetts Senator had proposed was an enormously complicated program run entirely by the federal government, with an annual price tag estimated even then as at least $100 billion—and perhaps twice as much," Carter charged in his memoirs. "Some of these federal expenditures would replace what was already being spent by private sources."[20]

In addition to imposing a substantial increase in federal spending, the Kennedy-Waxman bill would have required the government to contain health care costs by establishing an annual prospective budget. The Carter administration opposed the cost-containment provisions of the bill, arguing that it would result in excessive government regulation of the health care system. "To us, Kennedy's plan looked like an administratively unworkable and politically unachievable proposal, too much too fast in terms of cost and suffocating government regulation and bureaucracy," Joseph Califano noted in his memoirs. "It notably failed to take advantage of existing employer-employee relationships and private insurance systems."[21]

The Carter administration was not opposed in principle to federal regulation of health care costs. Indeed, Chapter 4 showed how the administration had fought hard from 1977 to 1979 in its unsuccessful campaign to secure passage of its own health care cost-containment program—the Hospital Cost Containment Act. However, the Kennedy-Waxman bill would have imposed far more stringent health care cost-containment measures than the Hospital Cost Containment Act. The Kennedy-Waxman bill would have limited the annual increase in health care spending to the average rate of growth in the GNP during the previous three-year period.[22]

Had the Kennedy-Waxman bill been in effect from 1980 to 1990, the average annual rate of growth in health care spending would have been 2.4 percent—equivalent to the average yearly rate of increase in the GNP during this period.[23] By contrast, health care spending actually rose at an average annual rate of 16.9 percent from 1980 to 1990.[24] The only way such a massive reduction in health care spending could have been achieved was through stringent rationing of medical resources. HEW Secretary Patricia R. Harris pointed this out in her appearance before two House committees on November 29, 1979.

This type of controlled, tight budgeting system . . . could work only in a highly structured health system which places severe limits on consumer access. Within the context of the U.S. health care system, a closed-end budget would inevitably result in an arbitrary rationing of health care services.[25]

The Hospital Cost Containment Act would have imposed far less stringent cost-containment measures than the Kennedy-Waxman bill. Unlike the Kennedy-Waxman bill, which would have contained the entire cost of health care, the Hospital Cost Containment Act would have been limited to hospital care, with all other medical services free of federal cost regulation. Moreover, the Hospital Cost Containment Act would have permitted a substantial rise in hospital costs. Chapter 4 noted that it would have allowed hospital costs to rise by 11.6 percent in 1979. From 1980 to 1989, the actual average annual rate of growth in hospital costs was 14.2 percent.[26] Had the Hospital Cost Containment Act been in effect during this period, and had annual hospital costs been allowed to increase by no more than 11.6 percent, the bill would have reduced hospital expenses by a fifth, representing nearly a 10 percent cut in overall health care costs.

The Kennedy-Waxman bill would have imposed a massive reduction in health care costs, resulting in stringent rationing of medical resources. By contrast, the Hospital Cost Containment Act would have instituted a more modest reduction in health care costs, leading to moderate rationing of medical resources. Opposed to any austere system of health care rationing, the Carter administration flatly rejected the Kennedy-Waxman bill, insisting that it would not accept anything more than the modest cost-containment provisions of the Hospital Cost Containment Act.

A final major reason why the Carter administration rejected the Kennedy-Waxman bill was that it was politically unfeasible. There was virtually no chance that the bill would be passed, since it would have resulted in more federal spending and regulation than the political system was willing to accept. As Califano declared at a press briefing on the National Health Plan following its introduction by Carter on June 12, 1979, "There's no more chance of passing Kennedy's plan than there is of putting an elephant through a keyhole."[27]

The Kennedy-Waxman bill was the latest effort by liberal Democrats to establish a federally mandated universal, comprehensive health insurance program. Truman and Kennedy had undertaken campaigns to institute such a program during the 1940s and the 1970s, respectively. And both campaigns had failed. The history of the politics of national health insurance convinced Carter that the only kind of program with a reasonable chance of being established was one that would build upon, rather than scrap and replace, the existing insurance system.

Kennedy's sponsorship of the Kennedy-Waxman bill reinforced Carter's belief that the senator was incapable of developing a national health insurance measure with a reasonable chance of being passed. In his memoirs, Carter argues that "Kennedy had the long-standing support of some labor leaders and senior-citizens organizations, but even after ten years or so, he had never been able to put his ideas into acceptable legislation that could be moved out of his own Senate committee."[28]

Carter accused Kennedy of taking an uncompromising position on national health insurance. As he saw it, Kennedy wanted a federally mandated universal, comprehensive health insurance program or no plan at all. Carter rejected the notion that the choice before the nation on the issue of health insurance lay between those two opposing extremes. Rather, he believed in seeking a middle ground, a plan that achieved universal coverage through the existing insurance system. In his remarks introducing his National Health Plan, Carter stated:

There are those who sincerely believe that we must insist upon a full-scale, comprehensive plan enacted all at once. The idea of all or nothing has been pursued now for almost three decades. But I must say in all candor that no child of poverty, no elderly American, no middle-class family has yet benefited from a rigid and unswerving commitment to this principle of all or nothing.[29]

Kennedy countered the Carter administration's opposition to the Kennedy-Waxman bill by making objections to the National Health Plan. He charged that the plan failed to provide the public both adequate health insurance coverage and equitable access to health care, while containing medical costs in the process.

By permitting substantial patient cost-sharing requirements, Kennedy argued, the National Health Plan failed to adequately reduce the powerful financial barriers impeding public access to health care. Those barriers could be fully lifted only when the public was relieved of the financial burden of having to meet patient cost-sharing requirements. Since the Kennedy-Waxman bill would have provided the public with comprehensive health insurance coverage, without any patient cost sharing, the measure would have given the population better access to health care than that granted by the National Health Plan.

By allowing health care costs to be determined largely by market forces, as is currently the case, Kennedy claimed that the National Health Plan would do nothing to contain soaring medical expenses. To do so adequately required that health care costs be determined by the government through a prospective budget. Unlike the National Health Plan, the Kennedy-Waxman bill would have established such a budget, as we have seen. This is why the Kennedy-Waxman bill would have been more effective in containing health care costs than the National Health Plan.[30]

Kennedy especially opposed the fact that the National Health Plan would have established two health insurance programs: an employment-based plan for working families and a federal plan, HealthCare, for low-income families, the elderly, and the disabled. It would have required doctors treating HealthCare patients to accept reimbursement through federal fee schedules, which would be the same as those used by Medicare. Doctors would have had to agree to the federal government's approved charges as payment in full for all services rendered to their HealthCare patients. They could not bill those patients for any additional charges. On the other hand, doctors would have been free to charge whatever the market would bear in providing services to their privately insured patients.[31]

Kennedy charged that the National Health Plan would create a two-tier health care system. Doctors stood to lose financially by treating HealthCare patients, since they would have had to accept lower reimbursement than they might otherwise charge. Moreover, they could not recover their financial losses by billing their HealthCare patients for the difference. In 1989 only 40.7 percent of doctors participated in Medicare, accepting its approved charges as payment in full for all services rendered under the program. The remaining 59.3 percent of all doctors refused to participate in the program, reserving the right to bill their Medicare patients for additional charges.[32]

Since HealthCare would have used the same fee schedules as those utilized by Medicare, it is safe to assume that only a minority of doctors would have agreed to participate in HealthCare. As a result, they would have refused to treat HealthCare patients. They would have treated only privately insured patients, since they could charge whatever they wished for services provided through the private sector. A two-tier health care system would have resulted, in which privately insured patients had access to all the best doctors available, while publicly insured ones were limited to the minority of physicians willing to treat them.[33]

Unlike the National Health Plan, the Kennedy-Waxman bill would have established a single health insurance program providing coverage to all, rich and poor, working families and those not employed. Doctors would have been required to accept reimbursement through state fee schedules, which would be the same as those used by Medicare. They could not bill their patients for any additional charges.

Also unlike the National Health Plan, the fee schedules established by the Kennedy-Waxman bill would have applied to all patients, not just those insured by the government. All third-party payers would have been prohibited from reimbursing any doctor who refused to participate in the Kennedy-Waxman plan.[34] As a result, doctors would have had no choice but to participate in the plan. Few, if any, patients would have been willing to go to doctors who refused to participate, since they would not receive any insurance coverage for the services provided by those physicians.

Unlike the National Health Plan, doctors would gain no financial advantage by favoring the treatment of privately insured over publicly insured patients under the Kennedy-Waxman bill. Rather, they would receive reimbursement under the same fee schedule for treating all patients. Moreover, they would have strong financial incentives to participate in the Kennedy-Waxman plan, since to do otherwise would result in a substantial loss of patients and income. Under the Kennedy-Waxman bill, all individuals—rich and poor, working, retired, and unemployed families alike—would have the same access to all doctors, assuring that no two-tier health care system developed.

Kennedy was strident in his denunciation of the National Health Plan, charging that its establishment would undermine the health care system.

By failing to set a national budget, by inadequately controlling hospital costs, by failing to control doctors' fees in the private sector, by creating two separate and unequal systems of care, the President's plan may well become the straw that breaks the back of the American health care system.[35]

EDWARD M. KENNEDY AND NATIONAL HEALTH INSURANCE

Perhaps no political leader has displayed a deeper and more passionate commitment to health care reform than Edward Kennedy. National health insurance was an important issue for him politically. It served to solidify his credibility as leader of the liberal wing of the Democratic Party. Kennedy could not abandon his commitment to a sweeping and ambitious national health insurance program without sacrificing his leadership role of the Democratic Left.

National health insurance fit nicely into Kennedy's overall social welfare policy agenda. Kennedy eschewed means-tested and race-specified social welfare programs. The taxes to fund them come largely from the white middle class. The benefits are distributed mostly to the nonwhite poor. Means-tested and race-specified programs tended to polarize society between white middle-class taxpayers and nonwhite welfare recipients.

Kennedy wanted to secure the development of a welfare state that could unite the white middle class and nonwhite poor. He sought to forge bonds of solidarity between the two groups, and he saw national health insurance as the issue that could do this. Because health care remains a privilege of employment and income, the ability of nonrich families to secure access to medical services remains tenuous and cannot be guaranteed. All families, regardless of their income or race, have a stake in assuring their access to health care, which can be achieved only through national health insurance.

National health insurance is not a means-tested and race-specified program targeted to benefit the nonwhite poor. Rather, it is a universal program that would benefit all families, rich and poor, white and nonwhite, alike. Kennedy saw national health insurance as an issue that could appeal to all nonrich Americans. It could obliterate the polarization between white middle-class taxpayers and nonwhite welfare recipients that means-tested and race-specific programs have traditionally created. As James MacGregor Burns put it in his 1976 biography of Kennedy:

He has chosen health as his cornerstone issue for institutional change in the seventies, in part because it is an issue in which white, black, Chicano, and others have common cause. . . . Health, in this sense, is a safe issue. If the Senator became a national leader, one Kennedy staff person said that it was very possible that he would have "no antipoverty program" as such, no program easily identified as black or Chicano. The intent is to define issues in terms of universal "human rights" that touch all the oppressed regardless of race.[36]

Burns goes on to note that Kennedy found it difficult to secure the establishment of any social welfare program unless there is "a little something for everybody." As one Kennedy staff member explained, a white middle-class individual will not object if "some fellow down the line gets something as long as he does, too." Health insurance is that kind of program and that is perhaps the primary reason why Kennedy has invested so much energy on it," Burns concludes. "The issue cuts across all social and economic boundaries," notes S. Philip Caper, a Kennedy health care policy adviser.[37]

Kennedy's desire to use national health insurance as an issue to appeal to the white middle class is explained by Theo Lippman:

It was always understood that health care was Kennedy's middle-class-white issue. He was becoming identified with the various minority groups—blacks, Chicanos, youths, the very poor. He needed something to show the great middle-working-class that he was on its side. And everybody had medical expenses.[38]

JIMMY CARTER AND NATIONAL HEALTH INSURANCE

Carter was torn over national health insurance, perhaps more so than on any other issue he confronted as president. On the one hand, he supported the program. However, he also had deep misgivings concerning the political and fiscal wisdom of establishing it. Carter "clearly thought NHI was good politics, but he was not, personally, enthusiastic about it," Jonas Morris explains. "He came to endorse it slowly, and somewhat reluctantly, and his ideas on national health insurance were distinctly different from those generally espoused by the Democratic Party, particularly the liberal northern wing as represented by organized labor and Ted Kennedy.[39]

Carter's thinking on national health insurance changed dramatically during 1976–1977. On June 12, 1976, Carter appeared before the Democratic national convention's platform committee to endorse a federally-financed universal insurance program: "We need a national health insurance program financed by general tax revenues and employer/employee shared payroll tax which is universal and mandatory."[40] However, when Carter entered the White House, he completely reversed himself, insisting that any national health insurance program must build upon the existing voluntary employment-based insurance system.[41]

How can we explain Carter's change of attitude on national health insurance during 1976–1977? The answer lies in the dire economic conditions that plagued the United States during the Carter administration, as the American economy became mired in sluggish economic growth, high inflation, and mounting federal deficits. By 1978, Carter had come to the conclusion that any national health insurance program, even one mostly financed by the private sector, would wreak havoc on the economy and federal budget. This made him disinclined to press ahead with a program. However, during the 1976 presidential campaign, Carter had promised the public, especially the UAW, that he would work for the establishment of the program. He felt he had to honor his campaign pledge, despite his deep misgivings about doing so. On June 1, 1978, Carter outlined the dilemma he faced to his cabinet.

I have already made a number of commitments—during my campaign and subsequently to the UAW and to Senator Kennedy. At the same time, there appears to be no significant additional money for health care available in the budget in the next few years and I will not do anything to undermine the current effort to control inflation.[42]

The administration itself was deeply divided over national health insurance. Secretary of the Treasury Michael Blumenthal; James McIntyre, director of the Office of Management and Budget; Charles Shultze, chairman of the Council of Economic Advisers; and Robert Strauss, Carter's special trade representative, urged the president to abandon his commitment to the program. They shared his concerns about the negative fiscal and economic consequences of the program. McIntyre and Shultze warned Carter that the program would require a tax increase.

On the other hand, Califano and Stuart Eizenstat, director of the White House Domestic Affairs and Policy Staff, urged Carter to pursue his commitment to national health insurance.[43] Califano believed that the health care system was

politically and economically unsustainable given the existence of a large uninsured population and soaring medical costs.[44] "We could not afford the health
care system as it stood," he told Carter in a November 9, 1977, meeting.[45]
Carter agreed. In the June 1, 1978, meeting with his cabinet, Carter denounced
the health care system as "horrible and very soon . . . unsupportable."[46]

Given his commitment to health care reform and his need to act upon his
promise to the UAW, Carter ultimately broke free of his misgivings over national
health insurance, agreeing to recommend its establishment. He had a completely
free hand in developing a program of his own choice. True, he had promised
the UAW that he would press for its establishment. However, he never committed
himself to any particular program. Carter in fact was the only major Democratic
presidential candidate in 1976 who had refused to endorse the UAW-sponsored
Health Security Act.[47] His freedom to develop any national health insurance
program of his choice was an important asset for him. It allowed him to design
a modest and limited national health insurance program, the National Health
Plan, that would have imposed only a marginal increase in federal spending.

Carter's determination to adhere rigidly to a fiscally conservative course on
national health insurance was largely due to congressional pressure. Key congressional Democratic leaders were strongly opposed to the program, fearing that it
would boost the deficit and fan inflation. Leaders who shared this view included
House Ways and Means Committee Chairman Al Ullman of Oregon; Daniel
Rostenkowski, chairman of Ways and Means Health Subcommittee; Senate Finance Committee Chairman Russell B. Long of Louisiana; Herman Talmadge
of Georgia, chairman of Finance's Health Subcommittee, and Senator Abraham
Ribicoff of Connecticut, an influential committee member. Those leaders lobbied
Carter and Califano not to send any national health insurance bill to Congress.
Kennedy and Waxman were virtually the only congressional leaders pressing
them to recommend a bill.[48] Congressional support for the program was so weak
that in a March 2, 1978, Oval Office meeting, Califano told Carter:

There is little stomach on the Hill for any national health insurance legislation this year,
except for Kennedy. The congressmen I talk to . . . won't get involved in more taxes to
finance national health insurance, that's too much of a political liability for them in an
election year. And that could kill your chances of passing any national health bill.[49]

Due to congressional opposition to national health insurance, Califano urged
Carter to delay his recommendation of the program until 1979—advice the
president followed.[50]

THE 1980 PRESIDENTIAL CAMPAIGN AND THE ELECTION
OF RONALD REAGAN

Neither the Kennedy-Waxman bill nor the National Health Plan received
serious congressional consideration. Both bills were overshadowed by the 1980

presidential campaign. By the end of 1979, Kennedy and Carter were locked in a bitter struggle for the Democratic presidential nomination.

Kennedy's unsuccessful campaign for the 1980 Democratic presidential nomination did not end prospects for the establishment of national health insurance. Rather, after he defeated Kennedy to win the Democratic nomination, Carter reiterated his endorsement of national health insurance. He campaigned on a pledge to secure the establishment of the program, if reelected to a second term. "I think we ought to have [national health insurance]," Carter declared during a campaign stop in Youngstown, Ohio, on October 20, 1980. "I'm strongly in favor of it."[51]

Carter made health care reform a major issue during the 1980 presidential campaign. He repeatedly condemned his Republican challenger, former Governor Ronald Reagan of California, for his opposition to Medicare in 1965. In his October 28, 1980, debate with Reagan in Cleveland, Carter noted that "Governor Reagan, as a matter of fact, began his political career campaigning around this Nation against Medicare."[52] At a campaign rally in Newark, New Jersey, the following day, Carter pointed out that Reagan had opposed Medicare while serving "as spokesman for the American Medical Association and the anti-Medicare lobby."[53]

In his debate with Carter, Reagan attempted to defuse the president's attacks against him for his opposition to Medicare by humorously responding, "There you go again."[54] After inducing laughter in the audience, Reagan proceeded to explain away his opposition to Medicare by noting that he had not objected to the principle of providing health care to the elderly, but only to the specific Medicare bill that was passed.[55] In his memoirs, Reagan denied that he ever opposed Medicare, contradicting his acknowledgment that he had done so in his debate with Carter.[56]

No one should be fooled by the confused and contradictory statements Reagan has made on his past position on Medicare. The fact remains that Carter was correct in noting that Reagan had begun his political career by assisting the AMA in its campaign to defeat Medicare. In 1965 Reagan narrated an anti-Medicare record entitled "Ronald Reagan Speaks Out Against Socialized Medicine." The record was produced by the AMA as part of its campaign to defeat Medicare. The AMA distributed the record to a group of women supporters, known as the Woman's Auxiliary, whose responsibility was to play the record for guests in their homes. After the record was played, members of the Woman's Auxiliary would urge their guests to write to their senators and representatives, urging them to oppose Medicare.[57]

In "Ronald Reagan Speaks Out Against Socialized Medicine," the former actor denounced Medicare as "socialized medicine" that would lead to the outright establishment of socialism. "One of the traditional methods of imposing statism or socialism on a people has been by way of medicine," Reagan argued. "It's very easy to disguise a medical program as a humanitarian project."[58]

Reagan asked the public to write to their senators and representatives, demanding that they defeat Medicare.

Write those letters now; call your friends and tell them to write them. If you don't, this program, I promise you, will pass just as surely as the sun will come up tomorrow. And behind it will come other federal programs that will invade every area of freedom as we have known it in this country. Until one day . . . we will awake to find that we have socialism. And if you don't do this and if I don't do it, one of these days you and I are going to spend our sunset years telling our children and our children's children what it once was like in America when men were free.[59]

During his 1976 and 1980 presidential campaigns, Reagan was just as emphatic in his opposition to national health insurance as he had been to Medicare in 1965. In an article published in the August 1975 issue of *Private Practice*, the journal of the Congress of County Medical Societies, Reagan denounced national health insurance, erroneously arguing that

Virtually all Americans have access to excellent health care today. . . . Dwelling first on the illusion of massive lack of access to medical care on the part of Americans, the collectivist politicians and their bureaucratic camp followers would . . . implement the delusion that somehow government medicine (read it National Health Insurance) is the solution.

It is, in a word, a delusion to suppose that national health insurance is "the answer."[60]

Continuing his attacks against national health insurance, on February 15, 1976, Reagan told the *Kansas City Star* that the program was "a polite name for socialized medicine. You can't socialize the doctor without socializing the patient."[61]

Reagan reiterated his opposition to national health insurance during the 1980 presidential campaign. He charged that "federal intervention in the form of national health insurance" would be disastrous, arguing that such programs abroad had resulted in "a great reduction in the quality of medical care."[62] "I'm opposed to national health insurance," Reagan declared during the campaign. "There is no health crisis in America."[63] Reagan's election to the presidency ended whatever prospects might have existed for establishing national health insurance during a second Carter administration. As Jonas Morris notes, "Reagan was firmly against anything called national health insurance, equating any such program with socialized medicine."[64]

Consistent with his opposition to national health insurance, Reagan was committed to reduce federal involvement in the health care system, campaigning on a pledge to eliminate "unnecessary government regulation of hospitals and the medical profession."[65] Reagan's election ushered in a new era in health care policy, in which Washington practically ceased efforts, undertaken during the Carter administration, to expand federal regulation of the medical system.[66] As

Linda E. Demkovich put it, under the Reagan administration, there would be "no national health insurance [and] no mandatory hospital cost containment."[67]

Reagan's election provided the hospital industry with a welcome relief from the battles it had waged during the Carter administration to prevent federal containment of hospital costs. With a right-wing government firmly opposed to federal regulation of the health care system now in power, the industry was fully protected, at least for the foreseeable future, from further efforts by the political system to restrain the entrepreneurial freedoms and financial activities of hospitals, as well as other medical providers. In the FAHS's 1981 annual report, the interest group's president, Michael D. Bromberg, who had played a key role in the hospital industry's lobbying campaign against the Hospital Cost Containment Act, welcomed Reagan's assumption of the presidency. He praised Reagan for having established

an administration opposed to government regulation of our industry, opposed to comprehensive national health insurance, opposed to cost controls, opposed to planning, and receptive to new ideas. . . . We have never been in a better position in our history.[68]

Reagan's election abruptly ended efforts to achieve health care reform, which had been under way during the Carter administration. Health care reformers ceased their campaign to establish national health insurance, recognizing that the program stood virtually no chance of establishment as long as a right-wing president firmly opposed to any overhaul of the medical system resided in the White House. During the Reagan administration, practically no health care reform measures of any kind were adopted.[69]

The moratorium on health care reform continued following George Bush's election to the presidency. Bush endorsed Reagan's opposition to health care reform, but unlike Reagan, failed to keep health care reform off the national agenda during his presidency. As the United States entered the 1990s, pressure began to build for health care reform. This resulted in a renewed campaign to establish national health insurance during 1991–1992, which will be discussed in Chapter 8.

CONCLUSION

The effort to establish national health insurance during the late 1970s was dealt a fatal blow by the failure of Kennedy and Carter to agree on compromise health care reform plan. Agreement between the two was especially important in light of rising congressional opposition to national health insurance. Carter knew this all too well. In his White House meeting with Kennedy on July 28, 1978, Carter warned the Senator that "A split between us would doom prospects for health insurance."[70] Carter could not have been more correct. The failure of Kennedy and Carter to agree on a compromise health care reform plan gave congressional opponents of national health insurance an opportunity to seize the initiative in preventing the program from being placed on the legislative agenda during the Carter administration.

Agreement between Kennedy and Carter on a compromise national health insurance plan proved to be politically impossible because of the rigidlyinflexible positions each side took. Kennedy remained committed to a universal, comprehensive insurance program. He failed to take the existence of both fiscal constraints and political and intellectual opposition to federal regulation into account in his development of a national health insurance plan. He insisted on a plan that would have increased federal spending and expanded regulation of the health care system beyond levels the political system was willing to accept.

Carter was on the opposite extreme. While Kennedy was generally disinterested in taking the existence of both budgetary limits and political and intellectual opposition to federal regulation into account in developing a national health insurance plan, Carter refused to consider any program that resulted in a substantial increase in federal spending and stringent government controls over the health care system. The National Health Plan was designed less to improve the health care system than to avoid a tax increase and to assure that the private sector would continue to assume a dominant role in the financing of medical services.

In the end, Kennedy and Carter found themselves incapable of compromising their inflexible positions. They could not do so because compromise would damage their political credibility.

For Kennedy, national health insurance went to the heart of his political credibility as leader of the liberal wing of the Democratic Party. He was committed to developing a program that could improve access to health care among the middle class and the poor. He saw in national health insurance an issue that would allow the Democratic Left to build a constituency transcending all socioeconomic and racial barriers. It was important that he develop a universal, comprehensive health insurance program benefiting all individuals equally. To do anything less would undermine the credibility of his commitment to the well-being of all nonrich individuals, especially the white middle class, not just the poor and nonwhite. Kennedy approached the issue of national health insurance within an ideological context, seeking to develop a program that could boost the political fortunes of the Democratic Left, particularly with the white middle class.

For Carter, national health insurance went to the heart of his integrity as a fiscal and economic manager. Presiding over a nation plagued by high inflation and a mounting federal deficit, he was not about to accept any social welfare program that threatened to drive up inflation, substantially raise federal taxes and spending, or lead to stringent government regulation of any sector of the economy. Carter was sensitive to the need for health care reform, but only if it could be accommodated within the stringent limits on the fiscal and regulatory powers of government that determine the conduct of public policy. He approached the issue of national health insurance within a pragmatic context, seeking to develop a program within the realm of what he believed was politically possible.

Kennedy's ideological liberalism and Carter's political pragmatism turned out to be a deadly combination. They made compromise on national health insurance politically impossible, thus killing the final chance to establish the program before the onset of the Reagan presidency.

PART III

The Politics of National Health Insurance during the 1990s

CHAPTER 6

The Reemergence of National Health Insurance as a Major Political Issue

The United States is beginning a major debate on the financing of health care. The major stakeholders in health care services—physicians and hospital administrators, management and labor, insurers, suppliers of equipment and pharmaceuticals, elected officials, and the general insured population—are becoming increasingly dissatisfied with the current system....

Elected officials and private organizations have already advanced many and varied plans to reform health care financing.[1]

Henry J. Aaron, director, the Brookings Economic Studies Program

Three important reasons why the United States has no national health insurance are the intense and unrelenting opposition to the program mounted by the AMA, the lack of strong public support for the program, and the existence of an insurance system. AMA opposition to the program during the 1940s prevented its early establishment. During the 1940s and 1970s, the public was evenly divided in its preference between government and private insurance. Congress was unwilling to establish national health insurance over AMA opposition, especially in the absence of strong public support for it. This gave the AMA an opportunity to promote the development of private insurance as a politically acceptable alternative to a government program. The AMA joined other private organizations—the AHA, business, and organized labor—in fostering the growth of private insurance.

Employers assumed a critical role in the development of private health insurance through their contributions to group plans. The provision of federal tax subsidies for such contributions gave firms financial incentives to provide their working families with group coverage and to finance most of its cost. This stimulated the expansion of private insurance.

Because the provision of private health insurance is mostly employment-based, it serves primarily working families. As a result, only a relatively small share of individuals outside the labor market were privately insured. In 1965 only 56 percent of the elderly were.[2]

In 1965 Congress acted to rectify the gap in private health insurance coverage left by its failure to provide health care protection to most individuals outside the labor market. It established Medicare for the elderly and (in 1972) the disabled and Medicaid for the poor—the three largest groups that, for the most part, do not participate in the labor force. The existence of an insurance system, consisting of private plans, Medicare, and Medicaid, is the most important reason why the United States has no national health insurance. With 85.3 percent of the public insured as of 1991, Congress sees no urgent and compelling need for the program.[3]

A final reason why the United States has no national health insurance is that Congress was unwilling to establish health care cost-containment measures during the 1970s. By reducing financial barriers that impeded public access to health care, national health insurance promised to raise patient utilization of medical services, especially among the poor and uninsured, thereby increasing medical costs and the overall inflation rate. To the extent that an expansion in insurance coverage was achieved through the federal government, the program also was certain to raise the budget deficit. The fiscal and economic viability of national health insurance required the imposition of stringent health care cost-containment measures to assure that the program did not add appreciably to inflation and the deficit—both of which rose during the 1970s. Accordingly, Congress's refusal to impose such measures deprived the Carter administration of any rational basis to proceed with its plans to secure the establishment of a national health insurance program. Carter's attempts to obtain the adoption of national health insurance were further complicated by his deep differences with Senator Edward Kennedy over the kind of program that should be established. With Kennedy and Carter unable to reach agreement on a compromise health care reform plan they could jointly support, congressional opponents of national health insurance succeeded in keeping the program off the legislative agenda during the late 1970s.

THE RETURN OF NATIONAL HEALTH INSURANCE

However, despite the past failures to establish national health insurance, it is far from a dead issue. Quite the contrary; during the 1990s, national health insurance has returned to assume a prominent place on the political agenda for two reasons: the United States faces a severe and rapidly worsening health care crisis, which the political system can no longer ignore; and public support for the program has risen to an all-time high.

The Health Care Crisis

The United States currently confronts a severe and rapidly worsening health care crisis of unprecedented magnitude. A rapidly expanding uninsured population and soaring health care costs have severely undermined the foundations of the medical system. The United States spends substantially more on health care than any other nation, and yet remains the only advanced industrial democracy where a significant number of individuals are uninsured.

In the absence of far-reaching health care reform, it is doubtful that the medical system as we know it—capable of providing the overwhelming majority of the public with reasonably good access to health services—will survive beyond the 1990s. Rather, access to health care is increasingly becoming limited to the wealthy, who can afford to purchase private health insurance, and to the shrinking number of working families who are covered by group plans. To understand the origins of the health care crisis, we must comprehend how the current voluntary employment-based insurance system developed, and why it is increasingly failing to provide the overwhelming majority of the public with the reasonably good access to medical care that they once enjoyed.

The voluntary employment-based health insurance system was tied to the rise of large corporations, which dominated the American economy during the first four decades of the postwar era. During this period, a substantial share of the public was employed by large corporations, virtually all of which provided their working families with comprehensive group insurance coverage. Because the public had access to extensive group insurance benefits, it saw no urgent and compelling need for a government program. As a result, no political basis existed for the establishment of national health insurance.

However, far-reaching transformations in the American economy are wreaking havoc upon the voluntary employment-based health insurance system. Thrust into an increasingly competitive global marketplace, large American corporations are downsizing their operations, as they reduce costs by cutting the size of their labor forces. This has resulted in widespread layoffs of corporate workers with group insurance coverage. As unemployment rose, the tax base shrank, resulting in massive budget deficits. To balance their budgets, state and local governments have reduced their public services, resulting in massive layoffs of government workers with group insurance.

Many, if not most, of laid-off corporate and government workers have either remained unemployed or found jobs with small firms, which often do not provide them any group insurance. As a result, the ranks of uninsured are swelling. Reflecting the widespread layoffs of previously-insured corporate and government workers which have occurred during the Bush Administration, the share of the public covered by group plans declined from 59.3 percent in 1989 to 57.1 percent in 1991.[4]

The cost of a private health insurance plan providing even the most minimal

Table 6.1
The Employment and Income Status of the Uninsured in 1990

```
------------------------------------------------------------
Employment                              Percent of
Status                                  Uninsured
------------------------------------------------------------
Year-Round, Full-Time                   54.0
Year-Round, Some Unemployment           15.8
Part-Year                                8.0
Year-Round, Part-Time                    7.7
Unemployed                              14.5
------------------------------------------------------------
Income
------------------------------------------------------------
Under $5,000                            12.7
$5,000 to $9,999                        14.0
$10,000 to $14,999                      15.9
$15,000 to $19,999                      12.7
$20,000 to $29,999                      18.3
$30,000 to $39,999                      10.5
$40,000 to $49,999                       5.7
$50,000 or Over                         10.3
------------------------------------------------------------
Source: Julie Kosterlitz, "A Sick System,"
National Journal, February 15, 1992, p. 385.
```

coverage is beyond the financial reach of many, if not most, families. As a result, relatively few families without group insurance can afford to purchase their own private plans. Rather, practically the only means in which all but the wealthiest families can insure themselves is through their employers, who usually pay most of the cost of coverage for their working households.

Because the cost of private health insurance is beyond the financial reach of all but the wealthiest individuals, most uninsured persons are not unemployed and poor—many of whom receive Medicaid coverage, but rather, members of working middle-class families. Table 6.1 shows that in 1990 69.8 percent of the uninsured were members of year-round, full-time working families and 63. percent middle class, earning annual incomes of $20,00 to $50,000. Many, if not most, small businesses do not provide group insurance to their working families. As a result, in 1990 most uninsured workers were employed in small business, as Table 6.2 shows. Soaring health care costs have practically priced middle-class working families not covered by group plans, out of the insurance market, and forced many, if not most, to become uninsured.

Not all uninsured individuals are unable to afford the cost of private health insurance. Many uninsured individuals have the financial means to purchase

Table 6.2
Nonelderly Uninsured Workers in 1990

Number of Workers Firms	Percent of Workers Uninsured
Self-employed	13.6
Under 25	36.2
25-99	15.2
100-499	11.8
500-999	3.3
1,000 or More	20.0

Source: Christine Shenot, "Are Health Reforms at Hand?," Investor's Business Daily, November 18, 1991, p. 1.

private plans, but are not eligible, either because they have pre-existing medical conditions, or are for a specific reason considered uninsurable at any price.

Many families who are able and willing to purchase private health insurance choose not to do so because they have members with pre-existing medical conditions. To limit their financial liabilities, private plans exclude pre-existing medical conditions from the coverage they provide their subscribers. Pre-existing medical conditions are often the single greatest health care expense families incur. As a result, private plans that exclude such conditions from coverage are usually practically worthless. Families find it financially unfeasible to pay the high cost of private insurance when pre-existing medical conditions, their greatest single health care expense, are excluded from coverage. As a result, they have no alternative but to become uninsured.

Many individuals who can afford to purchase private health insurance are denied the opportunity to do so because they have chronic medical conditions that require continual and extensive treatment and thus make them uninsurable at any price. To limit their financial liabilities, private plans cherry-pick subscribers, agreeing to provide coverage to the healthiest individuals while denying health care protection to the sickest ones. By maintaining a relatively healthy subscriber base with minimal health care expenses, private plans are able to restrain the growth in their premiums, and remain competitive in the voluntary insurance market.

Unable either to afford the cost of private health insurance or to purchase a voluntary plan providing coverage for preexisting medical conditions—or even any health care protection at all because they have chronic medical conditions— the only recourse available to all but the wealthiest working families without a group plan is to seek either Medicare or Medicaid coverage. However, Medicare coverage is limited to three groups: the elderly, individuals who have received Social Security Disability Insurance benefits for over twenty-four months, and individuals who are undergoing kidney dialysis or have had a kidney transplant.[5]

Practically all working families are composed of nonelderly and able-bodied individuals. As a result, relatively few members of working families qualify for Medicare coverage.

Nonelderly, able-bodied individuals may qualify for Medicaid coverage if they meet a means test.[6] The cost of Medicaid has soared from $734 million in 1966 to $127.2 billion in 1992.[7] In 1992 the states, which determine eligibility requirements for Medicaid, financed 43 percent of its cost, with the remainder funded by the federal government.[8] The soaring cost of Medicaid represents a fiscal threat to the states, practically all of which are constitutionally required to have a balanced budget. As a result, the states have acted to reduce skyrocketing Medicaid costs by maintaining extremely tight eligibility requirements for the program that have left all but the very poor without any coverage.[9] Due to the existence of highly restrictive eligibility requirements, in 1987 only 42 percent of the poor received Medicaid coverage.[10]

An increasing share of the public cannot find employers willing to provide group health insurance, are too poor to purchase private plans, too "rich" to qualify for Medicaid, and too young and healthy to be eligible for Medicare. They are falling through the cracks of America's incomplete and underdeveloped insurance system, and are becoming uninsured. The share of the public who were uninsured rose from 13 percent in 1988 to 14.7 percent in 1991.[11] The number of uninsured individuals increased by nearly 2 million, from 33.6 million to 35.4 million during the same period.[12] As large corporations and government agencies which provide group insurance continue to lay off an increasing number of their workers, the percentage of the public who are uninsured is certain to rise during the 1990s in the absence of far-reaching health care reform.

Since practically all uninsured individuals lost their coverage with their jobs, their only means to regain health care benefits is to find an employer willing to provide them with group insurance. However, this often takes a long time, given the difficulty of finding a job, let alone one that provides group health insurance. As a result, most of the uninsured must go without coverage for long periods. As Table 6.3 shows, half the uninsured go without coverage for six months or more.

While 35.4 million individuals were uninsured in 1991, the number of uninsured persons is substantially larger if they are measured over a period extending beyond a single year. The Commerce Department conducted a health insurance survey over a thirty-month period from February 1985 to August 1987. It found that only 71.9 percent of the public was insured during the entire thirty-month period: 23.8 percent were uninsured for at least one month, and 4.3 percent were uninsured during the entire period.[13] The Commerce Department survey shows that a third of the public does not have secure health insurance coverage and periodically loses health care benefits during any given period of time.

The rising number of workers with group health insurance who are being laid off is not the only segment of society that is losing its coverage. Those workers with group insurance who are lucky enough to keep their jobs are losing an

Table 6.3
The Number of Months in which the Uninsured Go without Coverage

```
-----------------------------------------------------------
Percentage of the Uninsured     Months Without Coverage
-----------------------------------------------------------
            50                            2-5
            15                            6-9
             9                           10-13
             9                           14-21
             3                           22-29
            14                         30 or Over
-----------------------------------------------------------
Source: John Merline, "Who Really Lacks Health Care?,"
Investor's Business Daily, March 25, 1993, p. 1.
```

increasing share of their health care benefits. As a result of soaring health care costs, employer contributions to group insurance rose from $33 billion in 1977 to $186 billion in 1990.[14] The share of corporate operating profits spent on health care increased from 9 percent in 1965 to 40 percent in 1989.[15] The skyrocketing cost of group insurance threatens to drive even the largest and most profitable corporations out of business. As a result, corporations have had no alternative but to act to reduce the cost of their group insurance plans by cutting the coverage they provide for their working families and requiring them to shoulder an increasing financial burden for their health care expenses.

Labor Department surveys of firms employing 100 or more workers that provide group health insurance to 31 million employed families found that the share of households with coverage fully financed by the employer declined from 50 percent in 1982 to 31 percent in 1989. The average monthly employee contribution to the group plans provided by those companies rose form $27 to $72 during the same period—an increase of 178 percent. By contrast, average weekly wages increased only 25 percent during the same period.[16]

In addition to group health insurance, soaring health care costs have driven up Medicare spending, which rose from $4.5 billion in 1967 to $129.4 billion in 1992.[17] In 1982, 90.8 percent of the cost of Medicare was financed by the federal government and the remainder by beneficiaries.[18] To reduce soaring budget deficits, the federal government has acted to cut Medicare costs by slashing coverage to its beneficiaries and requiring them to shoulder a growing financial burden of their own health care expenses in much the same way corporations have done to their working families. From 1966 to 1992, the deductible for Part A of Medicare, Hospital Insurance, rose from $40 to $652, the deductible for Part B, Supplemental Medical Insurance (SMI), doubled from $50 to $100, and the SMI monthly premium nonpoor Medicare beneficiaries must pay grew from $3 to $31.80.[19] As a result of increases in Medicare patient cost-sharing requirements, the share of their income the elderly spent on health care rose from 15 percent in 1965 to 19 percent in 1989.[20] The elderly currently pay a greater share of their income on health care than they did prior to Medicare.

Soaring health care costs combined with the shrinkage of both public and private health insurance coverage, has created substantial financial barriers impeding public access to health care, especially for low-income individuals. Because they usually lack adequate coverage and financial resources, low-income individuals find it difficult to finance the cost of their care. During February to June 1992 the National Opinion Research Center of the Harvard School of Public Health, and the Henry J. Kaiser Family Foundation, jointly conducted a poll of 1,900 individuals earning annual incomes of under $20,000. The poll found paying for their health care was of the greatest concern to its respondents. Paying for health care ranked ahead of finding a job and paying the rent. Eighteen percent of the respondents said they worry most about paying for their health care.[21]

Because they have difficulty paying for their health care, low-income individuals, and even some members of the middle class, have financial incentives to avoid seeing the doctor, unless absolutely necessary. This has served to curtail patient utilization of health care among the middle class, and especially the poor. The segment of society most vulnerable to inadequate access to health care are obviously the uninsured, who utilize substantially less medical services than the insured. In 1977 the uninsured received 90 percent less hospital care and paid 54 percent fewer visits to the doctor than the insured.[22]

When illness or injury strikes, the uninsured have to avoid seeing the doctor due to the fact that they must pay all their health care expenses out of pocket, except for the uncompensated care they receive from charitable hospitals. A 1989 study found that uninsured adults were 54 percent less likely to utilize hospital care and 37 percent less likely to use physician services than their insured counterparts during any given year.[23] A report issued by the National Association of Community Health Centers in Washington on February 26, 1992 found that in 1990 40.5 million individuals lacked sufficient access to primary care because they had inadequate incomes and insurance coverage.[24]

Low-income, inadequately-insured individuals, who cannot afford the cost of their health services, have no alternative but to seek uncompensated care from charitable hospitals when they suffer either an illness or injury. However, uncompensated care is usually provided only by public hospitals. Because they are funded by state, county, and municipal governments, public hospitals do have the financial means to pay for the uncompensated care they provide.

By contrast, private hospitals are financed through the compensation they receive from either third-party payers or paying patients. They will go bankrupt if too much uncompensated care is provided. As a result, private hospitals avoid providing uncompensated care to low-income, inadequately-insured individuals, leaving public hospitals to assume this responsibility. Accordingly, a disproportionate share of uncompensated care is extended by public hospitals. In 1982 only 21.6 percent of all hospital care was granted by private hospitals, and only

78.4 percent by public hospitals. However, 40.6 percent of uncompensated care was given by public hospitals, compared to 59.4 percent by private hospitals.[25]

Because they must assume responsibility for providing a disproportionate share of uncompensated care, public hospitals are burdened with heavy patient loads, and they suffer from severe overcrowding. They lack the resources—adequate medical personnel and technology—to provide sufficient care to their low-income, inadequately insured patients. The ability of public hospitals to provide uncompensated care to such individuals is further undermined by the fiscal crisis states are facing.

The severe recession, which began in July 1990 and continues as of April 1993, has resulted in high unemployment, depriving states of the revenues they need to provide essential social services like public hospital care. As a result, states have had to reduce their financing for public hospital care, forcing public hospitals to cut their provision of uncompensated care to low-income, uninsured individuals. Meanwhile, a rising number of workers are being laid off due to the recession. They are losing the group health insurance that came with their jobs, forcing them and their families to become uninsured. As a result, public hospitals are reducing their provision of uncompensated care at the very time that the demand for such services is rising due to the increasing number of individuals who are becoming uninsured.

Faced with a continuing shrinkage of medical resources, public hospitals must stringently ration the uncompensated care they provide low-income, inadequately insured individuals. As a result, those persons usually must wait until their illnesses become catastrophic before they can receive uncompensated care from public hospitals. However, catastrophic illnesses are difficult, if not impossible, to treat. The health, and very lives, of low-income, inadequately insured individuals have been placed at grave risk because they usually cannot receive uncompensated care unless they develop catastrophic illnesses.

Faced with having to pay most, if not all, of their health care expenses out of pocket and deprived of adequate access to uncompensated care, low-income, inadequately insured individuals have financial incentives to avoid seeing the doctor unless absolutely necessary—if then. As a result, when either illness or injury strikes, they face the danger that their ailments may develop complications, leading to deformities, disability, or death. The insurance system has failed to provide 40.5 million low-income, inadequately insured individuals access to the primary care they need to remain healthy, and to medical care at the early stages of their illnesses before complications develop.

Public Support for National Health Insurance

Faced with the increasing likelihood that they will become uninsured, if they are not already, and with the health care crisis having a devastating effect upon public access to medical services, an overwhelming majority of the public support a national health insurance program that will guarantee universal access to af-

Table 6.4
**Domestic Public Opinion on Health Care Systems in Selected Advanced Industrial
Democracies in 1988 and 1990**

```
------------------------------------------------------------
    The Percentage of Respondents Who Believed That:
------------------------------------------------------------
```

	Only Minor Changes Are Needed In Their Health Care System	Fundamental Changes Are Needed In Their Health Care System	Their Entire Health Care System Should Be Rebuilt
Canada	56	38	5
Netherlands	47	46	5
France	41	42	10
Germany	41	35	13
Australia	34	43	17
Sweden	32	58	6
Japan	29	47	6
Britain	27	52	17
Italy	12	46	40
United States	10	60	29

Source: Erik Eckholm, "Rescuing Health Care," The New
York Times, May 2, 1991, p. A16. B12

fordable health care. Moreover, they oppose the current insurance system. Domestic public support for the American health care system is lower than in any
major advanced industrial democracy, with the possible exception of Italy. In
1988 and 1990 Louis Harris and Associates conducted a poll measuring public
backing of health care systems in various advanced industrial democracies. The
results of the Harris poll are in Table 6.4.

Why is the American health care system so unpopular with the public, compared with the Western European, Canadian, and Japanese medical systems?
The answer does not lie in the quality of health care services provided in the
United States. A 1990 *Los Angeles Times* poll found that over 90 percent of
those questioned were satisfied with their personal health care services.[26]

The answer is not that the United States does not spend a sufficient amount
of its income on health care. Quite the contrary; as Tables 6.5 and 6.6 show,
the United States spends substantially more of its income on health care, both
on a per capita basis and as a share of GDP, than any other nation in the world.
Yet domestic public support for the Western European, Canadian, and Japanese
health care systems is substantially higher than that for the American system.

It is easy to understand why the American health care system is so domestically
unpopular, compared with Western Europe, Canada, and Japan. The govern-

Table 6.5
Per Capita Health Care Spending in Selected Advanced Industrial Democracies in 1989 in American Dollars

United States	2,354
Canada	1,683
Switzerland	1,376
Sweden	1,361
Iceland	1,353
France	1,274
Norway	1,234
Germany	1,232
Luxembourg	1,193
Netherlands	1,135
Austria	1,093
Finland	1,067
Italy	1,050
Japan	1,035
Australia	1,032
Belgium	980
Denmark	912
Britain	836
New Zealand	820
Ireland	658

Source: Michael Wolff, Peter Rutten, and Albert F. Bayers III, Where We Stand: Can America Make It in the Global Race for Wealth, Health, and Happiness? (New York: Bantam Books, 1992), p. 126.

ments of those nations guarantee universal, comprehensive, cradle-to-grave health insurance coverage. No citizen or resident is allowed to go without adequate insurance at any time.[27]

Moreover, the governments of Western Europe, Canada, and Japan impose stringent cost-containment measures to assure that universal access to health care can be provided at an affordable cost.[28] As a result, those nations spend substantially less on health care than the United States does. The people have every reason to support their health care systems because they are guaranteed universal access to affordable medical services.

By contrast, the United States remains the only advanced industrial democracy where the government does not assume responsibility for assuring universal, comprehensive health insurance coverage, leaving a substantial share of its population uninsured. Since employers assume primary responsibility for providing insurance in the United States, all but the wealthiest Americans are just one job away from losing their coverage; and, should this occur, one illness away from being either financially bankrupted or denied access to health care because of its high cost. American public anxiety about the health care system was perhaps best summed up by Michael Wolff, Peter Rutten, and Albert F. Bayers III. ''No

Table 6.6
Health Care Spending as a Percentage of the GDP in Selected Advanced
Industrial Democracies in 1989

United States	11.2
Sweden	9.0
Canada	8.6
France	8.6
Netherlands	8.5
Austria	8.4
Germany	8.2
Iceland	7.8
Switzerland	7.7
Norway	7.5
Luxembourg	7.5
Finland	7.4
Ireland	7.4
Belgium	7.2
Australia	7.1
Italy	6.9
New Zealand	6.9
Japan	6.8
Portugal	6.4
Britain	6.1
Denmark	6.0
Spain	6.0
Greece	5.3

Source: Michael Wolff, Peter Rutten, and Albert F.
Bayers III, Where We Stand: Can America Make It in the
Global Race for Wealth, Health, and Happiness? (New
York: Bantam Books, 1992), p. 126.

developed country is as unhappy with its health-care system as the U.S. Public
disenchantment with the U.S. health-care system . . . reflects not so much doubts
about the quality of care as fears about the availability of any care at all.''[29]

Even if they were not threatened with the loss of their health insurance,
Americans would still be dissatisfied with the health care system due to soaring
medical costs. Families are paying a rising share of their earnings in taxes to
finance Medicare and Medicaid; are suffering wage reductions to pay increased
premiums to fund the cost of their group plans; and are paying for a growing
share of their health care out of pocket. From 1980 to 1987, the average real
personal income rose by 6.4 percent, totaling about $1,500. However, average
real health care costs increased by 35 percent, amounting to $1,412, during the
same period.[30] As a result, soaring health care costs wiped out over 95 percent
of the income gains families made during most of the 1980s. Health care costs
represent perhaps the single greatest danger to the American standard of living,

threatening all but the wealthiest families with financial ruin from a catastrophic illness. As *Money* magazine put it:

Competent affordable health care—this aspiration is linked to the biggest financial worry clouding the American dream, particularly for those approaching or in retirement. When we asked respondents what might stand in the way of achieving their dream, catastrophic illness came out at the top of the list, outranking such fears as recession and natural disaster. . . . Even the affluent know that one major illness could wipe them out.[31]

In addition to undermining the financial security of families, the health care crises poses a direct threat to the family as a social unit. Many individuals are working not so much because they need the income but because they need the health insurance their jobs provide. As a result, they are locked into jobs they do not want because they cannot afford to lose the insurance that comes with their employment.

Job lock prevents workers from tending to their family responsibilities. At the very least, workers need to take time off from their jobs to tend a sick child or parent, or a newborn baby. Some workers may even want to take additional time off to be with their children while they are growing up or with their parents in their twilight years. However, workers who take time off risk being fired and losing their health insurance, since the United States is the only advanced industrial democracy without a universal family leave program. As a result, many individuals have no alternative but to work in jobs they do not like, and neglect their family responsibilities in the process, simply to avoid losing their insurance. By promoting job lock, the insurance system has undermined the family as a social unit.

Threatened with the increasing likelihood that they will become uninsured, if they are not already, and with soaring health care costs posing a danger to their standard of living and their ability to tend to their family responsibilities, the public has every reason to be dissatisfied with the health care system and to be worried, if not alarmed, by the threat that the medical crisis poses to the financial and physical security of families. Reflecting their dissatisfaction, the overwhelming majority of the public support the establishment of a national health insurance program to guarantee universal access to affordable health care. Public backing for the program is currently higher than it has been at any time in recorded history.

During January 21–24, 1990, the *Los Angeles Times* asked 2,046 individuals the following question: "Even if it meant an increase in taxes, would you favor or oppose a comprehensive national health insurance plan?" Seventy-two percent supported national health insurance, 20 percent opposed it, and 8 percent did not know.[32] Public support for national health insurance, expressed in the 1990 *Los Angeles Times* poll, exceeded the previous record set in August 1944, when 57 percent of those surveyed in a National Opinion Research Center poll stated their willingness to paying higher taxes to finance the program.[33] A larger share of the public currently back national health insurance than favored Medicare prior to its establishment. In February 1965, 62 percent of the respondents in a Louis Harris poll supported paying higher taxes to finance Medicare.[34]

Why does an overwhelming majority of the public currently support the establishment of a national health insurance program? The answer lies in the fact that an equally overwhelming majority does not believe that it is possible to guarantee universal access to affordable health care unless there is a complete overhaul of the current medical system. During March 6–9, 1993, Peter Hart and Robert Teeter conducted a poll of 1,503 adults for *The Wall Street Journal* and NBC News. The poll asked whether "it is, or is not, possible to control costs and cover everyone without a complete overhaul of the current health-care system?" Seventy-four percent said it was not possible and 22 percent that it was possible.[35]

Polling data show that a majority of the public is willing to make two major sacrifices which would be required for the establishment of a national health insurance program: first, they are willing to pay higher taxes to finance the program; second, they are willing to accept limits on their access to health care in order to contain its cost.

During March 25–26, 1993, the Gallup Organization conducted a poll of 755 adults for *Newsweek*. The poll asked the following question: "Would you favor or oppose additional taxes to pay for reforming and expanding health care in the U.S.?" Fifty percent favored higher taxes and 47 percent opposed them.[36]

In addition, an overwhelming majority of the public is willing to pay sufficient taxes to provide coverage to the uninsured. During March 3–10, 1993, Louis Harris and Associates conducted a poll of 1,255 adults. The poll asked its respondents whether they were willing to support a "3% national sales tax on purchases other than food and medical care to move quickly to pay for health coverage for the uninsured." Fifty-eight percent of those questioned supported imposition of the tax and 40 opposed it.[37] A 3 percent national sales tax would provide the federal government an estimated $89.4 billion annually in revenues, which would be sufficient to provide coverage to the uninsured.[38] As a result, the Harris Poll shows that an overwhelming majority of the public is fully prepared to make the financial sacrifices required to guarantee universal health insurance coverage.

The public has every reason to support higher taxes to finance a national health insurance program. Given the fact the growing job insecurity facing the labor force, the public realizes that any individual can lose his or her job and the health insurance which comes with their employment. The overwhelming majority of the public who support higher taxes to assure universal coverage want to insulate themselves against the possibility that they will lose their insurance should they lose their jobs. They recognize that it will be well worth the cost of paying higher taxes in order to assure themselves against the loss of their coverage and the physical and financial catastrophe they may face should they become uninsured and ill.

Public dissatisfaction with the health care system is based upon the high cost, rather than poor quality or the lack of availability of medical services. The *Newsweek* poll asked its respondents the following question: "What is your biggest concern about health care?" Fifty percent said that their biggest concern was cost, 37 percent said quality, and 11 percent said availability.

Consistent with their concern over health care costs, a plurality of the public supports the imposition of stringent medical cost-containment measures. The *Newsweek* poll asked its respondents the following question: "Would you support legislation to control health-care costs even if it meant restricting people's options of doctors and medical services?" Forty-eight percent said they would support such legislation, and 46 percent would oppose it.[39]

The Wall Street Journal/NBC News Poll found additional evidence confirming the public's willingness to accept restrictions on their access to health care in order to contain its cost. The poll asked its respondents whether they were willing to accept "limits on the availability of expensive high-tech services?" Fifty-one said they were willing to accept such limits and 43 percent opposed them. The poll also asked its respondents whether they were willing to accept "limits on the right to choose your doctor?" Fifty-two percent said they were willing to accept such limits and 48 percent opposed them.[40]

Since 85.3 percent of the public is insured, the overwhelming majority of the population has reasonably good access to health care, and is satisfied with its availability, as the *Newsweek* poll shows. However, as we have seen, soaring health care costs have forced employers and the federal government to reduce the coverage they provide working families, the elderly, and disabled under group health insurance and Medicare. As a result, a rising share of the public is having to shoulder an increasing financial burden for the cost of their health care, making them more sensitive to soaring medical costs. Accordingly, half the public is concerned, if not alarmed, over soaring health care costs and support the imposition of stringent medical cost-containment measures, even if such action would result in restrictions in their choice of doctors and access to health care, especially high-technology hospital services.

The willingness of a majority of the public to accept the sacrifices—higher taxes and restrictions on access to health care—required for national health insurance paves the way for its establishment. To finance the program the federal government will, at the very least, have to provide coverage for those not eligible for either Medicare or Medicaid. It will also have to extend tax subsidies for small businesses in order that they can afford to purchase group insurance for their workers. This will incur additional federal spending. Given the magnitude of the budget deficit, the federal government can only finance this new spending through a tax increase. The willingness of an overwhelming majority of the public to pay higher taxes to finance coverage for the uninsured will make it politically feasible for the federal government to raise such taxes.

By reducing financial barriers to health care, a national health insurance program would raise patient utilization of health care, especially among the poor and uninsured. Patient utilization of health care, especially costly, high-technology hospital care, will have to be curtailed under the program to prevent the cost of medical services from soaring even further.

To further reduce health care costs, the federal government will have to reimburse doctors through a stringent fee schedule which will pay them substantially less than what they currently receive. As a result, some doctors will refuse to participate in any national health insurance program which is established. However, practically all individuals would be covered through the government under the program. Doctors refusing to participate in the program would not be reimbursed for any services provided to patients covered through the government. To assure that they would have coverage for the physician services they receive, those patients would have no choice but to go only to those doctors who participated in the program. As a result, doctors refusing to participate in national health insurance would lose access to a large number of patients and in turn, the income tied to the program. Ultimately, practically all of them could go out of business. However, some doctors would still refuse to participate in any national health insurance program established, and limit themselves to treating the small number of wealthy patients who could afford to pay for their own health care out of pocket. As a result, all but the wealthiest individuals could not expect to have access to all doctors, in private practice, under the program.

National health insurance will require that the public accept restrictions on their access to costly, high-technology hospital care and go only to those doctors willing to participate in the program. The willingness of a majority of the public to accept those restrictions on their access to health care will make it politically possible for the program to be established.

Despite their willingness to make sacrifices for the establishment of national health insurance, the public remains deeply divided over the kind of program it wants. The *Newsweek* poll found its respondents evenly divided over whether they wanted to maintain the current employment-based insurance system or scrap and replace it with a federally-financed insurance plan. The poll asked the following question: "Should health care be financed mostly by the federal government or employers and private citizens using private insurance?" Forty-nine percent chose private insurance and 44 percent the federal government.[41]

Additional polling data exists confirming the deep division over what kind of national health insurance program it wants. On March 22, 1993, *USA Today* published the results of a poll which asked 1,149 voters which of three opposing national health insurance programs they support: the first, a plan to provide tax credits to allow the uninsured to purchase their own private coverage; the second, a Canadian-style single-payer universal insurance plan financed and administered by the government; and the third, a mandatory employment-based plan which would require employers to provide group insurance to their working families, with the government extending coverage to those outside the labor market. Thirty-three percent supported a tax credit-based plan, 32 percent a single-payer plan, 28 percent a mandatory employment-based plan, 6 percent were not sure, and

3 percent preferred "leaving things as they are."[42] The poll showed that the public was evenly divided in their preference among a tax credit-based, single-payer, and mandatory employment-based insurance plan. Given the deep division among the public over what kind of national health insurance program it wants, health care reformers will have to work to build popular support for whatever health care reform plan they choose to establish.

CONCLUSION

Since the establishment of Medicare and Medicaid in 1965, employers and the government have shared responsibility for providing the overwhelming majority of the public coverage. Employers have extended coverage to their working families. The government has done the same to groups outside the labor market. With the overwhelming majority of the public insured through either their employers or the government, neither the population nor Congress has seen any urgent and compelling need for national health insurance.

However, the current health insurance system is in a state of disrepair, if not collapse. Neither employers nor the government can assume the financial burden for soaring health care costs. As a result, the ranks of the uninsured are beginning to swell, as an increasing number of individuals are unable to find employers who provide them coverage, and cannot meet the stringent eligibility requirements for either Medicare or Medicaid. In the meantime, those who are insured find their coverage shrinking as employers and the federal government act to reduce their costs by cutting back on the health care benefits they provide under group insurance and Medicare, respectively.

Faced with the growing prospects of becoming uninsured, if they are not already, an overwhelming majority of the public supports, and in some cases is demanding, health care reform. Henry J. Aaron argues that the current health care crisis and unpopularity of the medical system are certain to result in the establishment of a national health insurance program before the end of the 1990s.

Current arrangements for financing health care cannot endure. Clearly visible trends ensure the continuing erosion of support for the current financing system. Unless financing policy changes dramatically, the number of uninsured and spending on health care will both continue to grow. As a result, the national debate on the reform of health care financing that has already begun will lead to major legislation before the end of the decade.[43]

Is Aaron correct in his argument that the political system, which has repeatedly ducked the issue of health care reform since the 1940s, is finally willing and able to grant the public's wish for national health insurance? It is this question that we will explore in the remainder of this book.

CHAPTER 7

Play-or-Pay Health Insurance: A Dead End to Health Care Reform

[Bentsen] wants to do whatever there's a critical mass for [on health care reform]. But at this point, that's not play or pay.[1]
> A member of the staff of Senate Finance Committee
> Chairman Lloyd Bentsen of Texas

During 1991–1992, health care reformers launched a new campaign to establish national health insurance. In doing so, they faced the particularly thorny challenge of how to restructure the insurance system to guarantee universal access to affordable health care. The problem they faced was a conflict between economic efficiency and political feasibility. The most economically efficient means to achieve health care reform was to scrap private insurance and replace it with a single government plan. However, the establishment of a single-payer insurance plan remained politically unfeasible.

The attempt to balance the conflicting objectives of economic efficiency and political feasibility led health care reformers to adopt a compromise national health insurance plan, known as play or pay. It was designed to expand the role of the government in the insurance system, without eliminating private plans altogether. Health care reformers hoped that this arrangement would balance the conflicting objectives of economic efficiency and political feasibility in a way that would make the establishment of national health insurance possible.

WASTE AND INEFFICIENCY IN PRIVATE HEALTH INSURANCE

The most important challenge facing health care reformers is to eliminate private health insurance, which represents a major source of waste and inefficiency within the health care system, squandering tens of billions of dollars annually on excessive administrative costs. Consider a comparison between America's multiple-payer insurance system and Canada's single-payer insurance plan.

There are currently 1,500 private plans in the United States, each with its own bureaucracy and forms to process claims and pay providers.[2] As a result, there is excessive administrative overhead and paperwork within the private insurance industry which drives up health care costs.

The American private health insurance industry is intensely competitive. Fifteen hundred private plans must compete for business. To solicit business, they must spend substantial sums on marketing, advertising, and sales, which has further driven up administrative costs.[3]

To remain competitive in the health insurance market, all private plans must limit their financial liabilities. They must maintain large underwriting departments to review each application for coverage they receive. Underwriters must examine the health history of each applicant in order to assure that they are healthy at the time they enroll in the private plan. Underwriters will deny coverage for any pre-existing medical conditions their new subscribers may have and refuse to provide health care benefits to individuals with chronic ailments. The need to maintain larger underwriting departments to review each application for coverage adds substantially to the administrative costs of private insurance.

By contrast, each of the ten provinces and two territories of Canada represents a single third-party payer.[4] Private insurance is limited to providing supplemental coverage for those few health care services not financed by the government.[5] The existence of only twelve basic insurance plans to process medical claims and reimburse health care providers guarantees a minimum of administrative overhead and paperwork, which serves to restrain the growth in medical costs.[6]

In Canada cradle-to-grave public health insurance coverage is compulsory. The government does not spend a dime soliciting business. The cost of marketing, advertising, and sales is practically, if not virtually, nonexistent within the Canadian insurance system.

Every Canadian has a right to full and comprehensive health insurance coverage, regardless of his or her health status. There are no underwriting departments in Canada to review applications for coverage to determine the health history of each subscriber and the health care benefits they will receive. The absence of underwriting departments substantially reduces the administrative costs of health insurance in Canada.

A comparative analysis of the United States and Canada shows that public health insurance is efficient because the government acts as a single payer to keep administrative overhead and paperwork to a minimum. It provides coverage on a compulsory basis, avoiding expenditures on marketing, advertising, sales, and underwriting. By contrast, private insurance is wasteful and inefficient because the existence of a multiplicity of plans competing for business leads to excessive administrative overhead and paperwork, and generates additional costs for marketing, advertising, sales, and underwriting.

Just how wasteful and inefficient America's multiple-payer insurance system is in relation to Canada's single-payer insurance plan was revealed in two major studies published during the spring of 1991, which compared administrative costs of the two systems. The first study was written by Steffie Woolhandler and David U. Himmelstein; and the second by the General Accounting Office (GAO).

Woolhandler and Himmelstein estimate that health insurance administrative costs in the United States rose from 21.9 percent of health care spending in 1983 to 23.9 percent in 1987. By contrast, insurance administrative costs in Canada declined from 13.7 to 11 percent of health care spending during the same period. Woolhandler and Himmelstein argue that had the insurance system in the United States been as efficient as that in Canada in 1987, the cost of health care in the United States would have been from $69 billion to $83.2 billion lower than it actually was. This savings represented from 13.8 to 16.6 percent of health care spending in 1987. "Reducing our administrative costs to Canadian levels would save enough money to fund coverage for all uninsured and underinsured Americans," Woolhandler and Himmelstein claim. "Universal comprehensive coverage under a single, publicly administered insurance program is the sine qua non of such administrative simplification."[7]

The Woolhandler-Himmelstein study leads to one inescapable conclusion: The United States can guarantee universal health insurance coverage without spending an additional dime on health care. All the United States need do is establish a single-payer insurance program, based upon the Canadian system, and use the savings from the greater efficiency that would be achieved to provide coverage for the uninsured.

The Woolhandler-Himmelstein study was immediately denounced by the Health Insurance Association of America (HIAA), the largest interest group representing the private health industry, with 270 member firms. It charged that the study's conclusions were designed to reflect Woolhandler and Himmelstein's support for a single-payer insurance plan: "The blind faith of the committed ideologue is required in order to believe that [Woolhandler and Himmelstein's] figures represent anything close to reality."[8]

The HIAA was correct in one sense: Woolhandler and Himmelstein are not politically neutral social scientists. Rather, they are politically active health care reformers, and prominent members of Physicians for a National Health Program, a physician organization that supports the establishment of a single-payer health insurance plan.[9] As a result, Woolhandler and Himmelstein served as easy targets for the HIAA's efforts to discredit their findings concerning the waste and inefficiency of private insurance.

However, the HIAA's campaign against Woolhandler and Himmelstein received a setback on June 4, 1991, when the GAO released a report entitled

Canada's Health Insurance: Lessons for the United States. The report supported Woolhandler and Himmelstein's conclusions. It estimated that had the United States had a Canadian-style single-payer health insurance plan, its annual insurance administrative costs would have been reduced by $67 billion. The report also estimated that it would cost $64 billion to provide the uninsured with comprehensive coverage, completely free of charge, with no patient cost-sharing requirements of any kind.[10]

"If the universal coverage and single-payer features of the Canadian system were applied to the United States, the savings in administrative costs alone would be more than enough to finance coverage for the millions of Americans who are currently uninsured," the GAO report concluded. "There would be enough, left over to permit a reduction, or possibly elimination, of copayments and deductibles, if that were deemed appropriate." Accordingly, the report urged that the United States consider adopting the basic features of a Canadian-style insurance system. "Some elements of the Canadian system are worthy of consideration in a reformed U.S. system. These might include Canada's universal access, uniform payment system and expenditure controls."[11]

It was easy for the HIAA to attempt to discredit Woolhandler and Himmelstein's findings, given their commitment to health care reform. However, it was much harder to do the same against the GAO's conclusions, since the GAO is a politically neutral federal research organization, with no tie to any political group or commitment to any political cause. Nevertheless, HIAA President Carl Schramm attacked the GAO's findings. "The GAO has lost all objectivity as far as I am concerned," Schramm complained. He blasted the GAO for supporting consideration for the establishment of a single-payer health insurance plan. "I'm shocked. The GAO never makes advocacy statements as it has in this report."[12]

The studies by Woolhandler and Himmelstein and the GAO provide irrefutable empirical evidence that the most efficient means to achieve health care reform is to scrap and replace private insurance with a single government plan, and use the tens of billions of dollars saved through the elimination of voluntary plans to finance coverage for the uninsured. As Woolhandler put it, "The multiplicity of insurers not only raises overhead, it also buries hospitals and doctors in paperwork. What we really need to do is get the private insurance industry out of the health care business."[13]

Since the United States spends more on health care than any other nation in the world, a national health insurance program cannot be established on a fiscally and economically feasible basis if it adds to the already swollen costs of medical care. Such a program would reignite inflation, it would drive up the already massive budget deficit. To avoid doing economic and fiscal damage, a national health insurance program cannot be established if it adds to health care costs. Technically, the most painless and efficient means to establish a national health insurance program that does not add to health care costs, is to scrap and replace private plans with a single government program, and use the savings that would result from the elimination of the voluntary insurance industry to finance coverage for the uninsured.

However, while the establishment of a single-payer health insurance plan makes good economic sense, it is politically unfeasible. The private insurance industry is one of the most powerful interest groups in Washington, wielding substantial political and financial clout on Capitol Hill. As a result, it is virtually inconceivable that Congress would scrap and replace private insurance with a single government plan in the foreseeable future, regardless of how much economic sense such action would make.

In developing a national health insurance plan, health care reformers had to balance two competing objectives. On the one hand, they had to move toward the replacement of private insurance with a single government plan as the only economically feasible means by which they could reduce the waste and inefficiency permeating the health care system, and generate the savings required to finance coverage for the uninsured. On the other hand, they had to preserve a role for private plans in the health care system, since any wholesale attempt to eliminate the voluntary insurance industry would provoke a bruising battle with this politically powerful group, threatening chances for the achievement of health care reform.

THE EMERGENCE OF PLAY-OR-PAY HEALTH INSURANCE

The need to move toward eliminating private health insurance, while preserving a role for voluntary plans in the health care system, resulted in the development of a compromise national health insurance plan known as play or pay. Under play or pay, employers would be required either to provide their working families with group insurance or to pay a payroll tax to finance a government program to extend coverage to the uninsured.

The move toward the development of play-or-pay health insurance began in 1988 when Congress passed the Medicare Catastrophic Coverage Act. Among other things, the bill provided for the establishment of a fifteen-member U.S. Bipartisan Commission on Comprehensive Health Care. The commission was subsequently renamed in honor of its first chairperson, Representative Claude Pepper of Florida, following his death on May 30, 1989.[14]

The Pepper Commission was assigned the responsibility for conducting a study of the health care system in order to issue recommendations concerning how to guarantee "comprehensive health care services for all individuals in the United States."[15] On March 2, 1990, the commission recommended a play-or-pay plan in which employers would be required either to provide their working families with group insurance or to pay a payroll tax that the federal government would use to extend coverage to the uninsured.[16] However, the commission was far from unanimous in recommending such a plan. It voted to propose the plan by only the narrowest of margins—eight to seven. The vote divided largely along party lines. Of the fifteen commission members, twelve served in Congress, and the remaining three were nonpartisan presidential appointees. Of the eight Democrats on the commission, six supported the Pepper Commission plan. All four Republicans opposed it.[17]

Prospects for the establishment of national health insurance were strengthened by George Mitchell's assumption of the Senate majority leadership in 1989. Having served as chairman of the Subcommittee on Health of the Senate Finance Committee from 1987 to 1988, Mitchell has a strong interest in health care policy and a passionate commitment to medical care reform.[18] Acting upon this commitment, on June 5, 1991, Mitchell joined leading Senate Democratic health care policy makers in introducing the HealthAmerica Act. It was designed both to implement and to build upon the Pepper Commission's recommendations on national health insurance. In addition to Mitchell, sponsors of the bill included Edward M. Kennedy of Massachusetts, chairman of the Senate Labor and Human Resources Committee; John D. Rockefeller IV of West Virginia, who succeeded Pepper as chairman of the Pepper Commission; and Donald Riegle of Michigan, chairman of the Subcommittee on Health for Families and the Uninsured of the Senate Finance Committee.[19]

In announcing his introduction of the HealthAmerica Act at a news conference, Mitchell made it clear that the time for guaranteeing access to health care as a basic and fundamental right of American citizenship had finally come. "Access to affordable, quality health care should be a right of all Americans, not merely a luxury for those who have the economic means to purchase health insurance," Mitchell declared.[20]

The HealthAmerica Act would establish a play-or-pay health insurance plan. All employers would be required either to provide their working families with group insurance or to pay a payroll tax to finance the establishment of a state-administered insurance program, AmeriCare, which would replace the Medicaid program (except the coverage it extends for long-term care). If employers chose to grant their working families group insurance, they would be required to finance 80 percent of its cost for their full-time working families and half its cost for their part-time working households. Part-time working families would have the option to enroll in AmeriCare in lieu of a group plan.

Self-employed individuals who purchase private health insurance are currently able to deduct 25 percent of its cost from their taxable income. The Health-America Act would allow them to deduct the full cost of their private insurance. Private plans would be required to charge community-rated premiums for group insurance for small businesses. Firms employing fewer than sixty workers earning annual incomes of less than $20,000 that choose to provide their working families with group insurance would receive a tax credit to finance up to 25 percent of its cost. Those small businesses would also be able to deduct the full cost of the contributions they make to their group plans from their taxable income, as they and all other firms are currently entitled to do. Profitable small businesses in which an employer earns an annual income of over $53,400 would not receive any tax credit for providing working families with group insurance. Private plans would be prohibited from excluding preexisting medical conditions from the coverage they provide their subscribers. They would also be barred from denying any member of a small group coverage due to his or her health status.

All individuals not covered by either group health insurance or Medicare would be required to enroll in AmeriCare. Families with annual incomes below the poverty line would receive AmeriCare coverage completely free of charge, with no patient cost-sharing requirements of any kind. Families earning annual incomes between 100 and 200 percent of the poverty line would pay premiums, deductibles, and coinsurance charges on an income-related basis; the lower the income, the less they would pay. Families with annual incomes above 200 percent of the poverty line would pay premiums based upon a fixed percentage of their earnings.

AmeriCare and all private health insurance plans would be required to provide a comprehensive package of health care benefits. All AmeriCare beneficiaries earning annual incomes of 200 percent or above the poverty line and privately insured individuals would be required to pay no more than a $500 annual deductible and a 20 percent coinsurance charge. A stop-loss limiting maximum annual out-of-pocket health care expenses to $3,000 per family would also be imposed.[21]

PLAY-OR-PAY HEALTH INSURANCE: BALANCING THE COMPETING OBJECTIVES OF ECONOMIC EFFICIENCY AND POLITICAL FEASIBILITY

Play-or-pay health insurance was designed to balance the competing objectives of economic efficiency and political feasibility in the achievement of health care reform. By providing employers the option of paying a payroll tax to finance a government plan for the uninsured, play or pay was intended to expand the public insurance rolls. Since the government can provide insurance more efficiently than private plans, any enlargement of the public insurance rolls would reduce the waste and efficiency in the insurance system. This would generate the savings necessary to provide coverage for the uninsured.

However, play or pay also gave employers the option of providing their working families with private health insurance. As a result, it guaranteed a role for private plans in the insurance system. By doing so, Senate Democratic sponsors of the HealthAmerica Act hoped to make play or pay acceptable to the private insurance industry. This would avoid a bruising battle with the industry over health care reform, which was certain to come had Senate Democrats sponsored a single-payer insurance plan (which would have eliminated private plans).

In opting for play or pay as an alternative to single-payer health insurance, Senate Democratic sponsors of the HealthAmerica Act were willing to ignore public opinion. As Table 7.1 shows, a substantial plurality of those polled by

Table 7.1
Percentages of Public Support for Different Health Insurance Systems

	ABC News/ Washington Post Poll	NBC News/ Wall Street Journal Poll	Los Angeles Times/ Gallup Poll
Single-Payer Health Insurance	44	41	40
Play-or-Pay Health Insurance	32	31	34
Current Health Insurance System	20	19	22
Don't Know/ Other	3	9	4

Source: Julie Kosterlitz, "A Sick System," National Journal, February 15, 1992, p. 378.

various news organizations prefer single-payer over play-or-pay insurance, with support for maintaining the current insurance system running well behind either of the two opposing health care reform plans. However, Senate Democrats believed that it was better to design a health care reform plan that avoided a confrontation with the private insurance industry than one that satisfied public opinion. As Robert Blendon, a professor of health care policy at the Harvard School of Public Health, put it, "Play or pay is the in-town compromise with [health insurance] interest groups. It has mild support [from the public] but no passion. The passion is to get rid of the insurance industry." Blendon argues that the only advantage of play or pay is that it "will not get the $4 million media campaign against it" from the private insurance industry, since the program would preserve voluntary plans.[22]

Even harsher criticism of play-or-pay health insurance has come from Theodore R. Marmor, Jerry L. Mashaw, and Philip L. Harvey. They characterize play-or-pay insurance as a "timid" and "flawed" means to achieve health care reform because it would preserve the wasteful and inefficient private insurance industry. Marmor, Mashaw, and Harvey recommend that private insurance be scrapped and replaced by a single-payer public plan. "Single-payer government health insurance—not shoring up a failing private insurance system—is what is required," they argue.[23] Accordingly, they recommend American adoption of the Canadian insurance system. "Canadian Medicare offers an attractive, practical model for dealing with our medical-care woes, and many of our leaders know it," Marmor, Mashaw, and Harvey conclude.[24]

The arguments of Blendon, Marmor, Mashaw, and Harvey that play or pay represents a weak and timid approach to health care reform, designed more to preserve the private health insurance industry than to guarantee universal access to affordable medical services, is mistaken. Play or pay constitutes a far greater threat to the industry than they realize. It would severely restrict the role of private plans in the insurance system.

Because the administrative costs of public health insurance are relatively low, employers would have to pay a comparatively low payroll tax to allow the government to provide their working families with coverage under a play-or-pay plan. By contrast, because the administrative costs of private insurance are substantial, voluntary plans would have to sell employers comparable group coverage at significantly higher premiums than the payroll tax firms would pay for their working families to receive health care protection from the government. As a result, under a play-or-pay plan, most employers would choose to provide their working families public, rather than private, insurance.

The fact that play or pay would result in the expansion of public health insurance at the expense of private plans is confirmed by a study, commissioned by the Labor Department and jointly conducted by the Urban Institute and Rand Corporation, released on January 9, 1992.[25] The study estimated that a play-or-pay plan imposing a 7 percent payroll tax on firms which failed to provide group insurance to their working families would raise the number of publicly-insured individuals by 75.2 million to 112 million.[26] This would be in addition to the 35.5 million Medicare and 30.1 million Medicaid beneficiaries who existed in 1992.[27] Fifty-two million individuals currently covered by group insurance, representing 35 percent of the total population receiving employment-based health care protection, would be transferred from private to public insurance because their employers opted to pay a payroll tax to enroll them in a government program in lieu of continuing to provide them group coverage.[28]

Accordingly, a play-or-pay plan could result in as many as 177 million individuals covered by public health insurance, representing 69 percent of the population. This stands in sharp contrast to the 65 percent of the public who currently are privately-insured. A play-or-pay plan would result in a complete reversal in the distribution between public and private insurance coverage. Two-thirds of the public is currently privately-insured. However, under a play-or-pay plan up to two-thirds of the population would be publicly-insured. Play-or-pay insurance would establish a quasi-single-payer system in which the government assumed responsibility for providing coverage to the overwhelming majority of working families, as well as all retired, unemployed, and self-employed individuals who are not enrolled in group plans.

Play-or-pay health insurance would not lead to the complete elimination of private plans, as Marmor, Mashaw, and Harvey are quick to point out. Some employers would opt to provide their working families with private insurance, regardless of how costly it might be. Moreover, many, if not most, affluent individuals would prefer to purchase private insurance rather than enroll in a public plan. The Urban Institute and the Rand Corporation estimates suggest that up to a third of the public would be privately insured under a play-or-pay plan.

Private health insurance is wasteful and inefficient, as the studies conducted by Woolhandler and Himmelstein and the GAO show. Nevertheless, steps can be taken to make private insurance more efficient and less costly for those individuals who would opt to keep their voluntary coverage under a play-or-pay plan. The HealthAmerica Act would do so. To reduce administrative costs within the insurance system, all public and private plans would be required to use standardized forms for processing medical claims and reimbursing health care providers, in order to cut down on their paperwork. To slash administrative overhead that results from the existence of a fragmented insurance system in which 1,500 private plans operate independently, each state would have one of two options: it could establish its own single-payer insurance plan to provide universal coverage to all its residents; or it could form a private insurance consortium composed of all private plans that have small shares of the insurance market.[29]

States opting to establish their own single-payer health insurance plan would have to provide the same comprehensive package of health care benefits required by the federal government under the HealthAmerica Act. They would be required to meet the national health care spending goals imposed by the Federal health Expenditure Board, a new government agency that would be established under the bill to contain medical costs.[30]

States opting to establish private health insurance consortia could require their public and all private plans to join. They would serve as single, unified insurance bureaucracies. Acting on behalf of their member plans, the consortia would use standardized forms to process medical claims and reimburse health care providers.

As a result, the establishment by the states of either single-payer plans or private insurance consortia would eliminate the duplication of administrative activities and paperwork that exists in the current multiple-payer insurance system. This would substantially reduce the administrative costs of private insurance.

Play or pay would greatly shrink the private health insurance market as an overwhelming majority of the public shifted from voluntary plans to a government program. Many, if not most, private plans would be driven out of business. Those private plans remaining would have to reduce their operations substantially and would suffer a significant loss of income. They would be required to consolidate and streamline their operations in order to function more efficiently. As a result, play or pay would have a devastating effect on the private insurance industry. Accordingly, the industry was determined to block passage of any play-or-pay insurance bill.

The private health insurance industry announced its opposition to play or pay when the program was first recommended by the Pepper Commission. The HIAA called the commission's recommendation "a blueprint for economic disaster." It charged that by requiring employers either to provide their working families with group insurance or pay a payroll tax to finance a government program to extend coverage to the uninsured, play or pay "could result in increased unemployment and additional burden on publicly funded [health insurance] programs."[31]

CONTAINING HEALTH CARE COSTS

The private health insurance industry is only one source of waste and inefficiency in the health care system. Even if the United States were to establish the most efficient insurance system available—a Canadian-style single-payer plan—it would have reduced health care costs in 1987 by no more than $83 billion, 16.8 percent of total medical spending, according to Woolhandler and Himmelstein's estimates. However, the United States spends more on health care than any nation in the world—28.5 percent more on a per capita basis in 1989 than the next largest health care spender (Canada), as Table 6.2 shows. As a result, there is substantial waste and inefficiency throughout the entire American health care system, going beyond the confines of the private insurance industry. If the United States is to establish effective health care cost-containment measures, it will have to eliminate the waste and inefficiency within its medical system.

Recognizing the need to contain costs throughout the health care system, the HealthAmerica Act would have required the Federal Health Expenditure Board to impose national medical spending goals. The board would convene a conference of health care providers and third-party payers to determine reimbursement rates designed to meet the medical spending goals set by the board. It would formulate its own recommendations on reimbursement rates to be used by health care providers and third-party payers in guiding their negotiations. Those recommendations would be binding if accepted by the providers and payers.[32] If they were not accepted, the board would impose its own binding reimbursement rates.[33] State insurance consortia could formulate their own reimbursements rates for health care providers and third-party payers, provided they were accepted by the board.[34] Senate Democratic sponsors of the HealthAmerica Act estimated that the health care cost-containment measures included in their bill would reduce medical spending by $6 billion the first year the measure was in effect, and by $78 billion over a five-year period.[35] By imposing stringent cost-containment measures, the HealthAmerica Act promised to reduce hospital and physician reimbursements, and to slash the incomes of health care providers.

THE HEALTH CARE INDUSTRY PREVENTS MEDICAL CARE REFORM

By shrinking, consolidating, and streamlining the private health insurance industry and imposing stringent cost-containment measures that would have reduced the incomes of health care providers, the HealthAmerica Act promised to impose financial losses upon three key medical interest groups: doctors, hospitals, and insurance firms. Should Congress have decided to broaden the cost-containment provisions of the HealthAmerica Act to include every segment of the health care system, the bill would have imposed financial losses upon three additional medical interest groups: dentists, and the pharmaceutical and nursing home industries. Given the financial threat posed by the HealthAmerica Act, all major interest groups within the health care system acted to prevent passage of the bill and any other medical reform plan that promised to reduce their incomes by imposing stringent medical cost-containment measures.

The health care industry was well-positioned financially to prevent passage of a medical reform bill in the One Hundred Second Congress. Since the beginning of the 1980s, the industry has established itself as a major political force on Capitol Hill through the massive campaign contributions its PACs have made to congressional candidates. Common Cause estimates that from 1981 to 1991 health care industry PACs contributed $60 million to congressional candidates. Interest groups representing the various health care professions contributed $27 million. The private health insurance industry contributed an additional $19 million.[36]

From 1989 to 1990 and again from 1991 to 1992, health care industry PACs increased their campaign contributions to congressional candidates by 32 percent. The rise in contributions from health care industry PACs far outpaced those of PACs as a whole. Contributions to congressional candidates from all PACs grew by 15 percent during the same period. The increase in contributions made by health care industry PACs from 1989–1990 to 1991–1992 was higher than for any other interest group maintaining a PAC. During 1991 to 1992, health care industry PACs contributed $14,406,370 to congressional candidates, representing 8 percent of all PAC contributions during the same period. Like all PAC contributions, practically all health care industry PAC money went to incumbent members of Congress. Table 7.2 shows that contributions from the industry were concentrated among nineteen key medical interest groups, led by the AMA, each of which had its own PAC.

The three dominant contributors to the 1992 congressional campaign within the health care industry were the AMA, the American Dental Association (ADA), and the American Chiropractic Association. During 1989–1990 to 1991–1992, the AMA increased its contributions to congressional candidates by 23 percent to $2.9 million; the ADA raised its contributions by 70 percent to $1.4 million; and the American Chiropractic Association increased its contributions by 234 percent to $628,000.[37]

The massive campaign contributions made to members of Congress by the health care industry during 1991 to 1992 were designed to increase its financial influence over lawmakers. The industry intended to use its substantial financial clout on Capitol Hill to influence members of the One Hundred Second Congress to take no action on health care reform. It had an urgent need to increase its

Table 7.2
The Nineteen Largest Health Care Industry PACs as Measured by Their
Campaign Contributions to Congressional Candidates during 1989 to 1991 in
Dollars

PAC Sponsor	Congressional Campaign Contributions During 1989 to 1990	Congressional Campaign Contributions and Cash on Hand in 1991
American Medical Association	2,647,981	6,102,938
American Dental Association	824,578	1,499,451
American Academy of Ophthamalogy	960,411	797,302
American Hospital Association	505,889	693,821
American Podiatry Association	256,750	536,754
American Health Care Association	262,880	384,944
American Chiropractic Association	230,025	292,579
Federation of American Health Systems	174,350	291,234
Metropolitan Life Insurance Corporation	259,212	257,623
American Optometric Association	329,600	254,788
Travelers Corporation	260,200	242,131
Blue Cross and Blue Shield Associations	235,635	222,855
CIGNA Corporation	171,225	202,006
Health Insurance Association of America	156,125	199,534
Prudential Insurance Company of America	207,170	194,907
Aetna Life & Casualty Company	195,029	180,381
Eli Lilly and Company	175,740	170,099
American Nurses Association	289,860	134,283
Abbott Laboratories	156,125	81,258
Total	8,298,785	12,738,888

Source: Carol Matlock, "Staking Out Turf," National
Journal, February 15, 1992, p. 390.

financial influence over the One Hundred Second Congress in order to blunt the momentum toward health care reform that gained substantial steam in 1991. The One Hundred Second Congress opened in 1991 with Mitchell declaring health care reform to be his top legislative priority. Consistent with his commitment to health care reform, on June 5, 1991 he introduced the HealthAmerica Act, vowing to pass a national health insurance bill in the One Hundred Second Congress. "It is my hope, my expectation and my intention to enact meaningful health-care reform in this Congress," Mitchell announced.[38]

Mitchell's hopes of passing a national health insurance bill in the One Hundred Second Congress received a temporary boost on January 22, 1992, when the Senate Labor and Human Resources Committee approved a slightly amended version of the HealthAmerica Act on a party-line vote. All ten Democratic committee members supported the bill; all seven Republican members opposed it.[39] Mitchell responded to the committee's approval of the HealthAmerica Act by reiterating his commitment to pass a national health insurance bill. "It is my intention to make every effort to see that comprehensive health care reform is passed in this Congress," he declared.[40]

However, Mitchell's hopes of passing a national health insurance bill quickly faded. To reach the Senate floor for a vote, the HealthAmerica Act needed to be approved by the Finance Committee, which shared jurisdiction over the bill with the Labor and Human Resources Committee. However, the Senate Finance Committee refused even to consider the bill. Its action blocked further Senate consideration of the bill, effectively killing it.[41]

The death of the HealthAmerica Act ended prospects for the passage of a national health insurance bill in the One Hundred Second Congress. Senate Finance Committee Chairman Lloyd Bentsen of Texas declared in a speech to the National Press Club on March 4, 1992, "I know we're not going to have comprehensive health-care reform this year."[42] Nevertheless, Bentsen did make a political concession to health care reformers by introducing legislation to impose modest, incremental changes in group insurance purchased by businesses employing from two to fifty workers. The reforms would prohibit private plans from excluding individuals employed in a small business from access to group insurance due to their health status. Private plans would also be banned in most cases from excluding preexisting medical conditions from the coverage provided to members of small groups. Annual increases in premiums for small group insurance would be limited to 5 percent. The federal government would impose an excise tax equal to 25 percent of the revenue received from small group insurance premiums on any private plan that violated the new insurance regulations. The share of the cost of private insurance self-employed individuals could deduct from their taxable income would increase from 25 to 100 percent. Bentsen's health insurance reform legislation was attached as an amendment to a tax bill, which was passed by the Finance Committee on a party-line vote of eleven to nine on March 3, and then was passed by the full Senate.[43]

Bentsen's health insurance market reform proposals were designed to eliminate the worst abuses in the insurance system, which have been directed against small groups. Given their small number of members, small groups have access to limited financial resources that they can contribute to finance the cost of their health care. As a result, private plans raise premiums substantially whenever catastrophic illness or injury strikes a member of a small group to finance the cost of his or her medical treatment.

In addition, the small group health insurance market is of little financial importance to the private insurance industry. Rather, the industry caters to the large group insurance market, where most of its revenue is earned. Given the lack of financial importance of the small group insurance market, the industry prefers not to insure small businesses, and will do so only if it is profitable. To assure that small group insurance is provided on a profitable basis, the industry must limit the financial liabilities incurred in financing the provision of health care for working families employed in small businesses. Private plans usually do this by denying coverage to members of small groups who are in poor health and by excluding preexisting medical conditions from the health care protection they provide those members.

Bentsen's proposals would have made it easier for members of small groups to purchase and maintain private health insurance coverage. However, on the whole, the proposals were still inadequate. At best, they would have provided coverage to the handful of uninsured individuals who are employed in small business, can afford insurance, but have been denied coverage due to their health status. The remainder of the uninsured population would have continued without any coverage. In addition, Bentsen's proposals included no health care cost-containment measures. Bentsen defended the inadequacy of his proposals by explaining that they represented the only health care reforms that had any chance of passage. "We tried to do what we could in the Finance Committee," he explained to the National Press Club.[44]

Due to their inadequacy, Bentsen's health insurance market reform proposals ran into heavy opposition from House Democrats. Leading the opposition to Bentsen's proposals were three powerful House Democrats: John D. Dingell of Michigan, chairman of the House Energy and Commerce Committee; Henry A. Waxman of California, chairman of the committee's Subcommittee on Health and the Environment; and William D. Ford of Michigan, chairman of the Education and Labor Committee. They rejected the modest, incremental changes in the small group insurance market sponsored by Bentsen, demanding comprehensive health care reform instead. The Energy and Commerce Committee, its Subcommittee on Health, and the Education and Labor Committee jointly exercised jurisdiction over health care reform in the House. As a result, opposition to Bentsen's health insurance market reforms by the chairman of those three bodies effectively blocked House approval of the Senate Finance Committee chairman's proposals.

House Democrats were especially opposed to Bentsen's health insurance market reforms because they feared that by eliminating the worst abuses in the insurance system, which are directed against small businesses, his proposals were designed to defuse pressure for comprehensive health care reform.[45] Bentsen heatedly denied the charge. "I do not look on it as a substitute for total health-care reform," he told the National Press Club. "I do not look on it as an obstacle to total health care reform."[46]

However, Bentsen's denial of any involvement in a campaign to thwart comprehensive health care reform fell on deaf ears. House Democratic members of the conference committee that wrote the final version of the tax bill deleted Bentsen's proposals before the tax measure was passed by Congress in March.[47]

The failure of Bentsen's efforts to secure passage of modest, incremental reforms in the small group health insurance market ended all Senate efforts to achieve health care reform in the One Hundred Second Congress. Instead, the political spotlight moved to the House. On April 2, House Ways and Means Committee Chairman Daniel Rostenkowski announced that he would draft a health care reform bill after Congress returned from its spring recess. Five days later Speaker of the House Thomas Foley of Washington told reporters that he hoped to bring a health care reform bill to a vote on the House floor by Memorial Day.[48] Pursuant to Foley's call for quick House action on health care reform, Rostenkowski ordered his Subcommittee on Health to approve legislation overhauling the medical system by the Fourth of July.[49]

Accordingly, Health Subcommittee Chairman Pete Stark of California drafted the Health Care Cost Containment and Reform Act.[50] It would have imposed a national health care budget. The government would establish reimbursement rates for doctors, hospitals, nursing homes, and prescription drugs. The CBO estimated that the bill would have reduced health care costs by $114 billion in 2002.

The Health Care Cost Containment and Reform Act would have prohibited private health insurance plans from denying coverage to individuals due to their health status. It also would have limited the duration for which private plans could exclude preexisting medical conditions from the coverage they provide their subscribers. Private plans would be required to use standardized forms for processing medical claims and reimbursing health care providers. The share of the cost of private insurance that self-employed individuals could deduct from their taxable income would be raised from 25 to 100 percent.[51]

By imposing stringent cost-containment measures throughout the medical system, the Health Care Cost Containment and Reform Act would have reduced reimbursement rates for doctors, hospitals, and nursing homes. Price controls would have been imposed on prescription drugs and medical equipment. Private health insurance plans would have been required to provide full coverage to all subscribers, regardless of their health status, thereby driving up their financial liabilities and reducing their revenues. The bill would have imposed substantial financial losses upon virtually every segment of the health care system. As a result, the health care industry mounted an intensive lobbying campaign to defeat the bill. As Stark put it, by imposing stringent health care cost-containment measures, "we've absolutely solidified our opposition [to the bill]. The doctor's don't like it. The hospitals don't like it. The drug companies don't like it, and the insurance companies don't like it."[52]

The Health Care Cost Containment and Reform Act stood no chance of serious congressional consideration, let alone passage, given the fact that members of the medical industry were united in their opposition to the bill. True, on June 30 the Subcommittee on Health of the House Ways and Means Committee approved the bill by a voice vote. However, the full committee refused to take any action on the bill, thus killing it. The death of the bill ended all further efforts to pass health care legislation in the One Hundred Second Congress.[53]

Why were congressional Democrats willing to defy their leaders, Senator Mitchell and Speaker of the House Foley, and reject their pleas to pass a health care reform bill? Why were they willing to ignore the demands of an overwhelming majority of the public, who support the establishment of national health insurance?

The answer remains the massive campaign contributions to members of Congress of both parties that flowed from the health care industry during 1991 to 1992. Had congressional Democrats passed a national health insurance bill, like the HealthAmerica Act, that imposed stringent cost-containment measures combined with the a shrinkage of the private insurance industry, it would have resulted in substantial financial losses to health care providers and third-party payers. The health care industry would have retaliated against congressional Democratic supporters of national health insurance by terminating all campaign contributions to them and would have used its massive financial resources to finance Republican challengers.

As a result, congressional Democrats could not have responded to Mitchell, Foley, and an overwhelming majority of the public's demand for passage of a health care reform bill without antagonizing the medical industry, and risking defeat the next time they ran for reelection. They had no choice but to ignore Mitchell and Foley's call for passage of a health care reform bill, handing them a stinging political setback and undermining their credibility as congressional leaders. For most congressional Democrats, serving the political interests of the health care industry took precedence over loyalty to their leaders and responsiveness to public opinion. Mitchell and Foley's failure to mobilize effective support for national health insurance in the One Hundred Second Congress suggests that passage of a health care reform bill will remain politically impossible as long as the medical industry continues to exercise substantial financial influence over lawmakers.

CONCLUSION

The current campaign to establish national health insurance opened in 1991 on a promising note. Leading Senate Democratic health care policymakers produced a compromise national health insurance plan, the HealthAmerica Act, designed to impose a fundamental overhaul of the health care system without incurring opposition from the medical industry. The bill would have achieved sweeping health care reform, contrary to the arguments of its critics. However, by imposing stringent health care cost-containment measures combined with shrinking, consolidating, and streamlining of the private insurance industry, the bill promised to impose substantial financial losses on the medical industry. As a result, the industry stepped up its campaign contributions to members of Congress in a successful effort to prevent health care reform.

In refusing to take action on health care reform, the Democratic majority in the One Hundred Second Congress was willing to defy the wishes of its leaders, who had made national health insurance their top legislative priority, as well as the desires of the overwhelming majority of the public, who supported the program. Congressional Democrats had no choice but to ignore the pleas of their leadership and public opinion for legislative action on health care reform. Any such action would have resulted in health care cost-containment measures and insurance market reforms, which would have imposed substantial financial losses upon the medical industry. The industry would have retaliated against congressional Democratic supporters of health care reform by using its substantial financial clout to defeat those lawmakers when they ran for reelection. To maintain their financial relationship with the industry, which was vital to retaining their seats, congressional Democrats could not take any action on health care reform. The financial power of the health care industry, not the wishes of the leaders of the Democratic majority in Congress and public opinion, dictate the legislative process on medical reform. And this will remain the case as long as the current congressional campaign finance system, which provides the industry with its political influence on Capitol Hill, remains intact.

CHAPTER 8

The Debate on Health Care Reform, 1991–1992

After nearly a three-decade hiatus, the time has come for fundamental reform of our medical care.[1]
Theodore R. Marmor and Lawrence R. Jacobs, political scientists

George Mitchell's unsuccessful efforts to pass a national health insurance bill in the One Hundred Second Congress occurred during a major national debate on health care reform that took place in 1991–1992. It began on November 5, 1991, when a little-known Democratic political novice, Harris Wofford, won a stunning upset victory in the Pennsylvania Senate election. Wofford's election was largely based upon his support for national health insurance, which he made the centerpiece of his campaign. His recipe for victory was followed by Governor Bill Clinton of Arkansas, who was elected to the presidency on a pledge to secure the establishment of such a program. Like Wofford, Clinton made the adoption of national health insurance a centerpiece of his campaign.

The 1991 Pennsylvania Senate election and the presidential contest the following year turned out largely to be referenda on national health insurance, with the Democratic nominees supporting the program and their Republican challengers opposing it. The Democratic victories in those two crucial elections are consistent with polling data which show that an overwhelming majority of the public supports national health insurance and, as we shall see in this chapter, is looking to the Democrats, and specifically Clinton, to secure the establishment of the program.

NATIONAL HEALTH INSURANCE AND THE ELECTION OF HARRIS WOFFORD

On November 5, 1991, national health insurance was suddenly catapulted to the forefront of the political agenda as a result of a Senate election in Pennsylvania. No single event in the seventy-five-year history of America's debate on health care reform did more to galvanize public interest in this issue and compel the political system to address the medical needs of the public than that Pennsylvania election. It pitted Democrat Harris Wofford against his Republican challenger, Richard Thornburgh. Wofford was a political unknown, an obscure state secretary of labor who had never run for public office when Governor Robert P. Casey appointed him in May 1991 to fill the unexpired Senate term of the late John Heinz.[2] Thornburgh, by contrast, was a prominent figure in both national and Pennsylvania politics, having served as a two-term governor of the state before becoming attorney general in the Reagan and Bush administrations.[3]

When the Pennsylvania Senate campaign opened in September, Wofford seemed a sure loser, trailing Thornburgh in the polls by 44 percent.[4] However, Wofford ended up scoring an upset victory, defeating Thornburgh by an overwhelming margin of 55 to 45 percent.[5] A major factor in Wofford's surprise victory was the issue of national health insurance. Wofford made national health insurance the centerpiece of his campaign, urging its immediate establishment. In one television campaign advertisement, he declared, "If criminals have the right to a lawyer, I think working Americans should have the right to a doctor."[6]

Thornburgh responded to Wofford's support for national health insurance by denouncing it as a costly program that would drive many small firms out of business, create higher unemployment, and require a substantial tax increase.[7] The Pennsylvania Senate election turned out to be largely a referendum on national health insurance, with Wofford supporting the program and Thornburgh opposing it.

By using his support for national health insurance to win his stunning upset election victory, Wofford served to highlight the rising public clamor for health care reform. As Edward Kennedy put it on the Senate floor the day following Wofford's election, "Harris Wofford's dramatic win in the Pennsylvania Senate campaign makes clear that the American people want comprehensive health care reform, and they want it now."[8] In the wake of Wofford's election, members of Congress recognized that they could no longer ignore health care reform without jeopardizing their political credibility and their hold on public office. As a result, after ignoring health care reform for a decade, members of Congress, both Democrats and Republicans, liberals and conservatives, responded to Wofford's election by staking out their positions on the issue. As E. J. Dionne, Jr., put it:

The 1991 upset victory of Democratic senator Harris Wofford abruptly put health care on every politician's list of critical concerns, which is where it should have been in the first place. By winning the election in Pennsylvania (and overcoming a 40-point deficit in the polls), Wofford effectively used the health care issue as a way of addressing the electorate's broader anxieties. It turned out that even people who had jobs and health insurance were worried about losing one or the other or both. In the wake of the Wofford campaign, conservatives and liberals moved from dodging a vexing question to arguing about the cheapest, fairest, most efficient ways of providing adequate health care to everyone. It will be a difficult debate, but at least the debate has begun.[9]

Wofford's election guaranteed that health care reform would continue to be a prominent issue on the political agenda through the foreseeable future.

POLLING DATA ON NATIONAL HEALTH INSURANCE

In his speech conceding the Senate election to Wofford, Thornburgh blamed his defeat on his failure to effectively address the issue of health care reform. "The uncertainty and anxiety about the cost and coverage of health care obviously went further than we anticipated," Thornburgh candidly admitted.[10] Polling data suggest that Thornburgh was correct: Wofford's election was largely based upon his support for national health insurance. A poll of 1,000 Pennsylvania voters commissioned by the Kaiser Family Foundation, designed by the Harvard School of Public Health, and conducted on November 5–6, 1991, asked its respondents "Which two issues mattered most in deciding how you would vote for senator?"[11] Fifty percent named national health insurance as one of the two issues. Voter concern with national health insurance ranked well ahead of all other issues, far outpacing taxes, the recession, and unemployment.[12] Seventy-five percent of the respondents cited cost as their most important concern relating to health care. Only 7 percent cited inadequate coverage and 5 percent inadequate access to health care.[13]

The fact that the overwhelming majority of Pennsylvania voters were concerned about health care costs, rather than medical coverage, suggests that most residents who considered national health insurance a determining factor in their vote were insured, and had reasonably good access to health care. Their concern with health care costs is indicative of the fact that soaring medical expenses have forced employers and the federal government to reduce the coverage they provide working families, the elderly, and disabled under group health insurance and Medicare. As a result, many Pennsylvanians, as well as Americans as a whole, are assuming an increasing financial burden for the cost of their health care, exposing them to the financial pain of soaring medical expenses. This has made them sensitive to skyrocketing health care costs. In addition, Pennsylvanians, like other Americans who are insured, fear losing their jobs and the coverage that comes with their employment. Fear of losing coverage was a major reason for half of all Pennsylvania voters to consider national health insurance a major issue in the Senate election.

Fear among Pennsylvanians about losing their health insurance and having to shoulder an increasing financial burden for their health care was perhaps best summed up by Fein.

Most Pennsylvanians who voted for Harris Wofford had insurance. They were voting their fears: their fear of losing jobs, and, thereby, insurance; their fear of cutbacks in benefits; their concerns about costs and the impact on potential wage increases. . . .
Pennsylvania demonstrates that health insurance has become a middle-class issue that focuses on costs and the fear of losing insurance more than the problem of the uninsured.[14]

While half of Pennsylvania voters polled cited national health insurance as among the issues they were most concerned about, they remained evenly split on what kind of program they wanted. Thirty-five percent of the respondents supported a play-or-pay insurance plan in which "businesses are required to provide coverage for all their employees or contribute to a fund that would cover all Americans." Thirty-two percent favored a single-payer insurance plan "run by the government, financed by taxpayers, that would cover all Americans." Only 17 percent wanted to "leave things the way they are."[15]

The results of the postelection poll in Pennsylvania are similar to nationwide surveys on national health insurance cited in Chapter 6. They show that while roughly 70 percent of the public supports health care reform, they remain divided over what kind of national health insurance to establish: single-payer or a play-or-pay plan. The results of the Pennsylvania poll were best summed up by Drew Altman, president of the Kaiser Family Foundation in Menlo Park, California. "This poll doesn't tell you what kind of plan the public wants. But it does tell politicians: You better have a plan, and the plan had better address cost. Solutions may vary, but politicians who fail to address this issue now do so at their own peril."[16]

The concern among Pennsylvania voters about health care is consistent with national polling data. From August 31 to September 2, 1992, USA Today, CNN, and the Gallup Organization jointly conducted a poll of 1,007 registered voters. The poll asked its respondents, "What are the most important issues facing the presidential candidates?" Seventy-five percent named health care as one of "the most important issues." Health care ranked fourth on a list of five issues respondents considered to be among "the most important," behind the economy, education, and the federal deficit.[17]

While the public considered health care to be an important issue in the 1992 presidential campaign, during the early 1990s only a small segment of the population thought it was either the most important issue facing the United States or an issue they cared about. The 1990 Los Angeles Times poll on health care cited in Chapter 6 found that only 14 percent of those surveyed considered health care to be the most important issue facing the United States.[18] A 1992 Election Day exit poll of 15,241 voters conducted by the news divisions of ABC, CBS, NBC, and CNN found that 19 percent of those surveyed said they cared about the issue of health care.[19]

Polling data show that the share of the public considering health care to be either the most important issue facing the United States or one they cared about rose from 1990 to 1992, though only slightly less than one in five individuals cited their concern over health care on Election Day, 1992. Nevertheless, polling data reveal that public concern over health care was higher in 1992 than two years earlier. The 1990 *Los Angeles Times* poll found health care ranked fifth in a list of issues its respondents believed to be the most important facing the United States, behind drugs, crime, the deficit, and the economy.[20] By 1992, public concern over health care had risen. The 1992 Election Day exit poll conducted by the news divisions of the three television networks and CNN found that health care now ranked third on the list of nine issues its respondents said they cared about, behind the economy and the deficit.[21]

How do we explain the rise in public concern over health care between 1990 and 1992, as revealed by the polls? The answer lies in the stubborn recession, which persisted during 1990–1992, and lingered into 1993. It shattered the voluntary employment-based health insurance system, which had served as a stable source of coverage for working families since the 1950s. Because insurance usually comes with a job, most working families have relied upon their employers for coverage. This arrangement was acceptable as long as workers had the job security that much, if not most, of the labor force enjoyed during the first four decades of the postwar period. Many, if not most, workers benefited from employment with large corporations and government agencies, virtually all of which guaranteed lifetime employment and provided their working families with group insurance. Those working families were insured for life. They could rely upon their employers to finance most, if not practically all, the cost of their health care.

However, the postwar era of job security ended with the recession, as both the public and private sectors struggled to cope with the devastating effects of the economic downturn plaguing the United States. To cut costs and maintain their competitiveness in the market, large corporations have downsized their operations by laying off a substantial number of their workers. By driving up unemployment and shrinking the tax base, the recession resulted in massive budget deficits, depriving state and local governments of the revenues they need to maintain their public services. Faced with constitutional requirements to balance their budgets, state and local governments have reduced their public services, which resulted in substantial layoffs of public sector workers.

Laid-off corporate and government workers have lost their insurance. Many have found jobs with employers who do not provide their working families with group insurance; others have remained involuntarily unemployed. Whether or not they have found new jobs, many, if not most, laid-off corporate and government workers without group insurance have remained uninsured because they lack the financial means to purchase their own private coverage, and fail to qualify for either Medicare or Medicaid.

With job security a casualty of the recession, workers can no longer rely upon their employers as a source of insurance. They can easily lose their jobs and the insurance that comes with their employment at any time. As a result, they and members of their families can easily lose their access to health care, and be prevented from securing medical treatment when they fall ill; or they could become financially bankrupted by the high cost of medical services. Fearful of losing their jobs, insurance, access to health care, or all their assets to pay for their medical services, for the first time in American history, an overwhelming majority of the public has developed a deep concern over the issue of health care in the 1990s.

As a result, a massive change in public opinion on health care had occurred in the two short years from 1990 to 1992. Considered only a peripheral issue in 1990, by 1992 the public had considered health care to be their third most important national concern, with an overwhelming majority opposed to the current health insurance system, and supporting its elimination and replacement with a program to guarantee universal access to affordable medical services. The change in public opinion on health care was perhaps best expressed by Daniel Yankelovich.

> The recession has many people terrified about job security, and much of this anxiety gets channeled into worry about health care. Typically, someone will say, "If I lost my job we could manage for a while, but what happens if I get sick and no longer have health insurance?" This concern is why almost four out of five Americans (79%) believe the health care system is in crisis. . . . The dominant sentiment is a panicky appeal to "Do something."[22]

Yankelovich, writing in 1992, goes on to note that while the debate on health care had raged for decades, it was really only in 1991 that medical care emerged as a dominant issue on the national agenda. "Although the health care issue has been kicking around for years, the public's consciousness of its importance and active readiness to do something about it has [sic] risen only in the past year or so."[23]

Wofford took political advantage of rising public concern with health care in making national health insurance the centerpiece of his 1991 Senate campaign. By doing so, he served to heighten public interest in health care, not just in Pennsylvania but throughout the United States, since his support for national health insurance received nationwide attention. He gave full expression to the public frustration, if not exasperation, with the rapid deterioration of the health care system and the popular clamor for medical reform. By using his support for national health insurance to score an overwhelming upset victory in the Pennsylvania Senate election, Wofford proved the political potency of health care reform as a "hot button" issue. He assured that health care would continue to be a dominant public concern and a prominent issue on the national agenda during the 1990s.

GEORGE BUSH AND THE CHALLENGE OF HEALTH CARE REFORM

George Bush entered the White House determined to pursue Reagan's policy of ignoring the issue of health care reform. Bush and John Sununu considered the issue to be, in the White House chief of staff's words, "a poison bill," because it would have required additional federal spending—something the president could not accept, given the magnitude of the federal deficit, which reached record levels during his administration.[24] Moreover, Bush could not accept a tax increase to finance a health care reform plan, since during the 1988 presidential campaign he had promised not to raise taxes.

True, in October 1990 Bush did negotiate a deficit-reduction agreement with Congress that included a substantial tax increase.[25] He therefore came under attack for breaking his pledge not to raise taxes: from right-wingers, who charged that the president had betrayed the conservative cause by agreeing to a tax increase, and from liberals, who claimed that the chief executive lacked credibility both because of the decision to break an important promise he made to the public—not to raise taxes—and to have made such a politically reckless and irresponsible pledge in the first place. Stung by criticism from all political quarters over his agreement to raise taxes, on March 2, 1992, Bush announced that his decision to increase taxes was the "biggest mistake" of his presidency, a statement that all but ruled out any further tax increases as long as he remained in office.[26] By refusing to agree to any further tax increases, Bush foreclosed the establishment during his presidency of any new spending programs, like national health insurance, that could be financed only through additional federal revenues.

Hobbled by the soaring federal deficit and his reluctance to raise taxes, Bush was incapable of undertaking any initiative to reform the ailing and failing health care system during his presidency. With the public clamor for health care reform rising, he had to find some way to insulate himself from political damage for ignoring the health care crisis. During its first three years, the Bush administration believed that it could mobilize public support for its opposition to national health insurance on ideological grounds, by denouncing the program as "socialized medicine." As one senior White House aide put it in August 1991, "All we have to do is to say that the Democrats are for socialized medicine and we're not."[27]

However, Wofford's success in using national health insurance as an issue to win his overwhelming victory against Bush's former attorney general forced the administration to reassess its policy of ignoring the issue of health care reform. As a senior administration official explained,

There are 1½ crucial things to learn from Wofford. The half is about how a sagging economy can be played to advantage by Democrats and about how easily a candidate perceived as an outsider can play the desire-for-change theme against an insider. The more important signal involves the sudden saliency of the health-care issue.[28]

As health care became an increasingly dominant issue in the 1992 presidential campaign, the Bush administration began to realize the political need to come up with a medical reform plan of its own. "It's an issue that works better as a statement of general principle and concern . . . but as others get down to detail, we'll be pushed to come up with our own [health care reform plan]," an administration official predicted. "Politically, it's hard to see the upside in any particular plan, but it would be worse if we sit on our hands and let the other side define the discussion."[29]

Wofford's election finally galvanized Bush into recognition of the need for presidential action on health care reform. The morning following Wofford's election, Bush informed Health and Human Services Secretary Louis Sullivan that he would introduce a health care reform plan in his upcoming State of the Union message.[30] Bush held two news conferences, in Washington on November 6, 1991, and in Rome two days later, in which he acknowledged that the election results from Pennsylvania showed the public wanted the federal government to "try to help people with health care."[31] Accordingly, he promised to introduce a "constructive" health care reform plan before the 1992 presidential election.[32]

Consistent with his promise, on February 6, 1992, Bush introduced his health care reform plan in a speech delivered in Cleveland to the Greater Cleveland Growth Association. He recommended that the federal government provide each poor family not covered by either Medicare or Medicaid an annual tax credit of $3,750 to purchase private health insurance. Each family earning an annual income from 100 to 150 percent of the poverty line would receive an income-related tax credit to do so; the higher the income, the lower the credit. The credit would be $375 for each family earning an annual income of 150 percent of the poverty line.

Each family earning an annual income from over 150 percent of the poverty line to $80,000 would receive either a $375 tax credit or a $3,750 tax deduction, whichever amount was greater, to purchase private health insurance. Low-income families whose annual taxes fell below the amount of the tax subsidies to which they were entitled to would receive their assistance in the form of a voucher. Self-employed families would be able to deduct the full cost of their private insurance from their taxable income or receive the tax subsidies to purchase voluntary plans, whichever amount was larger. All tax subsidies would be adjusted annually for inflation. Private plans would be prohibited from excluding preexisting medical conditions from coverage they provide their subscribers; and denying any individual coverage due to his or her health status.[33] Bush estimated that his plan would provide tax subsidies to 95 million individuals, including 30 million uninsured persons, to purchase private insurance.[34]

A major goal of Bush's health care reform plan was to make group health insurance more affordable for small business. As we saw in Chapter 3, most small businesses do not provide their working families with group insurance because it is very costly to provide coverage to small groups. To rectify the problem, Bush recommended the establishment of health insurance networks (HINs), composed of large numbers of small businesses. They would pool their resources to finance coverage for all their working families.[35]

The establishment of HINs would allow group health insurance to be provided to small businesses on the same basis as large corporations, with coverage made affordable by having the cost of health care spread among large numbers of individuals. Because insurance is affordable when purchased by large groups, virtually all big businesses provide coverage for their working families, as we saw in Chapter 3. Accordingly, the formation of HINs would increase the number of small businesses providing group insurance, resulting in a reduction in the number of uninsured individuals, many of whom are employed by small firms.

Bush's health care reform plan created a sharp polarization between the Democratic and Republican parties over the issue of medical care. Republicans responded with enthusiastic support for the Bush plan, while Democrats bitterly denounced it. The Bush plan won the immediate support of an influential group of Republican Senators: Senate Minority Leader Bob Dole of Kansas, Arlen Specter of Pennsylvania, Christopher Bond of Missouri, David Durenberger of Minnesota, John Chaffee of Rhode Island, Larry E. Craig of Idaho, and Alan Simpson of Wyoming.[36]

Speaking on the Senate floor the day Bush introduced his health care reform plan, Dole blasted the Democratic Party's program to mandate employer provision of health insurance for working families, charging that it would drive firms out of business and cost jobs. "We can help low- and middle-income families buy insurance on the free market, as the President has proposed, or we can bury our businesses under a mountain of new mandates," Dole warned. "Americans want affordable health care but they shouldn't have to pay for it with their jobs." Dole praised the Bush plan as a sensible alternative to achieving universal coverage. "By helping individuals purchase health insurance with tax credits, by curbing the explosive costs of medical malpractice, and by helping small businesses to provide coverage for their employees, President Bush has gone a long way toward addressing our health system's major problems."[37]

Bush's health care reform plan was immediately denounced by leading congressional Democrats. Leading the Democratic attack against the Bush plan was George Mitchell, who called the President's program "woefully inadequate."[38] "It won't control costs or guarantee access to health care," Mitchell stated.[39] He was especially critical of the Bush plan for failing to include any effective health care cost-containment measures. "The President's proposals will drive costs right through the roof" because it "fails to meet the first and most important test of any [health care reform] plan—that of controlling costs."[40]

Mitchell's attacks against Bush's health care reform plan were supported by

Representative Fortney H. ("Pete") Stark of California. "The President's health plan is terminally sick," Stark said. "It fails to get everyone health insurance."[41]

THE INADEQUACIES OF BUSH'S HEALTH CARE REFORM PLAN

Congressional Democrats had good reason to denounce Bush's health care reform plan. It was, in Mitchell's words, "woefully inadequate" for three reasons: It lacked a politically viable financing mechanism, it failed to provide universal coverage, and did not contain health care costs.

A major inadequacy of Bush's health care reform plan was that it lacked a politically viable financing mechanism. The Bush administration estimated that its plan to expand private health insurance coverage would have cost the federal government $100 billion from 1992 to 1996, and $35 billion in 1997. True, Bush did suggest that his plan be financed through reductions in federal spending on Medicare and Medicaid.[42] However, federal spending on Medicare and Medicaid would have had to be sharply reduced to allow the government to produce the savings required to finance the Bush plan.

Had Bush's health care reform plan been in effect in 1992, it would have resulted in $20 billion in additional federal spending. In 1992 the government spent $129.4 billion on Medicare and an additional $127.2 billion on Medicaid.[43] As a result, the federal government would have had to reduce Medicare and Medicaid spending by nearly 10 percent to generate the savings necessary to finance the Bush plan. This would have resulted in a sharp reduction in Medicare and Medicaid coverage, depriving the elderly, disabled, and poor of needed health care. Bush would have provided the uninsured access to health care by reducing medical services for the elderly, disabled, and poor—in Jay Rockefeller's words, "robbing from a very poor Peter to pay an already poor Paul."[44] This is hardly a rational means to achieve health care reform.

A second deficiency of Bush's health care reform plan is that it failed to provide adequate financial assistance to families not covered by group health insurance, Medicare, or Medicaid to purchase private plans. Poor families would receive $3,750 annually in either vouchers or tax credits to do so. Nonpoor families would secure the same amount in tax deductions. Lower-income nonpoor families paying a 15 percent federal income tax rate would obtain $563 in deductions; higher-income families paying a 28 percent tax rate would receive $1,050.

However, the tax subsidies secured by poor and nonpoor families alike under Bush's health care reform plan would cover only a fraction of the cost of the average annual private health insurance premium. Consider the cost of insurance in two cities—Los Angeles and Augusta, Maine. In January 1992 the average premium for private insurance providing comprehensive family coverage was $7,296 in Los Angeles and $4,242 in Augusta.[45] The Bush plan failed to provide families not covered by group insurance with sufficient tax subsidies to purchase private plans extending even the most minimal coverage, let alone comprehensive health care protection.

As a result, Bush's claim that his health care reform plan would provide 30 million uninsured individuals coverage lacked credibility. Indeed, in October, 1992 a bipartisan commission issued a report on the Bush plan concluding that had it been in effect, 27 million individuals would have remained uninsured in 2000, compared with 35.4 million persons who had no coverage in 1991.[46] As a result, the Bush plan would have reduced the number of uninsured individuals by only a quarter during the 1990s.

Three-quarters of the uninsured population would have remained without coverage under Bush's health care reform plan because they still would have been unable to afford private health insurance, given the paltry amount of tax subsidies they would receive through the president's program. The only uninsured individuals likely to be able to afford private insurance under the Bush plan were the poor—who would receive annual vouchers of $3,750—and the affluent, who have the incomes to afford voluntary plans. However, the poor (who earn annual incomes of less than $10,000) represent only 26.7 percent of the uninsured. The affluent (who make $50,000 or more) constitute only 10.3 percent of the uninsured. The remaining 63 percent of the uninsured are middle class. They cannot afford the high cost of private insurance. And the Bush plan would, at most, provide them only $1,050 in tax subsidies, a seventh the cost of a premium for comprehensive insurance coverage in Los Angeles.

Bush's health care reform program would not have provided middle-class uninsured individuals the financial assistance they need to purchase private insurance, even plans providing the most minimal coverage. As a result, it would have left most, if not practically all, of the two-thirds of the uninsured who are middle class without coverage. The middle class would have represented the overwhelming majority of the 27 million individuals who would have remained uninsured under the Bush plan.

Moreover, even the poor, whom Bush's health care plan is designed to help the most, would not have been well served under the president's program. The $3,750 in vouchers the poor would receive to purchase private health insurance would still have been only half the cost of a voluntary plan providing comprehensive coverage in Los Angeles. As a result, the tax subsidies they would receive under the Bush program would have been sufficient to allow them to afford private plans providing only the most minimal coverage.

By leaving a substantial segment of the public inadequately insured, Bush's health care reform plan would have failed to alleviate the medical crisis. Tens of millions of individuals would have continued to be deprived of sufficient access to primary care due to inadequate income and insurance coverage. Their health, and very lives, would have continued to be placed at grave risk by their inability to receive needed health care.

A third shortcoming of Bush's health care reform plan is that it included no effective health care cost-containment measures but only a few minor, piecemeal ones. To reduce administrative costs related to excessive paperwork, the insurance industry would be encouraged to use standardized forms to process medical claims and reimburse health care providers. The public would be induced to enroll in more efficient and less costly managed-care insurance plans, especially HMOs.

The most important cost-containment measure in Bush's health care reform plan concerned medical malpractice law. The United States has more malpractice suits per physician, its courts impose a higher average malpractice award, and American doctors pay larger malpractice insurance premiums than in any other nation.[47] To protect themselves against malpractice suits, American doctors practice defensive medicine. Many, if not most, doctors order more services than they otherwise would without the fear of lawsuits. This reduces the possibility that doctors may be sued for failure to order services their patients may subsequently claim they needed.[48]

The high cost of malpractice insurance, combined with the practice of defensive medicine, generates waste and inefficiency in the health care system. Doctors must pass on the cost of malpractice insurance to their patients and third-party payers in the form of inflated fees. Many of the services doctors order are medically unnecessary. Their only purpose is to insulate doctors from the possibility of being sued. By generating the delivery of unnecessary services, the practice of defensive medicine drives up health care costs.

To reduce the cost of malpractice insurance and curtail the practice of defensive medicine, Bush's health care reform plan would have encouraged states to revise their malpractice laws to discourage patients from filing lawsuits against their doctors. Parties to a medical dispute would be induced to submit to binding arbitration. Plaintiffs who rejected binding arbitration, pursued their malpractice suits in court, and lost their cases would have to pay the legal costs of the defendants. This would make malpractice suits financially risky and discourage patients from suing their doctors. Stringent limits would also be imposed upon malpractice punitive damage awards.[49] This would both reduce the overall amount paid out in malpractice damage awards and curtail financial incentives for patients and their lawyers to sue doctors in the hope of winning exorbitant damage settlements. By making malpractice suits financially risky and curbing the financial incentives for such suits to be filed, the Bush plan would have resulted in fewer malpractice suits.

With doctors facing fewer lawsuits and the courts imposing lower damage awards, insurance companies would reduce the premiums they charge physicians for malpractice insurance, thus allowing them to cut their fees. In addition, doctors would have less need to practice defensive medicine, thereby reducing the unnecessary services they provide. Reductions in the cost of malpractice insurance, combined with the curtailment of the practice of defensive medicine, would result in a decline in health care costs.

However, Bush's emphasis on reducing the cost of malpractice insurance, curtailing the practice of defensive medicine, and lowering health care costs through malpractice law reform was misplaced. Malpractice insurance and defensive medicine are insignificant sources of soaring health care costs. Joseph Newhouse estimates that malpractice insurance premiums represent only 2 percent of health care costs. The practice of defensive medicine accounts for only an additional 1 percent of health care costs.[50] Even if Bush's health care reform plan had succeeded in completely eliminating malpractice insurance and the practice of defensive medicine, it would have reduced medical costs by only 3 percent.

Bush's health care reform plan promised to address only the most insignificant sources of soaring health care costs—malpractice insurance premiums and the practice of defensive medicine—while completely ignoring the major and overriding factors in skyrocketing medical expenses. It contained no provisions for either curbing the proliferation of costly medical technology or containing the runaway cost of hospital care, physician services, and prescription drugs. By providing an increased number of individuals access to health care, the Bush plan promised to raise patient utilization of health care. In the absence of any effective cost-containment measures, health care expenses were sure to rise under the Bush plan.

Moreover, as noted, Bush estimated that 95 million individuals, including 30 million uninsured persons, would take advantage of the tax subsidies provided by his health care reform plan to purchase private insurance. As a result, the Bush plan promised to drive up health care costs by using federal funds to expand the existing private insurance industry, adding to the tens of billions of dollars wasted each year in administrative inefficiency within the medical bureaucracy. The Bush plan was designed more to provide additional federal tax subsidies to aid this industry than to provide universal, comprehensive coverage. As Stark put it, "[The Bush plan] is a gift of billions of dollars to the insurance companies and the bloated health care system."[51] Mitchell agreed. "[The Bush plan] ought to be called the Health Insurance Company Protection Act," he said.[52]

Bush wanted to have it both ways. In his 1992 State of the Union address, he noted that the United States would spend over $800 billion on health care that year, and $1.6 trillion by 2000.[53] "We simply cannot afford this," Bush declared.[54] And yet, despite his alarm over America's staggering and soaring health care bill, the president recommended no effective measures to curb skyrocketing medical costs.

Given its woeful inadequacies, Bush's health care reform plan stood virtually no chance of being passed. In fact, a formidable coalition of congressional Democrats, many of them powerful leaders on Capitol Hill, lined up against the Bush plan: Mitchell, Kennedy, Rockefeller, Wofford, Bentsen, Foley, Stark, Alan Cranston of California, Paul Wellstone of Minnesota, Brock Adams of Washington, Bob Kerrey of Nebraska, Thomas Daschle of South Dakota, and Jeff Bingaman of New Mexico.[55] The Democratic case against the Bush plan was best summed up by Kennedy. Speaking on the Senate floor the day following the introduction of the Bush plan, Kennedy declared, "No health reform is worthy of the name unless it meets two basic tests. It must guarantee coverage for every American, and it must put in place a tough program to control rising costs. The Bush plan does neither."[56]

Given the fact that the formidable congressional Democratic opposition to his health care reform plan made its passage virtually impossible, the president would have abandoned his program if he were truly interested in health care reform. He would have attempted to reach agreement with leading Senate Democratic health care policymakers on a compromise program both sides could support. However, he steadfastly refused to do so.

Bush's intransigence on the issue of health care reform suggests that he had no intention of addressing the medical crisis. Rather, his health care reform plan represented a cynical ploy designed less to respond to the medical crisis than to allow the president to use the issue for his own political advantage. Indeed, after all but ignoring the health care crisis during the first three years of his administration, Bush was forced to introduce his medical reform plan to create the appearance that he was confronting the issue of health care when Wofford's election made such action politically necessary. Given its woeful inadequacies, Bush's health care reform plan was more designed to insulate the president from charges that he was failing to address the medical crisis than it was to reverse the breakdown of the health care system. As Mitchell put it, "This is not a proposal to deal with the problem of health care. This is a proposal to deal with the perception that the President doesn't care about health care."[57]

Bush's decision to reverse his previous policy of ignoring the health care crisis and introduce a medical reform plan of his own was motivated purely by partisan politics and represented a cynical exercise in presidential deception. Bush realized that health care was a politically popular issue the Democratic Party could use to defeat him in the 1992 presidential election. To prevent this, he had no alternative but to recommend a health care reform plan of his own. However, Bush really did not want health care reform. Accordingly, he introduced a plan so inadequate that it had virtually no chance of being passed. Moreover, he opposed the major alternative to his health care reform plan sponsored by leading Senate Democrats—play-or-pay health insurance. He stood ready to veto any play-or-pay insurance bill the Democratic Congress might pass.

Bush was determined to have it both ways. By introducing his health care reform plan, he could identify himself with the politically popular cause of national health insurance, undermining efforts by the Democratic Party to use the issue to defeat him in the 1992 presidential election. At the same time, he could prevent the achievement of health care reform by refusing to accept anything more than the inadequate and unacceptable plan he had introduced, thereby effectively preventing the establishment of national health insurance during his presidency.

THE BUSH ADMINISTRATION OPPOSES NATIONAL HEALTH INSURANCE

By recommending that expanded health insurance coverage be achieved through federal tax credits rather than either the government or mandates on employers, the Bush administration placed itself in direct opposition to national health insurance. Accordingly, it acted to mobilize public and congressional support for its health care reform plan by attempting to discredit national health insurance. The first salvo fired by the administration against national health insurance came from Louis Sullivan, who directed his attacks against a play-or-pay plan. He outlined the administration's opposition to such insurance in an article appearing in the January 13, 1992, *Los Angeles Times*.

In the article, Sullivan charged that play-or-pay health insurance would impose an onerous financial burden upon the business community by requiring all employers either to provide group coverage to their working families or to pay a payroll tax to allow the federal government to do so. Sullivan based his arguments on the study of a play-or-pay insurance plan imposing a 7 percent payroll tax upon business, conducted by the Urban Institute and Rand Corporation. They estimated that such a play-or-pay plan would raise annual business costs by nearly $30 billion, as firms not providing their working families with group coverage would be required to extend health care protection to their employed households under either public or private insurance. Unable to assume the financial burden of providing their working families with insurance, Sullivan charged, many small firms not currently providing their employed households with group coverage would be driven out of business by a play-or-pay plan, forcing their employees onto the unemployment lines. In addition, Sullivan noted that the imposition of a 7 percent payroll tax on business would be insufficient to finance public health insurance for working families not covered by group plans. As a result, the Urban Institute and Rand Corporation estimated that the federal government would have to spend $36.4 billion annually to finance the cost of public insurance not covered by the payroll tax.

Finally, the guarantee of universal, comprehensive health insurance coverage, as provided for under a play-or-pay plan like the HealthAmerica Act, would remove financial barriers that impede public access to health care. This would result in a substantial rise in patient utilization of health care, driving up its cost. The HealthAmerica Act would impose stringent cost-containment measures to assure that universal access to health care could be provided on an affordable basis. However, Sullivan denounced those measures, charging that they would result in severe health care rationing.

Sullivan concluded by charging that play-or-pay health insurance would be an unmitigated disaster for the health care system.

The truth is that "pay or play" would result in the worst of all possible worlds: closed businesses, lost jobs, huge new expenses for both the private sector and the taxpayer, and an enormous new bureaucracy. It would start us down the road to a nationalized health insurance system and lead eventually to the rationing of health care and long waits for medical care—something that the American people won't, and shouldn't, tolerate.[58]

Sullivan's attacks against national health insurance were echoed by Bush in remarks he made in support of his health care reform plan. Bush opened his campaign against national health insurance during his 1992 State of the Union message and in speeches he made introducing his health care reform plan on February 6 and 7 in Cleveland and San Diego, respectively. Echoing Sullivan's charges, Bush claimed that play-or-pay insurance would result in "higher taxes, fewer jobs, and eventually a [health care] system under complete Government control."[59] He charged that play-or-pay insurance would require small businesses not providing their working families with group coverage to choose among three unpalatable alternatives: they could reduce wages or raise prices in order to finance the cost of insurance for their working families; or they could lay off workers in order to relieve themselves of the financial burden of having to provide them insurance. He argued that play-or-pay insurance would result in a massive rise in unemployment as small firms either laid off workers because they could not afford the cost of providing insurance coverage, or were driven out of business altogether by the financial burden of having to extend health care protection to their employed households, leaving their employees without jobs.

Moreover, Bush predicted that play-or-pay health insurance would create "a back-door route to nationalized health care."[60] Many employers providing their working families with group health insurance would opt to pay a payroll tax to enroll them in a government program instead. Since the payroll tax businesses paid would be insufficient to cover the full cost of public insurance for their working families, the federal government would be required to finance the difference.[61]

Bush denounced "nationalized health care" as "a prescription for disaster."[62] A "nationalized health care system" would "restrict patient choice in picking a doctor and force the Government to ration services arbitrarily," resulting in "long waiting lists for surgery [and] shortages of high-tech equipment responsible for the miracles of modern medicine."[63] And what we'll get is patients in long lines, indifferent service, and a huge new tax burden."[64] Bush warned that by requiring the government to assume primary responsibility for financing medical services, "a nationalized health care system" would result in an additional $250 billion to $500 billion in taxes.[65] He vowed to fight any effort by congressional Democrats to establish a "nationalized health care system." "I will not allow those people to give America a prescription for failure," he declared. "I am going to fight against a nationalized, socialized medicine approach for this country."[66]

THE POLITICS OF NATIONAL HEALTH INSURANCE:
CLINTON VERSUS BUSH

Following the introduction of Bush's health care reform plan, the issue of medical care faded from the national agenda—but only briefly. As the presidential election campaign opened in July 1992, health care reform emerged as a major issue. Both Clinton and Bush used the issue to define their political and ideological differences, attack and discredit each other, and mobilize public support for their campaigns. The opening volley in the battle between the two presidential nominees over the issue was fired by Clinton.

In his speech to the Democratic national convention in New York, accepting the party's presidential nomination, Clinton pledged to establish "an America in which health care is a right, not a privilege. In which we say to all our people: your government has the courage—finally—to take on the health care profiteers and make health care affordable for every family."[67] Clinton blasted Bush for his opposition to national health insurance. "He won't take on the big insurance companies and bureaucracies to control health care costs and give us affordable health care for all Americans," Clinton stated. "But I will."[68]

On August 2 Bush responded to Clinton's attacks against the president for his failure of leadership in health care policy. His response came in a speech delivered at a fund-raising brunch in Rosemont, Illinois, for Republican Senate nominee Rich Williamson in which he called the issue of health care reform "the Grand Canyon of philosophy" dividing him from Clinton.[69] At the time, Clinton had not introduced any national health insurance plan of his own. Instead, he limited himself to declaring his support for play-or-pay insurance, including the imposition of stringent health care cost-containment measures.[70] As a result, Bush assumed that Clinton would attempt to secure the establishment of play-or-pay insurance if elected to the presidency. Acting upon this assumption, Bush touted his health care reform plan while denouncing play-or-pay insurance as "a prescription for disaster."

In his speech, Bush explained in stark terms the differences, as he saw them, between his health care reform plan and play-or-pay insurance.

The other plan will dump 52 million Americans into a new Government [health insurance] bureaucracy, and my plan will help 90 million Americans afford private health insurance to take care of their health care needs. The other plan will slap at least a 7-percent payroll tax on middle-income Americans, and my plan would provide tax relief to Americans to help them pay for their own health care.[71]

Bush charged that by imposing a payroll tax that would force small businesses either to lay off workers or go out of business altogether, play-or-pay health insurance would result in the loss of 700,000 jobs.[72] By contrast, he claimed that his health care reform plan would result in job gains by providing federal tax subsidies to help firms finance the cost of group insurance for their working families. In addition, he charged that the stringent health care cost-containment measures that Clinton recommended would result in severe medical care rationing, as hospitals would be forced to reduce services to meet the cost controls the Democratic presidential nominee would establish. "The other plan will create lines at hospitals so long you'll think you were selling Bears tickets inside," Bush declared, referring to the popular Chicago football team. He assured the public that his health care reform plan would avoid health care rationing while containing medical costs in the process. "My plan will allow you to get the care you need when you need it, and my plan would preserve the quality of care in this country," Bush claimed. "And my plan attacks the root causes of rising costs: faulty insurance, too much paperwork, far too many frivolous lawsuits out there."[73]

Bush concluded his speech by warning that Clinton's election would be an unmitigated disaster for the health care system, given his Democratic opponent's support for play-or-pay health insurance. "Understand what's at stake here," Bush warned. "If the Governor of Arkansas is elected with a new Democratic Congress . . . within a year the Government will run health care in this country. Our health care system will combine the efficiency of the House post office with the compassion of the KGB. I am not going to let that happen."[74] Bush repeated another version of this line at the 1992 Republican national convention in Houston. In his speech accepting the presidential nomination, he again touted his health care reform plan while blasting Clinton's support for play-or-pay insurance.

I have a plan to provide affordable health care to every American, controlling costs by cutting lawsuits and paperwork, and expanding coverage to the poorest of the poor.

We do not need my opponent's plan for a massive Government takeover of health care, which would ration care and deny you the right to choose a doctor. Who wants a health care system with the efficiency of the House Post Office, and the compassion of the KGB?[75]

By likening play-or-pay insurance to the scandal-ridden House post office and the corrupt and repressive KGB, Bush sought to incite public fear and outrage at his Democratic opponent's support for the program.

On August 2 and 3 Clinton held two news conferences at the governor's mansion in Little Rock to respond to the president's attacks on his support for play-or-pay health insurance. "I find that unbelievable after this administration and the one before it have presided over the biggest explosion of health care costs in the history of this country," Clinton said. "They don't have any credibility on the health care issue."[76] He was especially angered at Bush's comparison of national health insurance to the KGB, the symbol of communist repression. "He compared our common-sense effort to control health care costs with the police-state tactics of the KGB. Mr. Bush displays no passion for solving the health care crisis, but when somebody else has an idea for making health care available and affordable, he goes ballistic. Once again the Administration is trying to raise fears rather than solve problems."[77]

Clinton denounced Bush for failing to provide any presidential leadership in confronting the health care crisis.

For the past dozen years, he's done nothing while health care costs have risen like a patient's fever chart. The average cost of individual health insurance rose from $1,000 to $3,000 a year, but he did nothing. Our country's annual spending on health care increased in the decade of the '80s until last year, from $250 billion to $809 billion, but he did nothing. Thirty-five million Americans, mostly workers and their families, have no health insurance. Another 35 million don't have adequate coverage. Millions more live in fear that they'll have to pay more for less insurance or lose their insurance completely. And he's done nothing.[78]

Clinton concluded that the Bush Administration had failed to recommend any credible health care reform plan because of its desire to serve the financial interests of the medical industry: "They ought to come up with their own plan, which they haven't done because they don't want to take on the vested interests in the health care debate."[79]

On August 4 ten Democratic Senators called a news conference to join Clinton in blasting Bush on the issue of health care reform. Leading the news conference was Rockefeller, who denounced Bush for failing to provide any leadership on the issue. "I cannot understand how the President can be so callous, so indifferent, so unknowledgeable and take so little action" on the issue, Rockefeller said.[80] "President Bush does not give one whit about health care."[81]

Rockefeller assailed Bush's health care reform plan. In a reference to Bush's comparison of play-or-pay health insurance with the House post office and the KGB, Rockefeller pointed to the woeful inadequacies of the President's health care reform plan. "It combines the compassion of his antirecession policy with the efficiency of his savings and loan bailout," Rockefeller declared. "I look upon his actions with disdain."[82] By likening Bush's health care reform plan to his failed economic policy and the savings and loan fiasco, Rockefeller served to call public attention to the President's lack of leadership in health care policy.

On September 24, Clinton introduced his own national health insurance plan in a speech to workers at a Merck pharmaceutical manufacturing plant in Rahway, New Jersey.[83] The Clinton plan would require employers to provide private insurance to their working families. Unlike play-or-pay insurance, the Clinton plan would not give employers the option of enrolling their working families in a public insurance program. Moreover, the government would purchase private coverage for the poor and unemployed rather than extend them health care protection through a public plan.[84]

As a result, the Clinton plan would achieve universal coverage through private, rather than public, health insurance. This should have satisfied Bush, whose main complaint against play-or-pay insurance was that it would allow employers to enroll their working families in a public insurance program, requiring the government to assume responsibility for providing coverage to additional tens of millions of individuals. However, in a speech to the National Technology Initiative Conference in Chicago on September 25, Bush dismissed the Clinton plan as scarcely different from play-or-pay insurance. "It is the same old thing," Bush stated. He objected to the Clinton plan's requirement that employers finance the cost of group insurance for their working families, attacking such a mandate as a tax on business. He also denounced the Clinton plan's imposition of national and state limits on health care spending, repeating his warning that such action would result in "rationed health care."[85]

THE LACK OF CREDIBILITY OF THE BUSH ADMINISTRATION'S ARGUMENTS AGAINST NATIONAL HEALTH INSURANCE

As Clinton and Rockefeller claimed, Bush's (and Sullivan's) attacks on national health insurance were false and misleading. Their charge that the program would result in health care rationing is deceptive. By reducing financial barriers impeding public access to health care, the program would raise patient utilization of medical services, thus driving up their cost. The federal government would have to ration health care, especially the proliferation of expensive medical technology, in order to contain medical costs, as Bush and Sullivan argue.

However, health care is already being rationed in the United States on the basis of how much insurance coverage and income each individual has—a fact Bush and Sullivan chose to ignore. Affluent and well-insured individuals have access to all the health care they need. Low-income and inadequately insured individuals have access only to the health care they can afford or that they receive from charitable hospitals.

National health insurance would develop a more decent and humane way of rationing health care. All individuals would receive access to all medically proven and affordable health care they need, regardless of income. On the other hand, costly health care of questionable value, especially high-technology hospital care, would be strictly rationed. Bush and Sullivan ignored the fact that national health insurance would end the perverse way in which health care is currently being rationed, and develop a more dignified and honorable way to allocate society's scarce medical resources.

Bush's charge that national health insurance would restrict the right of patients to choose their own doctors is also false. No credible sponsor of the program would deny patients this right, which is fully guaranteed in virtually all the countries of Western Europe, and Canada, which have national health insurance programs.[86]

Bush and Sullivan's claim that national health insurance would result in an enormous tax increase—both to the business community and to individual taxpayers—is also false. Bush was especially adamant in his opposition to single-payer insurance, charging that by requiring the government to assume primary responsibility for financing health care, the program would impose a massive tax increase. However, he neglected to mention that the tax increase under the program would be offset by reductions in private insurance premiums that neither employers nor their working families would have to pay, since the government would replace voluntary plans as the dominant source of financing health care. Moreover, if the government provided more comprehensive coverage than private insurance does, then the program would result in reductions in out-of-pocket health care expenses. In addition, if the government imposed stringent health care cost-containment measures under single-payer insurance, it would result in an actual reduction in medical costs.

Finally, if single-payer insurance was financed through a progressive tax system, the wealthy would be required to assume a larger share of the financial burden for health care, allowing the middle class and the poor to pay less for their medical services. This stands in sharp contrast to the current insurance system, in which all individuals pay flat, nonincome-related premiums for their health care. The middle class and poor must pay the same premium for comparable coverage as the wealthy do, thereby requiring the nonrich to assume a substantial financial burden for the cost of their health care. As a result, the taxes the public, especially the middle class and the poor, would have to pay under single-payer insurance would be lower than the "taxes" they currently pay, in the form of private insurance premiums and out-of-pocket health care expenses.

Bush and Sullivan were especially critical of play-or-pay health insurance, charging that it would impose a substantial tax increase. Employers who chose not to provide their working families with group insurance would be required to pay a payroll tax to finance a public plan for the individuals not covered by group plans or Medicare. However, the payroll tax would be offset by the elimination of private insurance premiums that employers opting to enroll their working families in a public plan would no longer have to pay. Because of lower administrative costs, public insurance can be provided more cheaply than private plans, as we have seen. As a result, the payroll tax employers would have to pay for public insurance would be lower than the premiums they pay for private plans.

The only segment of the business community that would have to bear a tax increase under play-or-pay health insurance is employers not currently providing their working families with group plans. They would be required either to do so or to pay a payroll tax to finance public insurance for their working families. However, many, if not most, employers who do not provide their working families with group insurance are small businesses. The least profitable small businesses that employ primarily low-wage workers would receive tax subsidies to assist them in financing insurance for their working families under both the HealthAmerica Act and Clinton's national health insurance plan.

As a result, no segment of the business community would have to shoulder a substantial tax increase under play-or-pay health insurance. Accordingly, Bush and Sullivan's charge that small firms would be forced to lay off workers or would be driven out of business by the payroll tax the program would impose is false. And because no job layoffs or business failures would result from the plan, Bush and Sullivan's claim that it would lead to job losses is equally untrue. Their charge that play-or-pay insurance would result in massive business failures and job losses amounts to nothing more than a scare tactic designed to mobilize corporate and labor opposition to the plan.

Moreover, play-or-pay health insurance would not require any general tax increase on the public as a whole. True, the Urban Institute and Rand Corporation estimate that a 7 percent payroll tax would be insufficient to finance the full cost of universal coverage. As a result, the federal government would have to provide $36.3 billion in tax subsidies to make up the difference, as we saw earlier.

However, this would be more than offset by the $67 billion to $83.2 billion that Woolhandler and Himmelstein and the GAO estimate would be saved through the elimination of the wasteful and inefficient private insurance industry and the establishment of a Canadian-style single-payer plan. A play-or-pay plan would eradicate most of the private insurance industry through the establishment of a government program to provide coverage to most of the population. As a result, federal tax subsidies to achieve universal coverage could easily be financed through the substantial savings that would come from scrapping and replacing most of the private insurance industry with a public plan. Additional savings could be achieved through health care cost-containment measures designed to eliminate waste and inefficiency in the medical system outside the private insurance industry. The savings that could be achieved through the eradication of waste and inefficiency throughout the health care system would be more than enough to offset the additional federal spending required to achieve universal insurance coverage. As a result, taxpayers would not have to pay an additional dime in taxes to finance national health insurance, whether based upon a play-or-pay or a single-payer plan.

Bush and Sullivan's charge that national health insurance would result in a government-controlled health care system represents an exercise in fearmongering. The charge was designed to exploit public distaste for big government in order to mobilize popular opposition to the program. The fact remains that public insurance is more efficient and less costly than private plans. As a result, if universal coverage is to be achieved without a tax increase, the federal government will have to eliminate most, if not all, of the private insurance industry. Such action would reduce or eliminate the administrative waste and inefficiency associated with private insurance, generating the savings necessary to finance coverage for the uninsured. Universal coverage cannot be achieved as long as the United States maintains a large private insurance industry that wastes tens of billions of dollars each year. Those dollars can be put to better use providing coverage for the uninsured.

Bush's insistence on preserving the existing private health insurance industry, whose waste and inefficiency are a major source of the excessive amounts the United States spends on health care, made no sense. By attacking public insurance and insisting on the preservation of the existing private insurance industry, Bush placed ideology above political pragmatism and economic efficiency. He allowed his ideological opposition to big government to blind him to the realization that the public sector can provide insurance more efficiently than the private sector.

As a result, Bush's attacks against national health insurance lacked credibility. They were based upon an emotional opposition to big government rather than a reasoned and pragmatic understanding of how to respond effectively to the challenge of health care reform. Accordingly, Bush provided no leadership in meeting this challenge. Instead, he used empty rhetoric against the alleged evils of "nationalized health care" as a substitute for sound and reasoned judgment concerning how the United States can meet the health care needs of its people during the 1990s.

Bush's likening of national health insurance to the communist repression of the KGB marked a new low in the debate on health care reform. The comparison showed a president desperate to insulate himself from blame for his failure to manage health care policy by distorting the issue and casting aspersions on good-faith efforts of others to address the medical crisis in a serious and rational manner—which the president was incapable of doing. The management of health care policy had fallen into disarray during the Bush administration because of the president's determination to distance himself from his failure to address the medical crisis and to use support among some Democratic congressional leaders for national health insurance as a means to discredit the Democrats as the party of big government. The disarray in health care policy came at the worst possible time: when the medical system is sinking into disrepair, if not collapse.

In 1992 the onus was on voters to elect a president who was willing to join, if not lead, the national consensus in support of the program. As we will see in Chapter 9, Clinton pledged to secure the establishment of national health insurance as an immediate top domestic policy priority of the presidency. His election suggested that the voters were finally ready to choose a president who promised to provide leadership on the issue of health care reform.

NATIONAL HEALTH INSURANCE AND THE 1992 PRESIDENTIAL ELECTION

Clinton succeeded in making the 1992 presidential election largely a referendum on national health insurance. He attempted to capitalize upon the existence of overwhelming public support for national health insurance by promising, if elected, to secure its establishment. He seized upon Bush's opposition to the program as evidence that the president was unwilling to address the health care crisis, an issue of paramount concern to the public. Clinton had good reason to use the issue of health care reform for his own political advantage. Perhaps no other issue politically benefited Clinton and the Democrats, and hurt Bush and the Republicans, more than health care. Polling data suggest that a major reason why voters elected Clinton president was his commitment to securing the establishment of national health insurance, in contrast to Bush, who remained adamantly opposed to the program.

A *USA Today*/CNN/Gallup poll conducted from January 31 to February 2, 1992, found that an overwhelming majority of the public disapproved of Bush's handling of health care policy. The poll asked 1,007 registered voters to assess Bush's performance on seven issues, including health care. Sixty-six percent disapproved, and only 29 percent approved, of Bush's handling of health care policy. Public disapproval of Bush's management of health care policy ranked third on the list of seven issues surveyed in the poll, behind only the economy and unemployment.[87]

Another *USA Today*/CNN/Gallup poll, conducted January 3–9, 1992, found that an overwhelming majority of the public preferred the Democrats to manage health care policy. The poll asked 1,400 adults whether Democrats or Republicans would do a better job in handling twelve issues, including health care. Sixty percent believed that Democrats would do a better job in handling health care policy, and only 27 percent said Republicans would do so. The Democrats' margin of approval over the Republicans' on health care was greater than for any of the eleven other issues surveyed in the poll, with the exception of only poverty and homelessness.[88]

Not only did an overwhelming majority of the public believe that Democrats can do a better job than Republicans in handling health care policy, an equally impressive majority also felt that Clinton could do a better job than Bush in managing health care policy. The September 1992 *USA Today*/CNN/Gallup poll cited earlier asked its respondents whether Clinton or Bush "would do a better job handling" five issues, including health care. Sixty-two percent believed that Clinton "would do a better job handling health care" and only 27 percent thought that Bush would do so. Clinton's margin of approval on health care was greater than for any of the four other issues surveyed in the poll.[89]

The public preference for Clinton over Bush on the issue of health care was essentially the same when people were asked which presidential nominee could better guarantee individuals access to affordable medical services. From August 20-21 1992, the *Los Angeles Times* asked 1,186 registered voters the following question: "Who do you think would do a better job providing affordable health care for most Americans?" Fifty-seven percent of the respondents chose Clinton, 22 percent Bush, 7 percent neither, 1 percent both, and 13 percent didn't know. Clinton's margin of approval over Bush on public access to health care was greater than for any of the other three issues surveyed in the poll.[90]

Consistent with their preference for Clinton on the issue of health care, majority of the public favored the Democratic nominee's medical care reform plan over the President's. From October 2–5, 1992, the *Los Angeles Times* asked 1,545 registered voters which of two health care reform plans they preferred: the plan, sponsored by Clinton, that required employers to provide group insurance to their working families and the government to extend coverage to the remainder of the public; or the public disapproval of Bush's management of health care policy ranked third on the list of seven issues surveyed in the poll, with the exception of poverty and homelessness.

The public preference for Clinton over Bush on the issue of health care reform was due to the fact that the Democratic nominee supported national health insurance, while the president opposed it. Since over 70 percent of the public support national health insurance, the people had no difficulty backing Clinton on this issue, given his commitment to the program.[91]

Polling data suggest that public support for Clinton on the issue of health care reform was a major source of his decisive election victory. On Election Day the *Los Angeles Times* asked 14,513 voters at 201 polling places the following question: "What issues were most important to you in deciding how to vote?" Twenty-eight percent of Clinton supporters responded that the issue of health care was "most important" to them in determining their vote; only 8 percent of Bush backers said the same. Health care ranked second on a list of twelve issues Clinton supporters said were "most important" in determining their vote, behind only jobs and the economy; it ranked eighth on the same list for Bush backers.[92]

The *Los Angeles Times*'s conclusions regarding the critical role played by health care reform in Clinton's decisive election victory are confirmed by the Election Day poll conducted by the news divisions of the three television networks and CNN. Of the 19 percent of those polled who cared about the issue of health care, 67 percent voted for Clinton, 19 percent for Bush, and 14 percent for independent presidential candidate Ross Perot. Among the nine issues on which those polled expressed a concern, those interested in health care ranked second in their share of votes cast for Clinton, behind only those concerned about the environment. By contrast, those concerned with health care ranked second to last in their share of votes cast for Bush, above only those interested in the environment.[93]

Polling data show that a substantial share of voters who supported Clinton were drawn to him by his support for health care reform. Those concerned about health care supported Clinton and opposed Bush more strongly than those concerned about every other major issue, with the exception of the environment. As a result, Clinton had a rational political interest in supporting national health insurance, since polling data suggest that he won a significant number of votes for favoring the program. He had an especially strong political incentive to support national health insurance because he could exploit Bush's opposition to the program to win votes from individuals angry at the president for his failure to back health care reform. The fact that so few voters were drawn to Bush on the issue of health care is indicative of the fact that the president had failed to introduce any credible medical care reform plan. As a result, supporters of health care reform had no alternative but to vote for Clinton, who unlike Bush, presented

a viable medical reform plan during the presidential campaign, which he introduced shortly after he entered the White House, as we will see in Chapter 9.

The importance of national health insurance as an issue in the 1992 presidential
campaign was a major reason why Clinton made his support for the program a
centerpiece of his domestic policy agenda. This is especially true, given the fact
that Clinton's margin of approval over Bush on health care policy was greater
than for practically every other major issue. By emphasizing his support for
national health insurance, Clinton identified himself with the issue that gave him
perhaps the greatest political advantage in his campaign against Bush.

CONCLUSION

The issue of health care reform played a major role in the 1992 presidential
campaign. Clinton succeeded in capitalizing upon the rising public clamor for
health care reform to highlight his support for national health insurance. He
seized upon Bush's opposition to the program as evidence that the president was
incapable of providing leadership in achieving health care reform. Polling data
show that Clinton drew a substantial share of his votes from the large segment
of the public having a strong and passionate commitment to health care reform,
thus providing him a clear and unmistakable mandate to secure the establishment
of national health insurance. As Theodore R. Marmor and Lawrence R. Jacobs
put it:

Many Americans have demanded far-reaching changes in access to and the financing of
our troubled [health care] system and Gov. Bill Clinton made the problems of American
medicine a major feature of his campaign. Rarely has a President been swept into office
with so clear a mandate for change [in health care] as Clinton. . . . Democrats in Congress
and the White House have a glorious opportunity . . . to establish the basic rules for a
health system Americans can be justly proud of.[94]

Will Clinton be able to use the mandate for health care reform that his election
gave him to secure the establishment of national health insurance? Will his
election finally break the stalemate that has prevented every effort to achieve
health care reform since the beginning of the 1970s? It is to those questions that
we will now turn.

CHAPTER 9

Bill Clinton and the Challenge of Health Care Reform

It may be the fate of every U.S. president to become bogged down in a dismal swamp. Lyndon Johnson had Vietnam. Richard Nixon had Watergate. George Bush wrestled with the double-dip recession. And Bill Clinton will have the U.S. health care system.[1]

Susan Dentzer, journalist, *U.S. News & World Report*

Clinton assumed the presidency with the health care crisis looming as perhaps the most urgent issue confronting the United States. Polling data showed substantial public dissatisfaction with the health care system. During January 8–11, 1993, *USA Today*, CNN, and Gallup jointly conducted a poll of 1,000 adults. The poll measured public satisfaction on seven conditions affecting the military security of the United States and the socioeconomic conditions of its citizens, including availability of "affordable health care for all." Only 23 percent of those polled expressed satisfaction with the availability of "affordable health care for all." Public satisfaction with the availability of "affordable health care for all" was lower than for any of the other conditions surveyed in the poll, with the exception of the nation's progress in "reducing poverty and homelessness."[2]

Given the existence of widespread dissatisfaction with the health care system, the public believes that medical care reform should be one of Clinton's top priorities. During January 12–13, 1993, Princeton Survey Research Associates conducted a poll for *U.S. News & World Report*. The poll asked 1,005 adults "What are the top-priority problems that Clinton should address quickly?" Thirty-one percent of those polled said that health care reform was the top priority problem. Health care reform ranked second on the list of six issues that respondents considered top priority problems, behind reducing the deficit.[3]

CLINTON'S NATIONAL HEALTH INSURANCE PLAN

Clinton assumed the presidency fully prepared to take action on health care reform. During the 1992 presidential campaign, he made it clear that health care reform would be one of the top priorities, if elected. "The American health-care system costs too much and does not work," Clinton said. "It leaves 60 million Americans without adequate health insurance and bankrupts our families, our businesses, and our federal budget." Clinton blamed the federal government for the health care crisis. "Instead of putting people first, Washington favors the insurance companies, the drug companies, and the health-care bureaucracies."

"Health care should be a right, not a privilege," Clinton declared. Accordingly, he promised that "in the first year of a Clinton-Gore Administration . . . we will send a national health-care plan to Congress, and we will fight to pass it." The Clinton plan would "make health care affordable and accessible for every American."[4]

Clinton acted quickly in launching his drive to fulfill his campaign pledge to secure the establishment of national health insurance. Just five days following his inauguration as president, he established the President's Task Force on National Health Reform, composed of a number of high-level members of his administration.[5] The purpose of the task force was to recommend a national health insurance plan for Clinton to propose during the middle of 1993.

Clinton appointed his closest and most influential adviser, First Lady Hillary Clinton, to chair the task force. Her appointment is a historic and unprecedented act; it marks the first time in American history that a first lady has assumed a formal policymaking position in the executive branch.[6] By appointing his wife to chair the task force, Clinton made two things clear: first, that health care reform would be the top priority of his Presidency; and second, that the White House would assume direct responsibility for securing establishment of a national health insurance program.

The importance of Hillary Clinton's appointment as Chairwomen of the President's Task Force on National Health Reform was perhaps best summed up by Marmor.

The appointment of Hillary Rodham Clinton to this responsible position . . . leaves no doubt that the universalization of [health insurance] coverage and the control of [health care] costs are top priorities of the Clinton Administration and that the President's concept of reform, not that of experts or interest groups, will guide what he presents to Congress. Having Hillary Clinton as the President's agent of [health care] reform . . . gives us good reason to believe that this new Administration takes seriously its commitment to universalize coverage and to restrain the skyrocketing costs of care.[7]

In announcing the establishment of the President's Task Force on National Health Reform, Clinton declared that the time for achieving a sweeping overhaul of the medical system had finally come.

There is an overwhelming knowledge that we have to move and move now [on health care reform]. . . . And we are going to work constantly, day and night, until we have a health care plan ready to submit to the Congress that we believe we can pass. . . . We've talked about [health care reform] long enough. The time has come to act.

By committing himself to achieving health care reform, Clinton placed himself in direct opposition to the medical industry, which is certain to fight any effort to establish national health insurance. Nevertheless, Clinton vowed that he would surmount opposition from the industry to secure the adoption of a national health insurance program: "Powerful lobbies and special interests may seek to derail our efforts, and we may make some people angry. But we are determined to come up with the best possible solution [to the health care crisis]."[8]

The national health insurance plan that Clinton intends to recommend during the middle of 1993 contains three elements: a guarantee of universal access to affordable health care, insurance market reforms to make coverage affordable for small business, and stringent medical cost-containment measures.

Guaranteeing Universal Access to Affordable Health Care

Clinton intends to recommend that all employers be required to provide their working families with group health insurance and finance 75 percent of its cost, with the remainder funded by their employees. Self-employed individuals would be required to purchase their own private insurance.[9] The government would purchase private insurance for all Medicaid beneficiaries and unemployed individuals.[10]

All private health insurance plans and Medicare would be required to provide their beneficiaries a minimum package of health care benefits, which would be determined by a Health Standards Board, a new federal agency composed of representatives of consumers, health care providers, business, labor, and the government.[11] Private plans would be prohibited from both excluding pre-existing medical conditions from the coverage they provide their subscribers and denying any individual coverage due to his or her health status. To reduce insurance administrative costs associated with excessive paperwork, all private plans and Medicare would be required to use standardized forms for processing medical claims and reimbursing health care providers.[12]

Reforming the Private Health Insurance Market

A major goal of Clinton's national health insurance plan is to make group health insurance affordable for small business. As we saw in Chapter 3, many, if not most, small businesses do not provide their working families with group insurance for two reasons: the cost of group insurance for small business is high; and small firms usually lack the income to afford group insurance, regardless of how low the premiums might be.

The cost of group health insurance is currently based upon experience-rated premiums. Groups pay premiums based upon the cost of providing health care for their members.[13] The experience rating of group insurance premiums hurts small businesses, since the cost of health care for small groups is confined to limited numbers of individuals. As a result, they have only limited financial resources they can contribute to their group plans. Given the limited availability of resources, when catastrophic illness or injury strikes a member of a small group, that group's insurance premium must be raised substantially to finance the cost of treatment for the sick member. This has made group insurance unaffordable for small businesses.

Clinton would reform the private health insurance market in order to make coverage affordable for small businesses. He would prohibit private health insurance plans from charging their subscribers experience-rated premiums. Instead, they would be required to charge community-rated premiums. Group insurance premiums would reflect the cost of providing health care to the entire community in which the small group resides.[14]

Since private health insurance serving entire communities includes tens of thousands, hundreds of thousands, or even millions of individuals, who collectively contribute substantial amounts to their voluntary plans, they have sufficient resources to finance the cost of catastrophic illnesses and injuries for sick residents. As a result, private plans serving entire communities have no reason to raise premiums substantially whenever catastrophic illness or injury strikes one of their subscribers. Given the availability of extensive financial resources, the cost of providing health care for communities can be controlled, regardless of how many catastrophic illnesses and injuries their residents suffer. Community-rated premiums would assure that group insurance would be affordable for small businesses, allowing them to purchase coverage for their working families, as they would be required to do under Clinton's national health insurance plan.

Small businesses have difficulty affording group health insurance, since they tend to employ low-wage workers. As we saw in Chapter 3, large employers finance the cost of group insurance through reductions in wages. However, small businesses cannot do the same because the wages they pay are generally too low. As a result, small businesses lack the discretionary income to provide their working families with group insurance. To rectify this problem, Clinton would extend tax credits to small businesses, to help them purchase group insurance for their working families.[15]

Containing Health Care Costs

Clinton pledged to finance his national health insurance plan by imposing stringent health care cost-containment measures. The federal gvernment would use the savings from those measures to provide coverage to the uninsured. The Clinton administration estimates that it will cost $90 billion annually to provide coverage to the uninsured, over a tenth of the amount spent on health care in 1992.[16] As a result, Clinton will have to impose stringent health care cost-containment measures to assure that universal coverage does not add to the already soaring cost of medical services.

Clinton intends to contain health care costs through a combination of regulatory measures and reforms in the private health insurance market. He will recommend that mandatory limits on health care costs be imposed.[17] In addition, Clinton will propose that the private health insurance market be reformed by promoting managed competition within the health care system. He would establish health insurance purchasing cooperatives (HIPCs), consisting of tens of thousands, hundreds of thousands, or even millions of members. All individuals covered by government-financed private insurance would be required to join HIPCs. Employers providing group insurance to their working families would have the option of enrolling them in HIPCs. Self-insured individuals could join HIPCs voluntarily. HIPCs would negotiate insurance contracts for their members with private plans.

HIPCs would substantially strengthen the bargaining power of consumers in the private health insurance market. Given their small numbers, families and groups do not have the capacity to bargain effectively with the private insurance industry. Each family or group represents only a fraction of the insurance market and lacks the power to secure the most comprehensive coverage possible at the lowest conceivable cost. Rather, families and groups must accept whatever insurance private plans have to offer, regardless of how inadequate, inefficient, and costly such coverage might be.

However, this would not be the case with HIPCs. Because they would be composed of tens of thousands, hundreds of thousands, and even millions of members, HIPCs would exert substantial market power in negotiating with private health insurance plans. To restrain the growth in their costs and maintain their competitiveness in the private insurance market, HIPCs would have financial incentives to contract only with voluntary plans that finance and provide health care most efficiently and at the lowest possible cost.

HIPCs would use their substantial market power to provide their members the most comprehensive private insurance possible at the lowest conceivable cost. As a result, most, if not practically all, individuals would join HIPCs. Private plans that failed to secure insurance contracts from HIPCs would have few, if any, subscribers and would go out of business. To survive, private plans would have to secure insurance contracts from HIPCs by providing their members comprehensive, efficient, low-cost coverage. In addition to HIPCs, Clinton would promote the development of managed-care networks, composed of large groups of health care providers, each organized and sponsored by a private plan. Managed-care networks would compete for business with HIPCs by agreeing to provide health care most efficiently and at the lowest possible cost.[18] By containing health care costs through a combination of regulatory measures and reforms in the private insurance market, Clinton intends to establish a fiscally and economically viable basis for the establishment of a national health insurance program.

CLINTON, MANAGED COMPETITION, AND PRIVATE
HEALTH INSURANCE

By requiring that universal health insurance coverage be achieved through voluntary plans, Clinton's health care reform program was designed to preserve the private insurance industry. This stands in sharp contrast to previous health care reform plans—based on either single-payer or play-or-pay insurance—which would have scrapped and replaced either all or most private insurance with a government program. By preserving voluntary plans, Clinton hoped his health care reform program would be acceptable to the private insurance industry.

The private health insurance industry supports the concept of managed competition in which third-party payers would compete for business by providing health care most efficiently and at the lowest possible cost. Many, if not most, insurance firms own HMOs. Because they provide more efficient, lower-cost health care than traditional private insurance does, HMOs would thrive under a system of managed competition, in which the federal government provided the public incentives to enroll in voluntary plans that extended medical services on a competitive basis. As a result, insurance firms that own HMOs stand to earn substantial income under a system of managed competition.

However, the private health insurance industry opposes Clinton's recommendation that stringent limits on national and state health care spending be imposed. By reducing health care spending, those limits would impose substantial financial losses upon every segment of the medical industry, including private insurance. Rather, the private insurance industry insists that health care costs must be contained by market forces alone, absent any federal regulation.[19] The industry's rejection of any federal containment of health care costs assures that it will oppose Clinton's national health insurance program, despite the fact that the president's program poses no threat to the existence of the private insurance industry.

POLLING DATA ON CLINTON AND NATIONAL HEALTH
INSURANCE

As we have seen, Clinton's national health insurance plan is based upon three basic reforms: 1.) a requirement that employers provide group coverage to their working families; 2.) the imposition of stringent health care cost containment measures; and 3.) the establishment of HIPCs to bargain with the private insurance industry to provide the public the most comprehensive coverage available at the lowest possible cost. An overwhelming majority of the public supports each of those three reforms. The 1993 Harris Poll cited in Chapter 6 found that 63 percent of its respondents support requiring "employers to buy health insurance for full-time employees," 55 percent favor the imposition of "limits on price increase of health insurance premiums," and 54 percent back the formation of "purchasing cooperatives to bargain for lower insurance rates for businesses and employees."[20]

In addition to their support for basic reforms contained in Clinton's national health insurance plan, an overwhelming majority of the public believes that the President will achieve his goal of guaranteeing universal access to affordable health care. During January 12–14, 1993, the *New York Times* and CBS News jointly conducted a poll of 1,179 adults. The poll measured public expectations concerning Clinton's ability to accomplish seven major goals he promised to achieve either during or following the end of the 1992 presidential campaign, including making "significant progress in getting health insurance for all Americans." Sixty-six percent of those polled believed that Clinton would "make significant progress in getting health insurance for all Americans." A greater share of those questioned believed that Clinton would "make significant progress in getting health insurance for all Americans" than for any of his other six campaign or post-campaign promises surveyed in the poll.[21]

The *New York Times*/CBS News findings were confirmed by another poll jointly conducted by *USA Today*, CNN, and the Gallup Organization during February 26–28, 1993. The poll asked 1,005 adults whether or not the "Clinton administration would be successful in reforming health care." Sixty-one percent said that the administration would be successful and 33 percent said it would not be.[22]

Given the existence of widespread popular confidence in Clinton's ability to secure the establishment of a national health insurance program, an overwhleming majority of the population is optimistic about prospects for expanding public access to medical services. The January 1993 *USA Today*/CNN/Gallup Poll cited earlier asked its respondents about prospects for an improvement in the seven conditions affecting the military security of the United States and the socio-economic conditions of its citizens contained in the survey, including the availability of "affordable health care for all." Fifty-four percent of those polled believed that the availability of "affordable health care for all will improve." Twenty-eight percent thought it "will stay the same" and only 15 percent that it "will get worse." The availability of "affordable health care for all" ranked second on the list of seven conditions respondents believed would improve, behind only "the state of the economy."[23]

THE POLITICS OF NATIONAL HEALTH INSURANCE, FEBRUARY–MARCH 1993

Clinton initiated his campaign to secure the establishment of national health insurance during his first presidential address to Congress on February 17, 1993. He warned Congress that soaring health care costs posed a grave economic and fiscal threat to the United States:

In 1992, we spent 14 percent of our income on health care, more than 30 percent more than any other country in the world and yet we were the only advanced nation that did not provide a basic package of health care benefits to all of its citizens. Unless we change the present pattern, 50 percent of the growth in the deficit between now and the year 2000 will be in health care costs. By the year 2000 almost 20 percent of our income will be in health care. Our families will never be secure, our businesses will never be strong, and our Government will never again be fully solvent until we tackle the health care crisis.

Given the economic and fiscal threat to the United States posed by soaring health care costs, Clinton warned Congress that "all of our efforts to strengthen the economy will fail unless we . . . take this year, not next year, not 5 years from now but this year, bold steps to reform our health care system. . . . We must do it now." Accordingly, Clinton promised to recommend passage of a national health insurance plan in the spring "that finally will bring [health care] costs under control and [guarantee] that no one is denied the coverage they need."[24]

However, Clinton's plea for swift congressional action on national health insurance fell upon deaf ears on Capitol Hill. On March 3, Daniel Rostenkowski of Illinois, Chairman of the Ways and Means Committee, which exercises partial jurisdiction over health care reform in the House, warned that "it would be extremely difficult" to pass a national health insurance bill in 1993. Rostenkowski suggested that Congress would not be able to do so until 1995, at the very earliest. James M. Jaffe, a spokesman for Congress, explained that "Rosty thinks that health-care reform is basically a two-year job. He thinks that it would legislatively and logistically be a real long shot to do it all this year.[25]

House Majority Leader Richard Gephardt of Missouri agreed with Rostenkowski that Congress would not pass a national health insurance bill in the immediate future. In an interview on "Meet the Press" on March 28, Gephardt argued that national health insurance will "be the toughest bill since the Social Security Act." Given the political difficulties of passing health care reform legislation, Gephardt said that Congress was in no rush to enact a national health insurance bill: "We're going to take our time to do it."[26] Rostenkowski and Gephardt's argument that Congress is incapable of taking swift action on health care reform is indicative of the fact that the Democratic majority on Capitol Hill has no intention of passing a national health insurance bill in the near-term future, as we will now see.

WHY CLINTON CANNOT AND WILL NOT ESTABLISH NATIONAL HEALTH INSURANCE IN THE NEAR-TERM FUTURE

As the polling data show, Clinton's assumption of the Presidency has raised public expectations that Washington will finally take action to reform America's sick and troubled health care system, after having repeatedly failed to do so since the beginning of the 1970s. However, the public is likely to be disappointed by the results of the debate on health care reform which will follow Clinton's introduction of his national health insurance plan. They will find that Clinton's assumption of the Presidency has done little, if anything, to advance near-term prospects for health care reform. Indeed, Clinton is unlikely to secure the establishment of national health insurance in the near-term future. Moreover, it is doubtful that Clinton would even want to obtain adoption of the program, even if he could do so.

Clinton will find it difficult to overcome the insurmountable political obstacles that have prevented every effort to establish national health insurance since the 1940s. Those obstacles remain based upon the political power of the health care industry, which wields enormous influence on Capitol Hill through the massive campaign contributions medical interest groups provide members of Congress. AMPAC contributions to members of Congress played a critical role in the House's rejection of the Hospital Cost Containment Act, depriving Carter of the means to establish national health insurance on an economically and fiscally viable basis. The massive increase in contributions to members of Congress from the health care industry during 1991 to 1992 derailed Mitchell's efforts to pass a national health insurance bill in the One Hundred Second Congress.

The health care industry is certain to oppose Clinton's national health insurance plan because it would result in the imposition of stringent cost-containment measures and inflict substantial financial losses upon every segment of the medical system. As a result, the industry will use its financial power on Capitol Hill to prevent passage of Clinton's national health insurance plan.

Indeed, the health care industry's most politically and financially powerful member, the AMA, did not wait for Clinton to introduce his national health insurance program before condemning the President's intention to recommend cost-containment measures as an essential part of his medical reform plan. On March 29, 1993 Raymond Scalettar, Chairman of the AMA's Board of Trustees, appeared before the President's Task Force on National Health Reform, which held hearings during the day on health care reform. Scalettar warned that the AMA would oppose the imposition of any health cost-containment measures. He charged that such measures would result in rationing, as doctors would be forced to withhold their services to some patients in order to assure that health care costs did not exceed the limits the federal government imposed. He made it clear that the medical profession was not prepared to cooperate with the federal government in this manner to reduce health care costs:

True effective cost control has never been achieved in this or any other economy through arbitrary caps on spending or price controls. They did not work in the 1970's, only delaying natural price increases and impeding supply of necessary goods and services. They also will not work in health care.

Price controls, or global budgets, mean arbitrary decisions that will, without basis, limit our ability to deliver needed medical care to our patients.

Scalettar concluded that health care cost-containment measures were unacceptable because they would limit "patients' access to medical care."[27]

As we have seen, since 1968, AMPAC has, for the most part, represented among the top two contributors to congressional campaigns among all PACs. As a result, the AMA has the financial power, in conjunction with the handful of other health care interest groups listed in Table 7.2, to singlehandedly kill the health care cost-containment provisions of Clinton's national health insurance plan. In the absence of health care cost containment, Clinton will be deprived of the means to establish national health insurance on an economically and fiscally viable basis, derailing his efforts to institute the program.

Congressional Republicans remain adamantly opposed to national health insurance. They will vehemently oppose Clinton's national health insurance plan once it is introduced in Congress. As a result, the Clinton plan cannot pass without the solid support of the Democratic majority in Congress. However, it is difficult to conceive of Clinton securing anything more than token congressional Democratic support for his national health insurance plan. The financial relationship between the health care industry and congressional Democrats is even stronger than with Republican lawmakers. Of the $14.4 million health care industry PACs gave to congressional candidates during 1991 to 1992, 61 percent went to Democrats and only 39 percent to Republicans.[28]

Why does the health care industry favor Democratic congressional candidates? The reason is certainly not politics. The health care industry is far more comfortable with the conservative philosophy of Republican members of Congress than it is with the more nonideological and pragmatic views of Democratic lawmakers.

The health care industry's tendency to favor Democratic congressional candidates is totally pragmatic. Interest groups which maintain PACs, like the health care industry, are concerned with gaining influence over Congress, not in promoting any particular political agenda. Since practically all incumbent members of Congress are reelected, interest groups must establish a close relationship with incumbent lawmakers in order to gain influence on Capitol Hill. To create such a relationship, interest groups must provide financial support for incumbent members of Congress, even if they might disagree with the political philosophy of those lawmakers. As a result, practically all PAC campaign contributions go to incumbent members of Congress.[29] Since Democrats usually maintain overwhelming majorities in both houses of Congress, most PAC campaign contributions go to Democrats.

Health care industry PACs are no different than other PACs. Practically all campaign contributions from the industry go to incumbent members of Congress, most of whom are Democrats. By providing substantial financial support to the Democratic majority in Congress, the industry has succeeded in wielding enormous political influence on Capitol Hill. The industry has used its influence to prevent the establishment of national health insurance because the program cannot be instituted on a fiscally and economically viable basis without the imposition of stringent cost-containment measures, which would inflict financial losses upon every segment of the health care system.

The Democratic majority in Congress is unlikely to pass a national health insurance bill in the near-term future, since such action would be opposed by the health care industry. The industry would retaliate against Democratic supporters of national health insurance by using its substantial financial power to attempt to defeat them when they run for reelection. To avoid a confrontation with the health care industry that could spell the end of their political careers, congressional Democrats will ignore Clinton's pleas for swift passage of his national health insurance plan. As a result, Clinton's campaign to secure the establishment of national health insurance is almost certain to end in failure as all previous such efforts have.

The single most important action which could be taken to advance prospects for the establishment of national health insurance would be the abolition of all PACs. During 1991 to 1992, PACs provided $181.1 million in campaign contributions to congressional candidates, practically all of whom were incumbent lawmakers.[30] Those massive contributions have allowed interest groups, like the health care industry, to wield enormous influence on Capitol Hill. The abolition of PACs would deprive interest groups of the ability to provide financial support for members of Congress, greatly diminishing the influence of pressure groups on Capitol Hill.

However, because practically all PACs contributions go to incumbent members of Congress, they usually raise far more money than their challengers. This allows incumbents to greatly outspend their challengers in congressional campaigns.[31] The financial advantage they receive from PACs is a major reason why practically all incumbents are reelected.

As a result, members of Congress cannot abolish PACs without jeopardizing their prospects for reelection. In the absence of PACs, the financial advantage incumbent members of Congress maintain against their challengers would be greatly diminished. Without this advantage, many more incumbents would be defeated for reelection than has been the case. To maintain their financial advantage against challengers which is crucial to their prospects for reelection, members of Congress are unlikely to abolish PACs through the foreseeable future.

Given the unwillingness of Congress to abolish PACs, interest groups, like the health care industry, will be able to retain the enormous political influence they wield on Capitol Hill through the massive campaign contributions they make to incumbent lawmakers. The health care industry will continue to use those contributions to prevent the establishment of national health insurance. As a result, it would seem that prospects for the adoption of the program in the foreseeable future remain bleak.

Nevertheless, Clinton could still take action that might improve prospects for the establishment of national health insurance, if not immediately, at least in near-term future. He could ask congressional Democrats to terminate their financial relationship with the health care industry. He could work to replace those

Democratic members of Congress who continue to maintain such a relationship with other Democrats committed to health care reform. If Clinton can substantially reduce the financial influence the health care industry maintains over the Democratic majority in Congress, he will succeed in securing the establishment of national health insurance. Without its financial relationship with the health care industry, the Democratic majority in Congress will have no reason not to pass a national health insurance program, since it has the support of the overwhelming majority of the public, especially the middle class and poor, who represent important Democratic constituencies.

However, congressional Democrats would jeopardize their prospects of re-election if they renounced their financial relationship with the health care industry and passed a national health insurance bill. The industry would retaliate against congressional Democratic supporters of national health insurance when they ran for reelection by sending its substantial campaign contributions to their Republican challengers. This could result in the defeat of many Democrats members of Congress.

However, voters are likely to respond favorably to Democratic passage of national health insurance legislation, given its popularity. Congressional Democrats could point to the establishment of national health insurance as a major and historic legislative achievement. They could be expected to secure many votes from the public for having taken bold and courageous action to reform America's ailing and failing health care system.

As a result, while congressional Democrats would lose substantial campaign contributions from the health care industry for passing a national health insurance bill, they could gain many votes from the overwhelming majority of the public, who are demanding legislative action to reform America's sick and troubled health care system. The losses congressional Democrats would sustain by antagonizing the health care industry could be more than offset by the gains they would make by having addressed the health care crisis, which represents one of the most important issues of public concern. On balance, congressional Democrats could gain politically by passing a national health insurance bill.

However, congressional Democrats would be taking a political risk in severing their financial relationships with the health care industry and passing a national health insurance bill. The industry has served as a secure and reliable source of financial support for congressional Democrats. It is not at all certain that the increased political support that congressional Democrats will gain from voters for passing a national health insurance bill will be sufficient to offset the political losses they will sustain from antagonizing the health care industry. As a result, many, if not most, congressional Democrats, will refuse to break their financial ties to the industry and pass a national health insurance bill.

To secure passage of his national health insurance plan, Clinton will have to greatly diminish the financial influence the health care industry maintains over the Democratic majority in Congress. To do so, Clinton will have to work to replace the many congressional Democrats who will insist on maintaining their financial relationship with the health care industry with other Democrats committed to medical reform. However, such action would place Clinton in open confrontation with the Democratic majority in Congress. Congressional Democrats, especially the party leadership, would resent any effort by Clinton to disrupt the financial ties existing between Democratic lawmakers and the health care industry. Clinton seems intent on avoiding such a confrontation. He seems eager to establish a close working relationship with the Democratic majority in Congress and is unlikely to take any action which opens a rift between the White House and Capitol Hill.

Given his unwillingness to engage in open confrontation with the Democratic majority in Congress, Clinton seems powerless to break the financial ties between Democratic lawmakers and the health care industry. And as long as this relationship persists, the establishment of national health insurance will remain a political impossibility. In the end, Clinton gives us no reason to believe that he is up to the politically arduous and daunting task of reforming America's critically ill health care system.

THE COMING COLLAPSE OF THE HEALTH CARE SYSTEM

Clinton's failure to secure the establishment of national health insurance will not end prospects for its adoption. Rather, the program is certain to be instituted in the not too distant future due to the threat to the health care system posed by soaring medical costs. During the 1990s, health care costs will soar completely out of control. Health care costs as a share of the GDP will rise from 14 percent in 1991 to 18 percent in 2000.[32] Per capita health care costs will more than double from $3,160 to over $6,500 during the same period.[33] Annual health care costs will also more than double from $838.5 billion in 1992 to $1,616 trillion in 2000.[34] During the 1990s, soaring health care costs will result from the same factors which have driven up medical expenses since the establishment of Medicare and Medicaid in 1965: the existence of an insurance system which has insulated the public from most of the cost of health care, resulting in an increase in patient utilization of medical services; the uncontrollable proliferation of medical technology, which is driving up hospital costs; and a rapidly aging population, which will utilize substantial amounts of health care.

Eli Ginzberg argues that the public will no longer be able to bear the increasingly onerous financial burden of soaring health care costs during 1995–2000, when he estimates that medical expenses will double from $1 trillion to $2 trillion. As Ginzberg put it,

We need to find a second trillion dollars between 1995 and the year 2000 to keep the [health care] system on its present trajectory. That translates into an outlay of $30,000 for health care in 2000 for a family of four—more than the family would have spent on food, clothing, housing and transportation combined in 1990. The second trillion will not be findable.[35]

As Ginzberg notes, soaring health care costs will make medical services virtually unaffordable during the 1990s. To avoid going bankrupt from sky-rocketing health care costs, government and business will have to terminate the group insurance they provide their working families, who represented 57.1 percent of the population in 1991. Unable to qualify for either Medicare or Medicaid, and lacking the financial means to purchase their own private insurance, working families losing their group insurance will have no alternative but to become uninsured.

With the collapse of group health insurance, the number of uninsured individuals will rise by the tens of millions. Doctors and hospitals will sustain tens of billions of dollars in financial losses from having to provide uncompensated care to the tens of millions of newly-uninsured individuals. Unable to shoulder this financial burden, many, if not most, doctors and hospitals will be forced to close, leaving hundreds, if not thousands, of communities without any access to health care.

In the absence of corrective action, soaring health care costs could result in a total collapse of the medical system. To avert this collapse, which would plunge many, if not most, of its members into financial bankruptcy, the health care industry will be forced to reverse its longstanding opposition to medical reform and join the public in urging Congress to establish a national health insurance program, which would guarantee universal access to affordable medical services. The industry's support for health care reform will remove the last remaining political roadblock to national health insurance, clearing the way for its adoption sometime during 1995 to 2000. It would seem that the United States will eventually have a national health insurance program—but not before the health care system edges toward the brink of total collapse which will occur by the turn of the twenty-first century. As C. Everett Koop, the Surgeon General during the Reagan and Bush Administrations, assessed the prospects for health care reform, "We are in crisis and not much will happen until we enter chaos."[36]

Notes

PREFACE

1. Richard Nixon, *Public Papers of the Presidents of the United States 1974* (Washington, D.C.: U.S. Government Printing Office, 1975), pp. 139–140.

2. Gerald R. Ford, *Public Papers of the Presidents of the United States 1974* (Washington, D.C.: U.S. Government Printing Office, 1975), p. 10.

3. Harry S. Truman, *Years of Trial and Hope* (Garden City, N.Y.: Doubleday, 1956), p. 23.

4. Jimmy Carter, *Keeping Faith: Memoirs of a President* (New York: Bantam Books, 1982), p. 87.

5. For a historical account of the AMA's campaign against national health insurance, see Paul Starr, *The Social Transformation of American Medicine* (New York: Basic Books, 1982), bk. 2., ch. 1.

6. For an analysis of the political power PACs wield on Capitol Hill, see Philip M. Stern, *The Best Congress Money Can Buy* (New York: Pantheon Books, 1988).

CHAPTER 1

1. Theodore R. Marmor, "National Health Insurance in the 1980s," in David J. Schnall and Carl L. Figliola, eds., *Contemporary Issues in Health Care* (New York: Praeger, 1984), p. 17.

2. Monte M. Poen, *Harry S. Truman Versus the Medical Lobby: The Genesis of Medicare* (Columbia: University of Missouri Press, 1979), p. 163.

3. The FSA was established by Congress in 1939 to administer federal health, education, and welfare programs. In 1953 Congress elevated the FSA to a cabinet-level agency, which became the Department of Health, Education and Welfare.

4. Poen, *Harry S. Truman Versus the Medical Lobby*, pp. 152, 179–180.

5. Odin W. Anderson, *Health Services in the United States: A Growth Enterprise Since 1875* (Ann Arbor, Mich.: Health Administration Press, 1985), p. 142; J. Rogers

Hollingsworth, *A Political Economy of Medicine: Great Britain and the United States* (Baltimore: Johns Hopkins University Press, 1986), p. 115; Herman Miles Somers and Ann Ramsy Somers, *Doctors, Patients, and Health Insurance: The Organization and Financing of Medical Care* (Washington, D.C.: The Brookings Institution, 1961), p. 548.

6. Rashi Fein, *Medical Care, Medical Costs: The Search for a Health Insurance Policy* (Cambridge, Mass.: Harvard University Press, 1989), p. 49.

7. For a full presentation of this argument, see W. Lance Bennett, *The Governing Crisis: Media, Money, and Marketing in American Elections* (New York: St. Martin's Press, 1992).

CHAPTER 2

1. Milton Friedman, *Capitalism and Freedom* (Chicago: University of Chicago Press, 1962), p. 150.

2. For an analysis of the campaign to establish national health insurance at the turn of the century, see Ronald L. Numbers, *Almost Persuaded: American Physicians and Compulsory Health Insurance, 1912–1920* (Baltimore: Johns Hopkins University Press, 1978), p. 25.

3. For an examination of the efforts to adopt national health insurance during the 1930s, see Daniel S. Hirshfield, *The Lost Reform: The Campaign for Compulsory Health Insurance in the United States from 1932 to 1943* (Cambridge, Mass.: Harvard University Press, 1970).

4. For an assessment of Truman's campaign to institute national health insurance, see Monte M. Poen, *Harry S. Truman Versus the Medical Lobby: The Genesis of Medicare* (Columbia: University of Missouri Press, 1979).

5. For an evaluation of the National Education Campaign, see Stanley Kelley, Jr., *Professional Public Relations and Public Policy* (Baltimore: Johns Hopkins University Press, 1956), ch. 3.

6. The effort to achieve health care reform continued during the 1950s and 1960s, even though national health insurance was off the political agenda during this period. However, health care reformers decided to pursue more modest objectives. Rather than campaigning to establish a universal insurance program, as they did during the 1940s, they sponsored a more limited program, known as Medicare, to provide coverage only to the elderly, the group most vulnerable to illness. The first Medicare bill was introduced by Representative Aime Forand of Rhode Island in 1957. Medicare became a top domestic policy priority of Presidents John F. Kennedy and Lyndon B. Johnson. Johnson won a landslide victory in the 1964 presidential election, campaigning on a pledge to secure the establishment of Medicare. With the Democratic Party controlling overwhelming majorities in both houses of Congress, in 1965 lawmakers finally passed a Medicare bill. For a history of the legislative development of Medicare, see Sheri I. David, *With Dignity: The Search for Medicare and Medicaid* (Westport, Conn.: Greenwood Press, 1985).

7. Grace Budrys, *Planning for the Nation's Health: A Study of Twentieth-Century Developments in the United States* (Westport, Conn.: Greenwood Press, 1986), p. 39.

8. Joel Havemann, "Diagnosis: Healthier in Europe," *Los Angeles Times*, December 30, 1992, p. A9; John K. Iglehart, "Canada's Health Care System Faces Its Problems," *The New England Journal of Medicine*, February 22, 1990, p. 565.

9. Elton Rayack, *Professional Power and American Medicine: The Economics of the American Medical Association* (Cleveland: World Publishing, 1967), p. 2.

10. *Congressional Quarterly Almanac 1949*, p. 293. The surgeon general would have administered the national health insurance program provided for by the November 1945 version of the Wagner-Murray-Dingell bill. The 1947 version of the bill would have established a five-member federal agency, similar to the National Health Insurance Board, to administer the program. See *Congressional Quarterly Almanac 1946*, p. 659; *Congressional Quarterly Almanac, 1947*, p. 585.

11. Richard Harris, *A Sacred Trust* (New York: New American Library, 1966), p. 43.

12. Poen, *Harry S. Truman Versus the Medical Lobby*, p. 148.

13. Numbers, *Almost Persuaded*, pp. 62–63.

14. Gary Land, "American Images of British Compulsory Insurance," in Ronald L. Numbers, ed., *Compulsory Health Insurance: The Continuing American Debate* (Westport, Conn.: Greenwood Press, 1982), p. 63.

15. Rashi Fein, *Medical Care, Medical Costs: The Search for a Health Insurance Policy* (Cambridge, Mass.: Harvard University Press, 1989), p. 48.

16. Land, "American Images of British Compulsory Health Insurance," p. 67.

17. Ibid., p. 68.

18. Ibid., p. 67.

19. Ibid., p. 70.

20. Fein, *Medical Care, Medical Costs*, p. 45.

21. Kelley, *Professional Public Relations and Political Power*, p. 77; Poen, *Harry S. Truman Versus the Medical Lobby*, p. 145.

22. Poen, *Harry S. Truman Versus the Medical Lobby*, p. 145.

23. Fein, *Medical Care, Medical Costs*, p. 45.

24. Kelley, *Professional Public Relations and Political Power*, p. 86; Poen, *Harry S. Truman Versus the Medical Lobby*, pp. 181–182.

25. Paul Starr, *The Social Transformation of American Medicine* (New York: Basic Books, 1982), pp. 282, 285.

26. Claude Castonguay, "The Quebec Experience: Effects on Accessibility," in Spyros Andreopoulous, ed., *National Health Insurance: Can We Learn from Canada?* (New York: John Wiley, 1975), p. 103.

27. Ibid., pp. 115–117.

28. Theodore R. Marmor, "Canada's Path, America's Choices: Lessons from the Canadian Experience with National Health Insurance," in Ronald L. Numbers, *Compulsory Health Insurance* (Westport, Conn.: Greenwood Press, 1982), p. 93.

29. James G. Burrow, *AMA: Voice of American Medicine* (Baltimore: Johns Hopkins University Press, 1963), p. v; Rayack, *Professional Power and American Medicine*, pp. 12–19.

30. Rayack, *Professional Power and American Medicine*, p. 71; U.S. Congress, Senate, Hearings on S. 1106, S. 1456, S. 1581, and S. 1679, pp. 201–202.

31. Polling data show that the overwhelming majority of doctors supported the AMA's opposition to national health insurance during the 1940s. In 1945 the Opinion Research Corporation asked a representative sample of doctors to state their position on the Wagner-Murray-Dingell bill. Seventy-five percent of the doctors opposed the bill, 13 percent supported it, 10 percent were neutral, and 2 percent had no opinion. See U.S. Congress, Senate, Committee on Education and Labor, *Hearings Before the Committee on Education*

and Labor on S. 1606, Seventy-ninth Congress, Second Session, April 2–July 10, 1946 (Washington, D.C.: U.S. Government Printing Office, 1946), p. 559.

32. Budrys, *Planning for the Nation's Health*, p. 40. A subsequent poll conducted by the National Opinion Research Center in 1963 found that the medical profession continued to rank second in occupational prestige, behind only the justices of the Supreme Court.

33. Ibid., p. 41. Subsequent Gallup polls conducted in 1962 and 1973 found that the medical profession continued to rank first among the careers the public would recommend to young men. In 1962, 23 percent of the respondents said that they would recommend that young men pursue a career in the medical profession. In 1973, 28 percent of the respondents said the same.

34. Kelley, *Professional Public Relations and Political Power*, p. 86.

35. Harris, *A Sacred Trust*, p. 46; Kelley, *Professional Public Relations and Political Power*, pp. 79–81.

36. Poen, *Harry S. Truman Versus the Medical Lobby*, pp. 148–149. Senator James Murray of Montana, a cosponsor of the Wagner-Murray-Dingell bill, released a letter from the Library of Congress's Legislative Research Service that concluded it was unable to locate any such statement by Lenin in any of his speeches or writings.

37. Starr, *The Social Transformation of American Medicine*, pp. 288–289.

38. *Congressional Quarterly Almanac 1949*, p. 293.

39. *Congressional Quarterly Almanac 1946*, p. 662.

40. Ibid.

41. Harris, *A Sacred Trust*, pp. 206–7.

42. David, *With Dignity*, p. 150.

43. Ibid.; Rayack, *Professional Power and American Medicine*, p. 2.

44. Harris, *A Sacred Trust*, pp. 207–208.

45. David, *With Dignity*, p. 150.

CHAPTER 3

1. Paul Starr, *The Social Transformation of American Medicine* (New York: Basic Books, 1982), p. 290.

2. *Congressional Quarterly Almanac 1949*, pp. 292–293.

3. Robert Pear, "Bush Health Plan Would Be Financed by Medicare Curb," *New York Times*, February 3, 1992, p. C10.

4. Harry S. Truman, *Public Papers of the Presidents of the United States* (Washington, D.C.: U.S. Government Printing Office, 1961), pp. 475–491.

5. *Congressional Quarterly Almanac 1946*, pp. 658–660.

6. Richard M. Coughlin, *Ideology, Public Opinion & Welfare Policy: Attitudes Toward Taxes and Spending in Industrialized Societies* (Berkeley: University of California, 1980), p. 79.

7. The House of Delegates is the AMA's supreme policymaking organization. Its members are appointed by the state medical societies. Each state medical society is entitled to appoint one member of the House of Delegates for every 1,000 AMA members residing in that state. AMA membership consists of those who belong to state and county medical societies. The House of Delegates meets for a few days biannually. For a description of the AMA's organizational structure, see Elton Rayack, *Professional Power and American Medicine: The Economics of the American Medical Association* (Cleveland: World Publishing, 1967), pp. 2–3.

8. Ibid., p. 179. The AMA's fifteen-member board of trustees serves as its supreme policymaking organization when the House of Delegates is not in session. The Council on Medical Service was established by the House of Delegates in 1943 to promote the development of Blue Shield.

9. U.S. Congress, Senate, Committee on Education and Labor, *National Health Program: Hearings Before the Committee on Education and Labor on S. 1606*, Seventy-ninth Congress, Second Session, April 27–July 10, 1946 (Washington, D.C.: U.S. Government Printing Office, 1946), p. 552.

10. James G. Burrow, *AMA: Voice of American Medicine* (Baltimore: Johns Hopkins University Press, 1963), p. 330.

11. Ibid., pp. 411–412.

12. For an analysis of the development of Blue Cross, see Sylvia A. Law, *Blue Cross: What Went Wrong?* (New Haven: Yale University Press, 1974).

13. Odin W. Anderson, *Health Services in the United States: A Growth Enterprise Since 1875* (Ann Arbor, Mich.: Health Administration Press, 1985), p. 134; Rayack, *Professional Power and American Medicine*, p. 47.

14. Herman Miles Somers and Ann Ramsay Somers, *Doctors, Patients, and Health Insurance: The Organization and Financing of Medical Care* (Washington, D.C.: The Brookings Institution, 1961), p. 548.

15. Richard Harris, *A Sacred Trust* (New York: New American Library, 1966), p. 42.

16. U.S. Congress, Senate, Committee on Labor and Public Welfare, *National Health Program, 1949: Hearings Before a Subcommittee of the Committee on Labor and Public Welfare on S. 1106, S. 1456, S. 1581, and S. 1679*, Eighty-first Congress, First session, May 23–June 29, 1949 (Washington, D.C.: U.S. Government Printing Office, 1949), p. 817.

17. Stanley Kelley, Jr., *Professional Public Relations and Political Power* (Baltimore: Johns Hopkins University Press, 1956), p. 77.

18. Anderson, *Health Services in the United States*, p. 134; J. Rogers Hollingsworth, *A Political Economy of Medicine: Great Britain and the United States* (Baltimore: Johns Hopkins University Press, 1986), p. 115; Somers and Somers, *Doctors, Hospitals, and Patients*, p. 548.

19. Somers and Somers, *Doctors, Patients, and Health Insurance*, p. 548.

20. Pear, "Bush Health Plan Would Be Financed By Medicare Curb," p. C10.

21. Joseph A. Califano, Jr., *America's Health Care Revolution: Who Lives? Who Dies? Who Pays?* (New York: Random House, 1986), p. 44.

22. Robert J. Vogel, "The Tax Treatment of Health Insurance Premiums as a Cause of Overinsurance," in Mark V. Pauly, ed., *National Health Insurance: What Now, What Later, What Never?* (Washington, D.C.: American Enterprise Institute, 1980), pp. 223–224.

23. Somers and Somers, *Doctors, Patients, and Health Insurance*, p. 548.

24. Rita Keintz, *National Health Insurance and Income Distribution* (Lexington, Mass.: Lexington Books, 1976), p. 60.

25. Kevin Phillips, *Boiling Point: Republicans, Democrats, and the Decline of Middle-Class Prosperity* (New York: Random House, 1993), p. 150.

26. Louis Uchitelle, "Insurance Linked to Jobs: System Showing Its Age," The *New York Times*, May 1, 1991, p. A14.

27. Julie Kosterlitz, "A Sick System," *National Journal*, February 15, 1992, pp. 380, 382.

28. Katherine Swartz, "Why Requiring Employers to Provide Health Insurance Is a Bad Idea," *Journal of Health Politics, Policy and Law*, Winter 1990, p. 783.

29. Ibid., p. 781.

30. Robert H. Blank, *Rationing Medicine* (New York: Columbia University Press, 1988), p. 30.

31. Carl J. Schramm, "Job-Based Care Works," *USA Today*, June 19, 1992, p. 10A.

32. Karen Davis, *National Health Insurance: Benefits, Costs, and Consequences* (Washington, D.C.: The Brookings Institution, 1975), p. 32; Kosterlitz, "A Sick System," p. 383.

33. Keintz, *National Health Insurance and Income Distribution*, p. 60; C. Everett Koop, *Koop: The Memoirs of America's Family Doctor* (New York: Harper Paperbacks, 1992), p. 381.

34. Henry J. Aaron, "Health Care Financing," in Henry J. Aaron and Charles L. Schultze, eds., *Setting Domestic Priorities: What Can Government Do?* (Washington, D.C.: The Brookings Institution, 1992), p. 36; Isaac Ehrlich, "On the Rationale of National Health Insurance: Where Did the Private Market Fail?," in Isaac Ehrlich, ed., *National Health Policy: What Role for Government?* (Stanford, Ca.: Hoover Institution Press, 1982), p. 238.

CHAPTER 4

1. Jimmy Carter, *Public Papers of the Presidents of the United States 1979* (Washington, D.C.: U.S. Government Printing Office, 1980), p. 384.

2. Rashi Fein, *Medical Care, Medical Costs: The Search for a Health Insurance Policy* (Cambridge, Mass.: Harvard University Press, 1989), pp. 145–146, 148–149; Paul Starr, *The Social Transformation of American Medicine* (New York: Basic Books, 1982), pp. 394, 413–414.

3. Fein, *Medical Care, Medical Costs*, pp. 145–146.

4. Odin W. Anderson, *Health Services in the United States: A Growth Experience Since 1875* (Ann Arbor, Mich.: Health Administration Press, 1985), p. 227.

5. Paul Starr, "Health Care for the Poor: The Past Twenty Years," in Sheldon Danziger and David H. Weinberg, eds., *Fighting Poverty: What Works and What Doesn't* (Cambridge, Mass.: Harvard University Press, 1986), p. 115.

6. Richard M. Coughlin, *Ideology, Public Opinion & Welfare Policy: Attitudes Toward Taxes and Spending in Industrialized Countries* (Berkeley: University of California, 1980), p. 82.

7. Robert Pear, "Health-Care Costs Up Sharply, Posing New Threat," The *New York Times*, January 5, 1993, p. A1; Diana Chapman Walsh and Richard Egdahl, *Payer, Provider, Consumer: Industry Confronts Health Care Costs* (New York: Springer-Verlag, 1977), p. 4.

8. Judi Hasson, "All Players Have Ideas to Overhaul Health Care," *USA Today*, January 27, 1993, p. 8A; Walsh and Egdahl, *Payer, Provider, Consumer*, p. 4.

9. Julie Kosterlitz, "A Sick System," *National Journal*, February 15, 1992, p. 383.

10. Robert H. Blank, *Rationing Medicine* (New York: Columbia University Press, 1988), pp. 5–8.

11. Henry J. Aaron, *Serious and Unstable Condition: Financing America's Health Care* (Washington, D.C.: The Brookings Institution, 1991), pp. 48–49.

12. Henry J. Aaron and William B. Schwartz, *The Painful Prescription: Rationing Hospital Care* (Washington, D.C.: The Brookings Institution, 1984), pp. 85–87.

13. Aaron, *Serious and Unstable Condition*, p. 49.

14. Blank, *Rationing Medicine*, pp. 11–13.

15. Aaron, *Serious and Unstable Condition*, pp. 42–43.

16. Karen Davis and Dianne Rowland, *Medicare Policy: New Directions in Health and Long-term Care* (Baltimore: Johns Hopkins University Press, 1986), pp. 7, 32.

17. Ibid., p. 7.

18. Blank, *Rationing Medicine*, pp. 11–13.

19. Elizabeth Bowman, "Health Insurance: Carter For, Ford Against," *Congressional Quarterly Weekly Report*, October 9, 1976, p. 2918.

20. Paul Light, *The President's Agenda: Domestic Policy Choice from Kennedy to Carter* (Baltimore: Johns Hopkins University Press, 1982), p. 74.

21. Ibid., pp. 136–137.

22. *Congressional Quarterly Almanac 1977*, pp. 501–502.

23. U.S. Congress, Senate, Committee on Human Resources, *Hospital Cost, Containment Act of 1977: Hearings Before the Subcommittee on Health and Scientific Research of the Committee on Human Resources on S. 1391*, Ninety-fifth Congress, First Session, May 24–July 7, 1977 (Washington, D.C.: U.S. Government Printing Office, 1977), p. 141.

24. *Congressional Quarterly Almanac 1977*, p. 502.

25. Carter, *Public Papers 1979*, pp. 387–388.

26. Elizabeth Wehr, "Congressional Reaction Mixed on New Hospital Cost Control Proposal," *Congressional Quarterly Weekly*, March 17, 1979, p. 476.

27. Carter, *Public Papers 1979*, p. 388. States imposing hospital cost-containment measures up to 1977 (with the year in parentheses) include New York (1969), New Jersey (1971), Rhode Island (1971), Maryland (1973), Washington (1973), Connecticut (1974), Wisconsin (1975), Massachusetts (1976), and Colorado (1977).

28. Aaron, *Serious and Unstable Condition*, p. 57; Gary S. Whitted and Paul Torrens, *Managing Corporate Health Care Expenses: A Primer for Executives* (New York: Praeger, 1985), p. 60.

29. *Congressional Quarterly Almanac 1977*, p. 500.

30. Aaron, *Serious and Unstable Condition*, p. 58.

31. Louise B. Russell, *Technology in Hospitals: Medical Advances and Their Diffusion* (Washington, D.C.: The Brookings Institution, 1979), pp. 3–4.

32. Kosterlitz, "A Sick System," p. 382.

33. Davis and Rowland, *Medicare Policy*, p. 32.

34. *Congressional Quarterly Almanac 1977*, pp. 506–507.

35. Interest groups within the hospital industry that participated in the lobbying campaign included the AHA, FAHS, American Catholic Hospital Association, American Protestant Hospital Association, Council of Teaching Hospitals, National Council of Community Hospitals, and National Council of Private Psychiatric Hospitals.

36. Anderson, *Health Services in the United States*, p. 222.

37. Ibid., pp. 222–224.

38. U.S. Congress, House of Representatives, Committee on Ways and Means, *National Health Insurance: Hearings Before the Subcommittee on Health of the Committee on Ways and Means, February 11–21, 1980* (Washington, D.C.: U.S. Government Printing Office, 1980), p. 336.

39. Anderson, *Health Services in the United States*, pp. 224–225.

40. House of Representatives, *National Health Insurance*, pp. 337–338.

41. Elizabeth Wehr, "Hospital Cost Control Compromise Squeaks Through Subcommittee," *Congressional Quarterly Weekly Report*, March 4,1978, pp. 595–598.

42. Sheri I. David, *With Dignity: The Search for Medicare and Medicaid* (Westport, Conn.: Greenwood Press, 1985), p. 57.

43. Carol S. Greenwald, *Group Power: Lobbying and Public Policy* (New York: Praeger, 1977), p. 156; Ronald J. Hrebenar and Ruth K. Scott, *Interest Group Politics in America* (Englewood Cliffs, N.J.: Prentice-Hall, 1982), pp. 76, 135–136; Judith Robinson, "American Medical Political Action Committee," in Judith G. Smith, ed., *Power Brokers: People, Organization, Money and Power* (New York: Liverright, 1972), p. 80; Philip Stern, *The Best Congress Money Can Buy* (New York: Pantheon Books, 1988), pp. 196, 277.

44. Amitai Etzioni, *Capital Corruption: The New Attack on American Democracy* (New York: Harcourt Brace Jovanovich, 1984), p. 44.

45. *Congressional Quarterly Almanac 1978*, pp. 621–622.

46. Joseph A. Califano, Jr., *Governing America: An Insider's Report from the White House and the Cabinet* (New York: Simon and Schuster, 1981), p. 144.

47. Stern, *The Best Congress Money Can Buy*, pp. 102–103.

48. Etzioni, *Capital Corruption*, p. 45.

49. *Congressional Quarterly Almanac 1978*, p. 623.

50. Elizabeth Wehr, "Administration Launches Last-Ditch Fight to Get Hospital Cost Control," *Congressional Quarterly Weekly Report*, September 16, 1978, pp. 2480–2481.

51. *Congressional Quarterly Almanac 1978*, pp. 623–624.

52. "Hospital Cost Control Legislation Dies," *Congressional Quarterly Weekly Report*, October 21, 1978, pp. 3074–3075.

53. Carter, *Public Papers 1979*, pp. 386–389.

54. U.S. Congress, Senate, Committee on Labor and Human Resources, *Hospital Cost Containment Act of 1979: Hearings Before the Subcommittee on Health and Scientific Research of the Committee on Labor and Human Resources on S. 570*, Ninety-sixth Congress, First Session, March 9–15, 1979 (Washington, D.C.: U.S. Government Printing Office, 1979), pp. 83–85.

55. *Congressional Quarterly Almanac 1979*, p. 513.

56. Senate, *Hospital Cost Containment Act of 1979*, pp. 87–88.

57. *Congressional Quarterly Almanac 1979*, p. 515.

58. Senate, *Hospital Cost Containment Act of 1979*, p. 64.

59. Theodore R. Marmor, "Coping with a Creeping Crisis: Medicare at Twenty," in Theodore R. Marmor and Jerry L. Mashaw, eds., *Social Security: Beyond the Rhetoric of Crisis* (Princeton: Princeton University Press, 1988), p. 190; Whitted and Torrens, *Managing Corporate Health Care*, p. 60.

60. *Congressional Quarterly Almanac 1979*, pp. 513–515.

61. Elizabeth Wehr and Peg O'Hara, "Floor Votes Ahead on Hospital Cost Control," *Congressional Quarterly Weekly Report*, September 8, 1979, pp. 1917–1918.

62. *Congressional Quarterly Almanac 1979*, p. 515.

63. Wehr and O'Hara, "Floor Votes Ahead on Hospital Cost Control," p. 1918.

64. *Congressional Quarterly Almanac 1979*, p. 516.

65. Carter, *Public Papers 1979*, pp. 2111–2112.

66. *Congressional Quarterly Almanac 1979*, p. 517.

67. Carter, *Public Papers 1979*, p. 2129.

68. Joseph A. Califano, Jr., *America's Health Care Revolution: Who Lives? Who Dies? Who Pays?* (New York: Random House, 1986), p. 21.

69. Senate, *Hospital Cost Containment Act of 1977*, p. 270.

70. *Congressional Record*, Ninety-sixth Congress, First Session (1979), p. 32673.

71. Califano, *Governing America*, p. 144.

72. Lindorff, *Marketplace Medicine: The Rise of the For-Profit Hospital Chains* (New York: Bantam Books, 1992), p. 23.

73. Charles O. Jones, *The Trusteeship Presidency: Jimmy Carter and the United States Congress* (Baton Rouge: Louisiana State University Press, 1988), p. 165.

74. John W. Kingdon, *Agendas, Alternatives, and Public Policies* (Boston: Little, Brown, 1984), pp. 54–55.

75. Ibid., p. 158.

76. Senate, *Hospital Cost Containment Act of 1979*, pp. 140–143, 176–178, 521–525.

77. Ibid., p. 150.

78. Jonas Morris, *Searching for a Cure: National Health Policy Reconsidered* (New York: Pica Press, 1984), p. 110.

79. *Congressional Record*, Ninety-sixth Congress, First Session (1979), pp. 32719–32720.

80. Franklin Tugwell, *The Energy Crisis and the American Political Economy: Politics and Markets in the Management of Natural Resources* (Stanford, Calif.: Stanford University Press, 1988), pp. 117, 121, 129–131; Murray Weidenbaum, *Rendezvous with Reality: The American Economy After Reagan* (New York: Basic Books, 1988), pp. 235–238.

81. *Congressional Record*, Ninety-sixth Congress, First Session (1979), p. 32676.

82. David A. Stockman and W. Philip Gramm, "The Administration's Case for Hospital Cost Containment," in Cotton M. Lindsay, ed., *New Directions in Public Health Care: A Prescription for the 1980s* (San Francisco: Institute for Contemporary Studies, 1980), pp. 110–124.

83. Ibid., pp. 126–128.

84. Jack A. Meyer and Rudolph G. Penner, "Impact of National Health Insurance Proposals on Budget," in Mark V. Pauly, ed., *National Health Insurance: What Now, What Later, What Never?* (Washington, D.C.: American Enterprise Institute, 1980), pp. 24–25.

85. Ibid., p. 25.

86. Alain C. Enthoven, *Health Plan: The Only Practical Solution to the Soaring Cost of Medical Care* (Reading, Mass.: Addison-Wesley, 1980), p. 99.

87. Ibid., pp. 99–100.

88. *Congressional Record*, Ninety-sixth Congress, First Session (1979), p. 32674.

89. Judith Feder, Jack Hadley, and John Holahan, *Insuring the Nation's Health: Market Competition, Catastrophic and Comprehensive Approaches* (Washington, D.C.: The Urban Institute, 1981), p. 122.

90. Enthoven, *Health Plan*, pp. 21–25.

91. Ibid., p. 100.

92. Starr, *The Social Transformation of American Medicine*, p. 414.

93. Lawrence D. Brown, *Politics and Health Care Organization: HMOs as Federal Policy* (Washington, D.C.: The Brookings Institution, 1983), pp. 265–267, 375.

94. Steven R. Eastaugh, *Financing Health Care: Economic Efficiency* (Dover: Auburn

House, 1987), p. 154; Tom Morganthau and Andrew Murr," "Inside the World of an HMO." *Newsweek*, April 5, 1993, p. 39.

95. Harold S. Luft, "Health Maintenance Organizations: Competition, Cost Containment, and National Health Insurance," in Mark V. Pauly, ed., *National Health Insurance* (Washington, D.C.: American Enterprise Institute, 1980), pp. 289–290.

96. Dean C. Coddington, David J. Keen, Keith D. Moore, and Richard L. Clarke, *The Crisis in Health Care: Costs, Choices, and Strategies* (San Francisco: Jossey-Bass, 1991), p. 82.

97. H. E. Frech III, "Preferred Provider Organizations and Health Care Competition," in H. E. Frech III, ed., *Health Care in America: The Political Economy of Hospitals and Health Insurance in America* (San Francisco: Pacific Research Institute, 1988), p. 359.

98. Harry Nelson, "HMOs Expanding to Streamline Operations and Bolster Quality," *Los Angeles Times*, December 17, 1991, p. A5.

99. Louise B. Russell, *Medicare's New Payment System: Is It Working?* (Washington, D.C.: The Brookings Institution, 1989), pp. 1–3.

100. Ibid., p. 2.

101. William B. Schwartz and Daniel L. Mendelson, "Hospital Cost Containment in the 1980s: Hard Lessons Learned and Prospects for the 1990s," *The New England Journal of Medicine*, April 11, 1991, p. 1039.

102. Ibid., p. 1041.

103. Kosterlitz, "A Sick System," p. 388.

104. Lindorff, *Marketplace Medicine*, p. 10; Marmor, "Coping With a Creeping Crisis," p. 190.

105. Aaron, *Serious and Unstable Condition*, p. 39.

106. Robert Pear, "Clinton May Seek Lid on Doctor Fees and Liability Suits," *The New York Times*, March 9, 1993, p. A8.

107. Henry J. Aaron, "A Prescription for Health Care," in Henry J. Aaron, ed., *Setting National Priorities: Policy for the Nineties* (Washington, D.C.: The Brookings Institution, 1990), p. 252.

108. Stern, *The Best Congress Money Can Buy*, p. 142.

109. Etzioni, *Capital Corruption*, pp. 44–47.

110. Larry J. Sabato, *PAC Power: Inside the World of Political Action Committees* (New York: W. W. Norton, 1984), p. 132.

111. Morris, *Searching for a Cure*, p. 142.

112. Califano, *Governing America*, p. 147.

113. Jimmy Carter, *Keeping Faith: Memoirs of a President* (New York: Bantam Books, 1982), p. 87.

114. Kingdon, *Agendas, Alternatives, and Public Policies*, p. 26.

115. Jones, *The Trusteeship Presidency*, pp. 162–63.

CHAPTER 5

1. Jimmy Carter, *Public Papers of the Presidents of the United States 1979* (Washington, D.C.: U.S. Government Printing Office, 1980), p. 1031.

2. *Congressional Record*, Ninety-sixth Congress, First Session (1979), p. 23273.

3. Jonas Morris, *Searching for a Cure: National Health Policy Reconsidered* (New York: Pica Press, 1984), pp. 92–95.

4. *Congressional Quarterly Almanac 1971*, p. 542; *Congressional Quarterly Weekly Almanac 1974*, p. 391; *Congressional Quarterly Almanac 1975*, p. 639.

5. Morris, *Searching for a Cure*, pp. 92–95.

6. Ibid., pp. 119–129.

7. *Congressional Record*, Ninety-fourth Congress, First Session (1975), p. 225.

8. Ibid.

9. Elizabeth Bowman, "Health Insurance: Carter For, Ford Against," *Congressional Quarterly Weekly Report*, October 9, 1976, p. 2918.

10. Ibid.; Morris, *Searching for a Cure*, p. 92.

11. Joseph A. Califano, Jr., *Governing America: An Insider's Report from the White House and the Cabinet* (New York: Simon and Schuster, 1981), p. 111.

12. Morris, *Searching for a Cure*, p. 119.

13. Ibid., p. 129.

14. *Congressional Quarterly Almanac 1979*, p. 537.

15. Ibid., p. 538.

16. U.S. Congress, House of Representatives, *National Health Insurance: Joint Hearing Before the Subcommittee on Health and the Environment of the Committee on Interstate and Foreign Commerce and Subcommittee on Health of the Committee on Ways and Means on H.R. 5191 and H.R. 5400*, Ninety-sixth Congress, First Session, November 29, 1979 (Washington, D.C.: U.S. Government Printing Office, 1980), pp. 503–505.

17. "Kennedy: 'We Can't Do It Piecemeal,' " *Newsweek*, May 28, 1979.

18. House of Representatives, *National Health Insurance*, pp. 451–454.

19. Ibid., pp. 520–521.

20. Jimmy Carter, *Keeping Faith: Memoirs of a President* (New York: Bantam Books, 1982), p. 86. Carter's charge that the Kennedy-Waxman bill would have raised annual federal spending by $100 to $200 billion is wildly exaggerated, since the measure would have increased government outlays by only $30.7 billion in 1980.

21. Califano, *Governing America*, p. 132.

22. Judith Feder, Jack Hadley, and John Holahan, *Insuring the Nation's Health: Market Competition, Catastrophic and Comprehensive Approaches* (Washington, D.C.: The Urban Institute, 1981), pp. 10–11.

23. *Encyclopedia Britannica* 1985–1992.

24. Charles L. Schultze, "Paying the Bills," in Henry J. Aaron and Charles L. Schultze, eds., *Setting Domestic Priorities: What Can Government Do?* (Washington, D.C.: The Brookings Institution, 1992), p. 299.

25. House of Representatives, *Joint Hearing on H.R. 5191 and H.R. 5400*, p. 482.

26. Aaron, *Serious and Unstable Condition: Financing America's Health Care* (Washington, D.C.: The Brookings Institution, 1991), p. 57.

27. Califano, *Governing America*, p. 135.

28. Carter, *Keeping Faith*, p. 86.

29. Carter, *Public Papers*, 1979, p. 1025.

30. Morris, *Searching for a Cure*, pp. 126–29.

31. House of Representatives, *Joint Hearing on H.R. 5191 and H.R. 5400*,

32. National Committee to Preserve Social Security and Medicare.

33. Morris, *Searching for a Cure*, p. 128.

34. Feder, Hadley, and Holahan, *Insuring the Nation's Health*, pp. 106–110.

35. *Congressional Record*, Ninety-sixth Congress, First Session (1979), p. 23273.

36. James MacGregor Burns, *Edward Kennedy and the Camelot Legacy* (New York: W. W. Norton, 1976), pp. 206–207.

37. Ibid., p. 223.

38. Theo Lippman, *Senator Ted Kennedy* (New York: W. W. Norton, 1976), p. 236.

39. Morris, *Searching for a Cure*, p. 92.

40. Ibid., p. 95.

41. Ibid., p. 119.

42. Califano, *Governing America*, p. 109.

43. Ibid., pp. 109–112.

44. Ibid., pp. 98–99.

45. Ibid., p. 99.

46. Ibid., p. 110.

47. Ibid., p. 100.

48. Ibid., pp. 104–108.

49. Ibid., p. 102.

50. Ibid.

51. Jimmy Carter, *Public Papers of the Presidents of the United States 1980–81* (Washington, D.C.: U.S. Government Printing Office, 1982), p. 2360.

52. Ibid., p. 2496.

53. Ibid., p. 2526.

54. Ibid., p. 2496.

55. Ibid., pp. 2496–2497. In his response to Carter's charge that he had opposed Medicare, Reagan pointed out that he had actually supported a measure opposing the Medicare bill—presumably Eldercare, which the AMA introduced as an alternative to Medicare. Unlike Medicare, which provides health insurance to practically all elderly individuals, rich and poor alike, Eldercare would have limited its coverage to poor senior citizens. For an explanation of the differences between Medicare and Eldercare, see Sheri I. David, *With Dignity: The Search for Medicare and Medicaid* (Westport, Conn.: Greenwood Press, 1985), pp. 123–146.

56. Ronald Reagan, *An American Life* (New York: Simon and Schuster, 1990), p. 221.

57. Max J. Skidmore, *Medicare and the American Rhetoric of Reconciliation* (University: University of Alabama Press, 1970), pp. 123–128.

58. Ibid., p. 123.

59. Ibid., p. 128.

60. Bob Rankin, "Candidates on the Issues: Health Insurance," *Congressional Quarterly Weekly Report*, March 20, 1976, p. 617.

61. Ibid.

62. Elizabeth Wehr, "Health Policy Is Low Priority Issue," *Congressional Quarterly Weekly Report*, March 8, 1980, p. 76.

63. Carter, *Public Papers 1980–81*, p. 2554.

64. Morris, *Searching for a Cure*, p. 172.

65. Wehr, "Health Policy Is a Low Priority Issue," p. 659.

66. The only major expansion of federal regulation of the health care system during the Reagan administration came on October 1, 1983, when Congress established the Medicare Prospective Payment System (PPS). As we saw in Chapter 4, PPS represents a federal regulatory measure to contain hospital costs under Medicare. For an analysis of PPS, see Louise B. Russell, *Medicare's New Payment System: Is It Working?* (Washington, D.C.: The Brookings Institution, 1989).

67. Linda E. Demkovich, "Reagan's Cure for Health Care Ills—Keep the Government's Hands Off," *National Journal*, December 13, 1980, p. 2124.

68. Dave Lindorff, *Medical Marketplace: The Rise of the For-Profit Hospital Chains* (New York: Bantam Books, 1992), p. 128.

69. The only health care reform measure established during the Reagan administration was the Medicare Catastrophic Coverage Act, passed by Congress in 1988. The bill provided Medicare beneficiaries with catastrophic health insurance coverage by imposing limits on their out-of-pocket health care expenses. It was financed through income taxes imposed upon affluent Medicare beneficiaries. However, practically all affluent Medicare beneficiaries already had catastrophic coverage through private supplemental plans, known as Medigap, which fill in many, if not most, of the gaps in Medicare protection. Those Medicare beneficiaries did not want to pay higher taxes for Medicare catastrophic coverage they did not need. They organized and lobbied Congress against the Medicare Catastrophic Coverage Act, which resulted in its repeal in 1989. For an examination of the Medicare Catastrophic Coverage Act, see Aaron, *Serious and Unstable Condition*, pp. 62–63.

70. Califano, *Governing America*, p. 114.

CHAPTER 6

1. Henry J. Aaron, *Serious and Unstable Condition: Financing America's Health Care* (Washington, D.C.: The Brookings Institution, 1991), pp. 1–2.

2. Theodore R. Marmor, "Coping with a Creeping Crisis: Medicare at Twenty," in Theodore R. Marmor and Jerry L. Mashaw, eds., *Social Security: Beyond the Rhetoric of Crisis* (Princeton: Princeton University Press, 1988), p. 177.

3. "Health Care Woes Deepen," *USA Today*, December 22, 1992.

4. Tamara Lewin, "High Medical Costs Hurt Growing Numbers in U.S.," The *New York Times*, April 28, 1991; Robert Pear, "Bush Plan Would Be Financed By Medicare Curb," *The New York Times*, February 3, 1992, p. C10.

5. U.S. Department of Health and Human Services, Health Care Financing Administration, *The Medicare 1992 Handbook*, p. 1.

6. Rashi Fein, *Medical Care, Medical Costs: The Search for a Health Insurance Policy* (Cambridge: Harvard University Press, 1989), pp. 111–12.

7. Robert H. Blank, *Rationing Medicine* (New York: Columbia University Press, 1988), p. 14; Judi Hasson, "Governors Applaud 'Do-Something Policy,' " *USA Today*, February 2, 1993, p. 4A.

8. Hasson, "Governors Applaud 'Do-Something' Policy, p. 4A.

9. Fein, *Medical Care, Medical Costs*, p. 116.

10. Maura Reynolds, "Pepper Commission Issues Final Medical System Report," *Los Angeles Times*, September 26, 1990, p. A17.

11. Aaron, *Serious and Unstable Condition*, p. 74; Alissa J. Rubin, "Reinvention of Health Care Is Key to Clinton Overhaul," *Congressional Quarterly Weekly Report*, March 13, 1993, p. 596.

12. "Economic State of the Union," *Los Angeles Times*, January 29, 1992, p. A12; "1 Million Among Middle Class Lost Health Benefits Last Year," *Los Angeles Times*, December 22, 1992, p. A22.

13. Aaron, *Serious and Unstable Condition*, p. 74.

14. Charles J. Dougherty, *American Health Care: Rights, Responsibilities, and Reforms* (New York: Oxford University Press, 1988), p. 18; Donald W. Naus, "Big Three Call for National Health Care System," *Los Angeles Times*, March 23, 1993, p. D2.

15. Michael Wolff, Peter Rutten, and Albert F. Bayers, *Where We Stand: Can America*

Make It in the Global Race for Wealth, Health, and Happiness? (New York: Bantam Books, 1992), p. 137.

16. Donald L. Barlett and James B. Steele, *America: What Went Wrong?* (Kansas City: Andrews and McMeel, 1992), pp. 125–26.

17. Fein, *Medical Care, Medical Costs,* p. 69; Annelise Anderson, "It's Federal Spending, Sweetheart," *USA Today,* February 17, 1993, p. 13A.

18. Karen Davis and Dianne Rowland, *Medicare Policy: New Directions in Health and Long-Term Care* (Baltimore: The Johns Hopkins University Press, 1986), pp. 43, 48.

19. Robert J. Myers, *Social Security* (Homewood: Richard D. Irwin, 1985), pp. 522, 552, 570; *The Medicare 1992 Handbook,* pp. 1, 13, 19.

20. Marmor, "Coping With a Creeping Crisis," p. 189; Robert Dvorchak, "Are Things Getting Worse? They Are, Index Says," *Los Angeles Times,* January 26, 1992, p. A31.

21. "Doctor Bills Are Top Concern of Nation's Poor, Study Says," The *New York Times,* January 4, 1993, p. A10.

22. Paul Starr, "Health Care for the Poor: The Past Twenty Years," in Sheldon Danziger and Daniel H. Weinberg, eds., *Fighting Poverty: What Works and What Doesn't* (Cambridge: Harvard University Press, 1986), p. 118.

23. John E. Schwartz and Thomas J. Volgy, *The Forgotten Americans* (New York: W. W. Norton, 1992), p. 48.

24. Sam Fulwood III, "Health Care Study Finds Many at Risk," *Los Angeles Times,* February 27, 1992, p. A25.

25. Judith Feder, Jack Hadley, and Rose M. Mullner, "Falling Through the Cracks: Poverty, Insurance Coverage, and Hospitals' Care to the Poor, 1980 and 1982," in Sally J. Rogers, Ann Marie Rousseau, and Susan W. Hesbitt, eds., *Hospitals and the Uninsured Poor: Measuring and Paying for Uncompensated Care* (New York: United Hospital Fund, 1985), p. 9.

26. Robert Steinbrook, "Most Americans Favor Reforms in Nation's Health Care System," *Los Angeles Times,* February 4, 1990, p. A1.

27. Wolff, Rutten, and Bayers, *Where We Stand,* p. 136.

28. Aaron, *Serious and Unstable Condition,* pp. 96–97.

29. Wolff, Rutten, and Bayers, *Where We Stand,* p. 110.

30. Ibid., p. 136.

31. Ibid., p. 137.

32. Steinbrook, "Most Americans Favor Reforms in Nation's Health Care System," A26.

33. Richard M. Coughlin, *Ideology, Public Opinion & Welfare Policy: Attitudes Toward Taxes and Spending in Industrialized Countries* (Berkeley: University of California, 1980), p. 77.

34. Ibid., p. 82.

35. Hillary Stout, "Most Americans Pledge Sacrifice to Help Fix the Health Care System," *The Wall Street Journal,* March 12, 1993, p. A1.

36. Melinda Beck, "Doctors Under the Knife," *Newsweek,* April 5, 1993, p. 30.

37. Judy Keen, Judi Hasson, and Mike Snider, "Price Controls and Cost Are Big Concerns," *USA Today,* March 24, 1993, p. 2A.

38. Ray Marshall and Marc Tucker, *Thinking for a Living: Education and the Wealth of Nations* (New York: Basic Books, 1992), p. 247.

39. Beck, "Doctors Under the Knife," p. 30.

40. Stout, "Most Americans Pledge Help to Fix the Health Care System," p. A4.

41. Beck, "Doctors Under the Knife," p. 30.

42. John D. Rockefeller IV, "Seize the Momentum for Change," *USA Today*, March 22, 1993, p. 13A.

43. Aaron, *Serious and Unstable Condition*, p. 2.

CHAPTER 7

1. Julie Rovner, " 'Play or Pay' Gains Momentum As Labor Panel Marks Up Bill," *Congressional Quarterly Weekly Report*, January 25, 1992, p. 174.

2. Janny Scott, "Hike in Medical Bureaucracy Costs Cited," *Los Angeles Times*, May 2, 1991, p. A18.

3. Rashi Fein, "A Model For Health Insurance: Can We Learn from the Canadian Example?," *Dissent*, Winter 1991, p. 16.

4. Milton Terris, "Lessons from Canada's Health Program," *Technology Review*, February/March 1990, pp. 28–29.

5. John K. Iglehart, "Canada's Health Care System Faces Its Problems," *The New England Journal of Medicine*, February 22, 1990, p. 562.

6. Fein, "A Model For Health Insurance," p. 16.

7. Steffie Woolhandler and David U. Himmelstein, "The Deteriorating Efficiency of the U.S. Health Care System," *The New England Journal of Medicine*, May 2, 1991, pp. 1255–56.

8. Janny Scott, "Hike in Medical Bureaucracy Costs Cited," p. A18.

9. Dave Lindorff, *Marketplace Medicine: The Rise of the For-Profit Hospital Chains* (New York: Bantam Books, 1992), p. 282.

10. "GAO Report Hails Canada Health System," *Los Angeles Times*, June 4, 1991, p. A20.

11. Phil Kuntz, "Embattled GAO Fights Back; Bowsher Denies Any Bias," *Congressional Quarterly Weekly Report*, July 27, 1991, p. 2048–50.

12. Philip J. Hilts, "Canadian-Style Health System Gains Support," The *New York Times*, June 4, 1991, p. A18.

13. Scott, "Hike in Medical Bureaucracy Costs Cited," p. A18.

14. *Congressional Quarterly Almanac 1989*, pp. 169–70.

15. Ibid., p. 170.

16. Julie Rovner, "After the Pepper Commission: Now the Real Work Begins," *Congressional Quarterly Weekly Report*, March 10, 1990, p. 749.

17. Julie Rovner, "Pepper Commission Splinters Over Health Financing," *Congressional Quarterly Weekly Report*, March 3, 1990, p. 668.

18. Julie Rovner, "Mitchell: New Priority," *Congressional Quarterly Weekly Report*, February 16, 1991, p. 421.

19. Julie Rovner, "Democrats Taking a Gamble on Health-Care Overhaul," *Congressional Quarterly Weekly Report*, June 8, 1991, p. 1507.

20. Ibid.

21. *Congressional Record*, One Hundred Second Congress, First Session (1991), pp. S7214–7216.

22. Rovner, " 'Play or Pay' Gains Momentum as Labor Panel Marks up Bill," p. 172.

23. Theodore R. Marmor, Jerry L. Mashaw, and Philip L. Harvey, "Political Handcuffs Hobble Debate," *Los Angeles Times*, October 3, 1991, p. B7.

24. Theodore R. Marmor, Jerry L. Mashaw, and Philip L. Harvey, "If We Want Real Reform, Canada Has an Example," *Los Angeles Times*, October 4, 1991, p. B7.

25. Louis W. Sullivan, " 'Pay or Play' Is a Losing Gamble," *Los Angeles Times*, January 13, 1992, p. B5.

26. John Merline and Thomas McArdle, "Should Business Fear Clinton?," *Investor's Business Daily*, July 16, 1992, p. 2.

27. George Hager, "Entitlements: The Untouchable May Become Unavoidable," *Congressional Quarterly Weekly Report*, January 2, 1993, p. 24.

28. Merline and McArdle, "Should Business Fear Clinton?," p. 2; Sullivan, " 'Pay or Play' Is a Losing Gamble," p. B5.

29. Congressional Record, One Hundred Second Congress, First Session, p. 7215; Julie Rovner, "Senate Bill Highlights," *Congressional Quarterly Weekly Report*, January 25, 1992, p. 173.

30. Rovner, "Senate Bill Highlights," p. 173.

31. Martin Tolchin, "Panel Says Broad Health Care Would Cost $86 Billion a Year," The *New York Times*, March 3, 1990, p. A9.

32. Congressional Record, One Hundred Second Congress, First Session, p. S 7215.

33. Rovner, "Senate Bill Highlights," p. 173.

34. Congressional Record, One Hundred Second Congress, First Session, p. S7215.

35. Rovner, "Democrats Taking a Gamble on Health-Care Overhaul," p. 1507.

36. John MacDonald, "Health Insurance Lobby Spends Millions on Debate Spin Control," *Los Angeles Times*, June 7, 1992, p. A27.

37. Robert Benedetto, "Health PACs' Giving Rises," *USA Today*, March 12, 1993, p. 4A.

38. Robert Pear, "Democrats Offer Wide Health Plan," The *New York Times*, June 6, 1991, p. A22.

39. Rovner, " 'Play or Pay' Gains Momentum As Labor Panel Marks Up Bill," p. 172.

40. Ibid., p. 174.

41. Ibid.

42. Julie Rovner, "Insurance Reforms Slide By Senate Finance in Tax Bill," *Congressional Quarterly Weekly Report*, March 7, 1992, p. 536.

43. Julie Rovner, "Health Provisions in Tax Bill," *Congressional Quarterly Weekly Report*, March 7, 1992, p. 538.

44. Rovner, "Insurance Reforms Slide By Senate Finance in Tax Bill," p. 536.

45. Julie Kosterlitz, "Democrats Split on Health Bill," *National Journal*, May 16, 1992, pp. 1186–87.

46. Rovner, "Insurance Reforms Slide By Senate Finance in Tax Bill," p. 536.

47. Kosterlitz, "Democrats Split on Health Bill," p. 1187.

48. Julie Rovner, "Details of Insurance Reform Keep Democrats Divided," *Congressional Quarterly Weekly Report*,

49. Kosterlitz, "Democrats Split on Health Bill," p. 1187.

50. Julie Rovner, "Democrats Take Two Paths to System Overhaul," *Congressional Quarterly Weekly Report*, July 4, 1992, p. 1964; Julie Rovner, "Ways and Means Bill Highlights," *Congressional Quarterly Weekly Report*, July 4, 1992, p. 1965.

51. Rovner, "Ways and Means Bill Highlights," p. 1965.

52. Rovner, "Democrats Take Two Paths to System Overhaul," p. 1966.

53. Ibid., p. 1964.

CHAPTER 8

1. Theodore R. Marmor and Lawrence R. Jacobs, "Don't Settle for Crumbs on Health Reform," *Los Angeles Times*, November 16, 1992, p. B7.

2. Michael Kramer, "The Voters' Latest Ailment: Health Care," *Time*, November 11, 1991, p. 51; Susan Mandel, "Pennsylvania's Harris Wofford: His Upset Senate Victory Made Health Care a Big Issue," *Investor's Business Daily*, February 3, 1992, p. 2.

3. Mandel, "Pennsylvania's Harris Wofford."

4. Kramer, "The Voters' Latest Ailment," p. 51.

5. Hedrick Hertzberg, "Making Tracks Toward '92," *Los Angeles Times*, November 10, 1991, p. M1.

6. E. J. Dionne, Jr., *Why Americans Hate Politics* (New York: Simon and Schuster, 1992), p. 358.

7. Michael deCourcy Hinds, "Senate Hopefuls Withhold Attacks," *New York Times*, November 5, 1991, p. A9. Robert Shogan, "Elections Today Air Themes Likely to Shape '92 Contests," *Los Angeles Times*, November 5, 1991, p. A23.

8. *Congressional Record*, One Hundred Second Congress, First Session (1991), p. S16001.

9. Dionne, *Why Americans Hate Politics*, pp. 357–58.

10. Hertzberg, "Making Tracks Toward '92."

11. Edwin Chen, "Survey Finds Health Care Top Vote Issue," *Los Angeles Times*, November 8, 1991, p. A26. Paula Dwyer and Susan B. Garland, "A Roar of Discontent: Voters Want Health Care Reform—Now," *Business Week*, November 25, 1991, p. 29.

12. Dwyer and Garland, "A Roar of Discontent," p. 29. Twenty-nine percent of Pennsylvania voters polled said that taxes were among the two issues that "mattered most" in determining their vote in the Senate election, 21 percent chose the recession and unemployment, and 14 percent the candidate's record.

13. Chen, "Survey Finds Health Care Top Vote Issue," p. A26.

14. Rashi Fein, "National Health Insurance: Telling the Good from the Bad," *Dissent*, Spring 1992, p. 158.

15. Dwyer and Garland, "A Roar of Discontent," p. 29.

16. Chen, "Survey Finds Health Care Top Issue," p. A26.

17. Richard Benedetto and Brian O'Connell, "Bush Rated Weak in Key Areas," *USA Today*, September 4, 1992, p. 8A. Eighty-nine percent of those polled said that the economy was "a very important issue facing the presidential candidates," 84 percent chose education, 77 percent the federal deficit, and 69 percent taxes.

18. Robert Steinbrook, "Most Americans Favor Reforms in Nation's Health Care System," *Los Angeles Times*, February 4, 1990.

19. Howard Fineman, "The Torch Passes," *Newsweek*, November/December 1992, p. 10.

20. Steinbrook, "Most Americans Favor Reforms in Nation's Health Care System." Sixty-four percent of those polled believed that drug abuse was the most important issue facing the United States; 26 percent, crime; 19 percent, the federal deficit; and 16 percent, the economy.

21. Fineman, "The Torch Passes," p. 10. Forty-three percent of those polled said they cared about the economy and jobs; 21 percent, the deficit; 15 percent, family values; 14 percent, taxes; 13 percent, education; 13 percent, abortion; 8 percent, foreign policy; and 6 percent, the environment.

22. Daniel Yankelovich, "How Public Opinion Really Works," *Fortune*, October 5, 1992, p. 103.

23. Ibid.

24. Michael Duffy and Dan Goodgame, *Marching in Place: The Status Quo Presidency of George Bush* (New York: Simon and Schuster, 1992), p. 98.

25. Ibid., pp. 220–221.

26. Ibid., pp. 257–259.

27. Ibid., p. 98.

28. Kramer, "The Voters' Latest Ailment," p. 51.

29. Ibid.

30. Duffy and Goodgame, *Marching in Place*, p. 98.

31. *Weekly Compilation of Presidential Documents*, November 11, 1991, p. 1595.

32. Ibid., pp. 1595, 1608.

33. Julie Rovner, "Bush's Plan Short on Details, Long on Ambition, Critics," *Congressional Quarterly Weekly Report*, February 8, 1992, pp. 305–07.

34. *Weekly Compilation of Presidential Documents*, February 10, 1992, pp. 219–20.

35. Rovner, "Bush's Plan Short on Details, Long on Ambition, Critics," p. 306.

36. *Congressional Record*, One Hundred Second Congress, Second Session (Washington, D.C.: U.S. Government Printing Office, 1991), pp. S1177–78, S1182–85, S1318–19.

37. Ibid., p. 1177.

38. Robert A. Rosenblatt and Edwin Chen, "Health Reform Actions Likely to Be Minimal," *Los Angeles Times*, February 7, 1992, p. A13.

39. Judi Hasson and Kevin Anderson, "Bush Unveils Health Care Plan," *USA Today*, February 7, 1992, p. 4A.

40. Rosenblatt and Chen, "Health Reform Actions Likely to Be Minimal," p. A13.

41. Hasson and Anderson, "Bush Unveils Health Care Plan," p. 4A.

42. Rovner, "Bush's Plan Short on Details, Long on Ambition, Critics," p. 307.

43. Annelise Anderson, "It's Federal Spending, Sweetheart," *USA Today*, February 17, 1993, p. 13A; Judi Hasson, "Governors Applaud 'Do-Something' Policy," *USA Today*, February 2, 1993, p. 4A.

44. Rosenblatt and Chen, "Health Reform Actions Likely to Be Minimal," p. A13.

45. George J. Mitchell, "First Quit Feeding the Monster," *Los Angeles Times*, February 21, 1992, p. B7.

46. *Weekly Compilation of Presidential Documents*, October 19, 1992, p. 1955.

47. Michael Wolff, Peter Rutten, and Albert F. Bayers III, *Where We Stand: Can America Make It in the Global Race for Wealth, Health, and Happiness?* (New York: Bantam Books, 1992), pp. 134–135.

48. Robert H. Blank, *Rationing Medicine* (New York: Columbia University Press, 1988), pp. 138–140.

49. Rovner, "Bush's Plan Short on Details," p. 307.

50. Joel Havemann, "Safety Net for Malpractice Has Fewer Holes in Europe," *Los Angeles Times*, December 31, 1992, p. A12.

51. Hasson and Anderson, "Bush Unveils Health Care Plan," p. 4A.

52. Ibid.

53. *Weekly Compilation of Presidential Documents*, February 3, 1992, pp. 174–175.

54. Ibid., p. 175.

55. *Congressional Record*, One Hundred Second Congress, Second Session (1991), pp. S1178–1179, S1183–1186, S1298–1301, S1305–1307, S1325–1326; Hasson and Anderson, "Bush Unveils Health Care Plan", p. 4A. Rosenblatt and Chen, "Health Reform Actions Likely to Be Minimal," p. A13. Christine Shenot, "Bush Takes Wraps off Health Reform Plan," *Investor's Business Daily*, February 7, 1992, p. 1.

56. *Congressional Record*, One Hundred Second Congress, Second Session (1991), p. S1305.

57. Rovner, "Bush's Plan Short on Details," pp. 305–306.

58. Louis W. Sullivan, " 'Play or Pay' Is a Losing Gamble," *Los Angeles Times*, January 13, 1992, p. B5.

59. *Weekly Compilation of Presidential Documents*, February 3, 1992, p. 175.

60. Ibid., February 10, 1992, p. 219.

61. Ibid.

62. Ibid., p. 218.

63. Ibid., February 3, 1992, p. 175; ibid., February 10, 1992, p. 218.

64. Ibid., February 13, 1992, p. 175.

65. Ibid., February 10, 1992, pp. 218–219.

66. Ibid., p. 225.

67. Bill Clinton and Al Gore, *Putting People First: How We Can All Change America* (New York: Times Books, 1992), p. 228.

68. Ibid., p. 223.

69. *Weekly Compilation of Presidential Documents*, August 10, 1992, p. 1370.

70. Robert Pear, "National Health Policy: How Bush and Clinton Differ," The *New York Times*, August 12, 1992, p. A13.

71. *Weekly Compilation of Presidential Documents*, August 10, 1992, p. 1370.

72. Bush's estimate of the number of job losses resulting from the establishment of play-or-pay health insurance is presumably based upon figures provided by the Employee Benefit Research Institute (EBRI). In 1992 the EBRI estimated that a federal mandate for employers to provide their working families health insurance would result in from 200,000 to 1.2 million job losses. However, like Bush, the EBRI failed to consider the fact that under both the HealthAmerica Act and Clinton's national health insurance plan the least profitable small businesses employing primarily low-wage workers would receive tax subsidies to finance the cost of insurance for their working families. This would insulate struggling small businesses from the financial burden of having to provide their working families insurance, and eliminate the prospect that federally-mandated employer-provided insurance would result in any job losses.

73. *Weekly Compilation of Presidential Documents*, August 10, 1991, p. 1370.

74. Ibid.

75. Ibid., August 24, 1992, p. 1467.

76. Kathleen Decker, "Clinton Defends Health Care Plan," *Los Angeles Times*, August 3, 1992, p. A14.

77. Decker, "Clinton Defends Health Care Plan," p. A14; Michael Kelly, "In Swift Counteroffensive, Clinton Moves Against Bush," The *New York Times*, August 4, 1992, p. A13.

78. Kelly, "In Swift Counteroffensive, Clinton Moves Against Bush."

79. *USA Today*, August 3, 1992, p. 4A.

80. Andrew Rosenthal, "GOP Tries to Seize a Democratic Issue," The *New York Times*, August 5, 1992, p. A10.

81. William J. Eaton and Douglas Jehl, "Bush Delivers Pep Talk to GOP Senators," *Los Angeles Times*, August 5, 1992, p. A5.

82. *USA Today*, August 5, 1992, p. 4A.

83. David Lauter and Robert Rosenblatt, "Clinton Spells Out His Plan to Curb Health Care Costs," *Los Angeles Times*, September 25, 1992, p. A1.

84. Ibid., p. A25.

85. *Weekly Compilation of Presidential Documents*, October 5, 1992, p. 1753.

86. Joel Havemann, "Diagnosis: Healthier in Europe," *Los Angeles Times*, December 30, 1992, p. A9; Milton Terris, "Lessons from Canada's Health Program," *Technology Review*, February/March 1990, p. 27.

87. Judy Keen and Jessica Lee, "Bush Set to Do 'What I Have to Do,' " *USA Today*, February 12, 1992, p. 4A. Seventy-six percent of those polled disapproved of Bush's handling of the economy, 67 percent of unemployment, 61 percent of taxes, 58 percent of foreign trade, 45 percent of abortion, and 32 percent of foreign affairs. Sixty-five percent approved of Bush's management of foreign affairs, 41 percent of abortion, 38 percent of foreign trade, 36 percent of taxes, 29 percent of unemployment, and 22 percent of the economy.

88. Richard Benedetto, "Democratic Candidates Still Unknown," *USA Today*, January 14, 1992, p. 11A. Sixty-two percent of those polled chose the Democrats on poverty and homelessness, 55 percent on unemployment, 51 percent on race relations, 48 percent on education and the environment, 46 percent on the economy, 44 percent on taxes, 39 percent on the budget deficit, 38 percent on drugs, 32 percent on foreign trade, and 26 percent on foreign affairs. Fifty-seven percent chose the Republicans on foreign affairs, 52 percent on foreign trade, 41 percent on the budget deficit, 40 percent on taxes, 39 percent on the economy and on drugs, 35 percent on education, 32 percent on the environment, 30 percent on race relations, 30 percent on unemployment, and 24 percent on poverty and homelessness.

89. Benedetto and O'Connell, "Bush Rated Weak in Key Areas," p. 8A. Fifty-five percent of thse polled chose Clinton on the economy, 54 percent education, 53 percent the federal deficit, and 50 percent taxes. Thirty-eight percent chose Bush on taxes, 35 percent education, 34 percent the economy, and 32 percent the federal deficit.

90. George Skelton, "Bush Rebounds, Slices Clinton Lead to 8 Points," *Los Angeles Times*, August 22, 1992, p. A17. Forty-eight percent of those polled chose Clinton on the economy, 31 percent on holding down taxes, and 18 percent foreign affairs. Sixty-nine percent chose Bush on foreign affairs, 44 percent on holding down taxes, and 39 percent the economy.

91. Ronald Brownstein, "As Voters Split on Issues, Clinton Comes Out on Top," *Los Angeles Times*, October 9, 1992, p. A15.

92. Ronald Brownstein, "Economic Concerns Fueled Clinton's Drive to Victory," *Los Angeles Times*, November 4, 1992, p. A11. Sixty-nine percent of Clinton voters said the economy and jobs were "most important" issues in determining their votes, 25 percent chose education, 11 percent abortion, 10 percent the federal budget deficit and the environment, respectively, 9 percent moral values, 5 percent poverty, 3 percent crime and drugs, 1 percent foreign affairs, and 2 percent none of the above. Forty-six percent of Bush voters said moral values was the "most important" issue determining their vote, 34 percent chose jobs and the economy, 21 percent taxes, 19 percent foreign affairs, 17

percent abortion, 13 percent education, 10 percent the federal budget deficit, 4 percent crime and drugs, 3 percent the environment, and 4 percent none of the above.

93. Fineman, "The Torch Passes," p. 10. Among those polled, Clinton received the support of 73 percent of those concerned about the environment, 60 percent about education, 52 percent about the economy and jobs, 37 percent about abortion, 36 percent about the deficit, 23 percent about family values, and 9 percent about foreign policy. Bush received the support of 86 percent of those concerned about foreign policy, 65 percent about abortion, 26 percent about the deficit, 25 percent about education, 24 percent about the economy and jobs, and 14 percent about the environment.

94. Marmor and Jacobs, "Don't Settle for Crumbs on Health Reform," p. B7.

CHAPTER 9

1. Susan Dentzer, "Clinton's Big Test," *U.S. News & World Report*, November 23, 1992, p. 26.

2. Richard Benedetto, "Hopes High for Next Term—Poll," *USA Today*, January 15, 1993, p. 5A. Eighty-seven percent of those polled expressed satisfaction with the nation's military security, 52 percent with the protection of the environment, 49 percent with the state of race relations, 43 percent with the quality of education, 25 percent with the state of the economy, and 22 percent with reducing poverty and homelessness.

3. Steven V. Roberts, "High Hopes," *U.S. News & World Report*, p. 32. Thirty-three percent of those polled said that reducing the deficit was the top priority that Clinton "should address quickly," 29 percent chose other economic problems, 28 percent, creating jobs, 25 percent, foreign policy crises, and 10 percent chose education reform.

4. Bill Clinton and Al Gore, *Putting People First: How We Can All Change America* (New York: Times Books, 1992), pp. 107–08.

5. They include Secretary of Defense Les Aspin, Secretary of the Treasury Lloyd Bentsen, Secretary of Veterans Affairs Jesse Brown, Secretary of Commerce Ronald H. Brown, Leon E. Panetta, Director of the Office of Management and Budget, Secretary of Labor Robert B. Reich, Robert E. Rubin, Chairman of the National Economic Council, HHS Secretary Donna Shalala, and Laura D'Andrea Tyson, Chairwoman of the President's Council of Economic Advisers.

6. Thomas L. Friedman, "Hillary Clinton to Head Panel on Health Care," *The New York Times*, January 26, 1993, p. A16.

7. Theodore R. Marmor, "Hillary Clinton on Health: Right Person, Right Place," *Los Angeles Times*, January 27, 1993, p. B7.

8. *Weekly Compilation of Presidential Documents*, February 1, 1993, p. 97.

9. Edwin Chen, "Big Firms May Have to Pay 75% of Health Plans," *Los Angeles Times*, March 19, 1993, p. A1.

10. Robert Pear, "Clinton Considers Stopping Medicaid Under Health Plan," *The New York Times*, March 29, 1993, p. A1.

11. Clinton and Gore, *Putting People First*, pp. 108–09; Robert Pear, "Clinton Health-Care Planners Are Facing Delicate Decisions," *The New York Times*, March 23, 1993, p. A9.

12. Ibid., pp. 22–23.

13. Rashi Fein, *Medical Care, Medical Costs: The Search for a Health Insurance Policy* (Cambridge: Harvard University Press, 1989), p. 24.

14. Dentzer, "Clinton's BIG Test," p. 28.

15. Chen, "Big Firms May Have to Pay 75% of Health Plans," p. A22.

16. Edwin Chen, "Panel Weighing 'Luxury Tax' on Health Benefits," *Los Angeles Times*, March 17, 1993, p. A14; Robert Pear, "Health-Care Costs Up Sharply, Posing New Threat," The *New York Times*, January 5, 1993, p. A1.

17. Edwin Chen, "Lid on Health Care Needed, Gore Says," *Los Angeles Times*, March 30, 1993, p. A1.

18. Pear, "Clinton Health-Care Planners Are Facing Delicate Decisions," p. A9.

19. Sara Fritz, "Big Insurers Cast Wary Eye on Clinton's Health Plans," *Los Angeles Times*, December 7, 1992, p. A16.

20. Judy Keen, Judi Hasson, and Mike Snider, "Price Controls and Cost Are Big Concerns," *USA Today*, March 24, 1993, p. 2A.

21. Adam Clymer, "Americans Have High Hopes for Clinton, Poll Finds," The *New York Times*, January 19, 1993, p. A7. Sixty-four of those polled believed that Clinton would "significantly improve education," 60 percent that he would "create a significant number of jobs," 54 percent that he would "make it harder for Government appointees to profit financially from the connections they made while in office," 51 percent that he would "significantly improve the environment," 26 percent that he would "reduce the budget deficit significantly," and 24 percent that he would "cut taxes on the middle class."

22. Richard Benedetto, "Clinton Winning Nation Over," *USA Today*, March 1, 1993, p. 8A.

23. Benedetto, "Hopes High Next Term—Poll," p. 3A. Among those polled who believed that conditions in the United States would improve, 55 percent thought so about the state of the economy, 53 percent about the protection of the environment, 53 percent about the protection of the environment, 52 percent about the quality of education, 47 percent about the state of race relations and reducing poverty and homelessness, respectively, and 23 percent about American military security.

24. *Weekly Compilation of Presidential Documents*, February 22, 1993, p. 218.

25. Robert Pear, "Passage of Health-Care Bill Seen as Unlikely This Year," The *New York Times*, March 4, 1993, p. A10.

26. Robert Pear, "Clinton May Not Meet Deadline on Health Plan," The *New York Times*, April 2, 1993, p. A12.

27. "Ideas From Those Who Give Health Care and Those Who Need It," The *New York Times*, March 30, 1993, p. A10.

28. Richard Benedetto, "Health PACs Giving Rises," *USA Today*, March 12, 1993, p. 4A.

29. Philip M. Stern, *The Best Congress Money Can Buy* (New York: Pantheon Books, 1988), p. 5.

30. Benedetto, "Health PACs' Giving Rises," p. 4A.

31. W. Lance Bennett, *The Governing Crisis: Media, Money, and Marketing in American Elections* (New York: St. Martin's Press, 1992), p. 94.

32. President Clinton's *New Beginning: The Complete Text, With Illustrations, of the Historic Clinton-Gore Economic Conference in Little Rock, Arkansas, December 14–15, 1992* (New York: Donald I. Fine, 1992), p. 56.

33. Judi Hasson, "All Players Have Ideas to Overhaul Health Care," *USA Today*, January 27, 1993; John D. Rockefeller IV, "Seize the Moment for Change," *USA Today*, March 22, 1993, p. 11A.

34. Robert Pear, "Health-Care Costs Up Sharply Again, Posing New Threat," The

New York Times, January 5, 1993; Rockefeller, "Seize the Moment for Change," *USA Today*, March 22, 1993, p. 11A.

35. Eli Ginzberg, "The Health Swamp," The *New York Times*, November 12, 1992, p. A15.

36. Ibid.

Select Bibliography

Aaron, Henry J. *Serious and Unstable Conditions: Financing America's Health Care.* Washington, D.C.: The Brookings Institution, 1991.

Aaron, Henry J., and William B. Schwartz. *The Painful Prescription: Rationing Hospital Care.* Washington, D.C.: The Brookings Institution, 1984.

Anderson, Odin W. *Health Services in the United States: A Growth Enterprise Since 1875.* Ann Arbor, Mich.: Administration Press, 1985.

Andreopoulous, Spyros, ed. *National Health Insurance: Can We Learn from Canada?* New York: John Wiley, 1975.

Blank, Robert H. *Rationing Medicine.* New York: Columbia University Press, 1988.

Brown, Lawrence D. *Politics and Health Care Organization: HMOs as Federal Policy.* Washington, D.C.: The Brookings Institution, 1983.

Budrys, Grace. *Planning for the Nation's Health: A Study of Twentieth-Century Developments in the United States.* Westport, Conn.: Greenwood Press, 1986.

Burrow, James G. *AMA: Voice of American Medicine.* Baltimore: Johns Hopkins University Press, 1963.

Califano, Joseph A., Jr., *America's Health Care Revolution: Who Lives? Who Dies? Who Pays?* New York: Random House, 1986.

Coddington, Dean C., David J. Keen, Keith D. Moore, and Richard L. Clarke. *The Crisis in Health Care: Costs, Choices, and Strategies.* San Francisco: Jossey-Bass, 1991.

David, Sheri I. *With Dignity: The Search for Medicare and Medicaid.* Westport, Conn.: Greenwood Press, 1985.

Davis, Karen. *National Health Insurance: Benefits, Costs, and Consequences.* Washington, D.C.: The Brookings Institution, 1975.

Davis, Karen, and Dianne Rowland. *Medicare Policy: New Directions in Health and Long-Term Care.* Baltimore: Johns Hopkins University Press, 1986.

Eastaugh, Steven R. *Financing Health Care: Economic Efficiency.* Dover: Auburn House, 1987.

Ehrlich, Isaac, ed. *National Health Policy: What Role for Government?* Stanford, Calif.: Stanford University Press, 1982.

Enthoven, Alain C. *Health Plan: The Only Practical Solution to the Soaring Cost of Medical Care*. Reading, Mass.: Addison-Wesley, 1980.

Feder, Judith, Jack Hadley, and John Holahan. *Insuring the Nation's Health: Market Competition, Catastrophic and Comprehensive Approaches*. Washington, D.C.: The Urban Institute, 1981.

Fein, Rashi. *Medical Care, Medical Costs: The Search for a Health Insurance Policy*. Cambridge, Mass.: Harvard University Press, 1989.

Harris, Richard. *A Sacred Trust*. New York: New American Library, 1966.

Hirshfield, Daniel S. *The Lost Reform: The Campaign for Compulsory Health Insurance in the United States from 1932 to 1943*. Cambridge, Mass.: Harvard University Press, 1970.

Hollingsworth, J. Rogers. *A Political Economy of Medicine: Great Britain and the United States*. Baltimore: Johns Hopkins University Press, 1986.

Keintz, Rita. *National Health Insurance and Income Distribution*. Lexington, Mass.: Lexington Books, 1976.

Law, Sylvia A. *Blue Cross: What Went Wrong?* New Haven: Yale University Press, 1974.

Lindorff, Dave. *Marketplace Medicine: The Rise of the For-Profit Hospital Chains*. New York: Bantam Books, 1992.

Lindsay, Cotton M., ed. *New Directions in Public Health Care: Directions for the 1980s*. San Francisco: Institute for Contemporary Studies, 1980.

Meyer, Jack A., ed. *Market Reforms in Health Care: Current Issues, New Directions*. Washington, D.C.: American Enterprise Institute, 1983.

Morris, Jonas. *Searching for a Cure: National Health Policy Reconsidered*. New York: Pica Press, 1984.

Numbers, Ronald L. *Almost Persuaded: American Physicians and Compulsory Health Insurance, 1912–1920*. Baltimore: Johns Hopkins University Press, 1978.

———, ed. *Compulsory Health Insurance: The Continuing American Debate*. Westport, Conn.: Greenwood Press, 1982.

Pauly, Mark V., ed. *National Health Insurance: What Now, What Later, What Never?* Washington, D.C.: American Enterprise Institute, 1980.

Pauly, Mark V., and William L. Kissick, eds. *Lessons from the First Twenty Years of Medicare: Research Implications for Public and Private Sector Policy*. Philadelphia: University of Pennsylvania Press, 1988.

Poen, Monte M. *Harry S. Truman Versus the Medical Lobby: The Genesis of Medicare*. Columbia: University of Missouri Press, 1979.

Rayack, Elton. *Professional Power and American Medicine: The Economics of the American Medical Association*. Cleveland: World Publishing, 1967.

Russell, Louise B. *Medicare's New Payment System: Is It Working?* Washington, D.C.: The Brookings Institution, 1989.

———. *Technology in Hospitals: Medical Advances and Their Diffusion*. Washington, D.C.: The Brookings Institution, 1979.

Schnall, David J., and Carl L. Figliola, eds. *Contemporary Issues in Health Care*. New York: Praeger, 1984.

Skidmore, Max J. *Medicare and the American Rhetoric of Reconciliation*. University: University of Alabama Press, 1970.

Somers, Herman Miles, and Ann Ramsay Somers. *Doctors, Patients, and Health Insurance: The Organization and Financing of Medical Care*. Washington, D.C.: The Brookings Institution, 1961.

Starr, Paul. *The Social Transformation of American Medicine*. New York: Basic Books, 1982.

Walsh, Dianna Chapman, and Richard Egdahl. *Payer, Provider, Consumer: Industry Confronts Health Care Costs*. New York: Springer-Verlag, 1977.

Whitted, Gary S., and Paul Torrens. *Managing Corporate Health Care Expenses: A Primer for Executives*. New York: Praeger, 1985.

Index

About the Author

NICHOLAS LAHAM specializes in the study of American politics and public policy.

ISBN 0-313-28745-7

HARDCOVER BAR CODE